Cambridge Life

Grace before Dinner, drawn by Bryan de Grineau, 1950

R. J. WHITE

Cambridge Life

EYRE & SPOTTISWOODE

LONDON · 1960

UXORI DILECTISSIMAE ET AMANTISSIMAE

AUCTOR HOC OPUSCULUM

D..D..D

MCMLX

First published in 1960 by
Eyre & Spottiswoode (Publishers) Ltd
22 Henrietta Street, London, W.C.2
© R. J. White 1960
Printed in Great Britain by
The Chiswick Press, London
Cat. No. 6/2414

Contents

Illustrations

Drawings in Text

Preface

This book is neither a history nor a guide, although it contains some history and some guidance. It is a partial portrait of life as it is lived in the University in the mid-twentieth century. Every book about Cambridge from within is bound to be partial because every man who belongs to the place has his own vision of life there, its inherent quality, its peculiar savour, its unique charm and its historic tendencies. There are certain ineluctable facts which explain the constitutional structure within which its abiding character has come to be what it is. Most of these can be gleaned from a guide like *The Student's Handbook*, or Sir Sydney Roberts' pithy little volume, *An Introduction to Cambridge*, and a good many facts of this kind are included in the present volume. But what has been attempted here is something more and something different – a prose portrait of Cambridge life as it is lived, and, presented with the aid of a number of fictitious characters and an imaginary college. These characters, dons, undergraduates, and college servants, are entirely imaginary, and so is the small collegiate society within which they live.

In attempting such a portrait, one encounters two recurrent problems. In the first place, the portrait painter himself is a part of the material in which he works. He sees it not only through his present pair of eyes, but also through the eyes of memory – in this case, rather more than thirty years of it. The light cast by personal memory tends to be a light that never was on land or sea. A certain ruthlessness in this regard has been exercised, but the danger of romanticism still remains. In the second place, the sitter refuses to sit still. To put it in another way: history insists on going on. While this book was being written, the debate about requirements for University entrance was in full swing. By the time it is published, the question of what is loosely called 'compulsory Latin' will almost certainly be settled, one way or another.

Again, it is very likely that the section on Matriculation will be out of date, at least as regards the ceremony thereof, by the same time. Even at the proof-stage of this book, the inclusion of the Central Hotel in a Cambridge itinerary had become anachronistic. For comfort in all this, I propose to appeal to the Vice-Chancellor who recently observed that 'one is always surprised at the changes in Cambridge – and then surprised at the way the place has remained the same'.

The structure of the book is indicated by the table of contents. It follows the pattern of the Academic Year, with two interludes concerning events that take place during the Christmas and Easter vacations – events that bring the University much more vividly into the public eye than most of what goes on during term. Michaelmas Term, being very much the Freshmen's term when the life of the University is being learnt by large numbers of newcomers, is treated at rather greater length than the other two, for it affords the best opportunity to describe and explain a large number of things that are likely to be of general interest. Lent Term is used to discover something of the life of men in mid-career, the second year men who are well and truly launched on the tide of University life. In this section, too, some history has been included, together with some consideration of modern developments in the life and character of both dons and undergraduates. The Easter, or Summer, Term concerns itself considerably with the joys and anxieties of the third year men, with examinations and degrees, with cricket and May Races and May Week. There is a short closing section in which certain current problems are briefly discussed, along with some prognostications about the future. Most of these problems are raised in the earlier sections in course of discussion by both senior and junior members of the University, but, since neither dons nor undergraduates are on their oaths at Hall dinner or after Feasts, it was felt that some more measured treatment of these problems should be undertaken, if not *sub specie aeternitatis*, at least beyond the hurly-burly of term-time.

I wish to thank all those who have helped me. I owe a great deal to Sir Sydney Roberts, whose watchful eye has saved me from many mis-statements; for those that may remain, I alone am responsible. My thanks are also due to the Master and Fellows of Downing College for allowing the reproduction of the drawing entitled 'Grace before

Dinner', and to Dr. Graham Smith for supplying me with the portrait of a Proctor and Bulldogs. Miss H. E. Peek, Deputy Keeper of the University Archives, was kindness itself in helping me to the use of illustrations of the 'Women's War.' Mr. R. B. Pugh, editor of *The Victoria History of the Counties of England*, kindly lent a block, and Mr. C. J. Webb, of the *Cambridge Daily News* was particularly helpful over photographs. Mr. John Bright-Holmes of Messrs. Eyre and Spottiswoode has been tireless, and infinitely patient, in both interrogation and correction. Mrs. Esther Carmichael not only typed my MS. under trying conditions, but made a number of helpful suggestions in the process. My debts to those more learned in the subject than I am will be evident to anyone who consults the books on Cambridge listed at the end.

Cambridge   R.J.W.
March 1960

CAMBRIDGE

Town

'In Cambridge there are sixteen Colleges that look like workhouses, and fourteen churches that look like little houses. The town is very fertile in alleys, and mud, and cats, and dogs, besides men, women, ravens, clergy, proctors, tutors, owls, and other two-legged cattle.'

So wrote the young Samuel Taylor Coleridge when he came up to Jesus College in 1791. He went on to speak of 'the quiet ugliness of Cambridge', and to compose a fragment 'left in a lecture-room' which began:

> Where deep in mud Cam rolls his slumbrous stream,
> And bog and desolation reign supreme . . .

He was never happy at Cambridge, save in sentimental retrospect. Indeed, in his second year, he ran away to enlist in the dragoons. And doubtless the place was ugly and uninspiring enough in those sunset years of the Age of Reason. Even Henry Gunning, that prize collector of Cambridge gossip, preferred to live out at Trumpington, or Thriplow, or Ickleton, whenever he could make his getaway. He found it 'surprising that any family should have resided at Cambridge who could live anywhere else'. Those were the days when the citizenry went through the foul streets after dark with a servant carrying a torch; when the Mohock undergraduates (those Teddy-boys of the eighteenth century) insulted foot-passengers and smashed their lanterns; when a thunderstorm could wash the household furniture of Newnham village into Silver Street. But even at that moment better things were on the way. The long-resisted[1] Cambridge Lighting and Paving Act came in 1788. Throughout the nineteenth century the congested lanes and alleyways were being opened up, the ancient huddles of little shops and houses and pot-houses which infested the east end of King's College

---

[1] It was resisted on grounds of expense, and as involving the setting back of house and shop-fronts.

chapel and the Market Place and the riverside between Magdalene and
St. John's were being pulled down, the high walls which shut from
view the Round Church and the lovely chapel of Peterhouse were being
levelled with the earth. The town was slowly becoming a place of frank
open façades and light airy thoroughfares. In short, Cambridge was
becoming what it is to-day, one of the loveliest[1] towns in Europe. It is
difficult to realize, now, how comparatively modern this loveliness is.
At last it is possible to go all the way from the Senate House to Hobson's
Conduit[2] along King's Parade and Trumpington Street, without alight-
ing upon a single inanimate object which offends the eye.

A place of light and air and noble vistas; yes, if one chooses one's
road, sticking to this main artery on foot, or to the Queen's Road along
the Backs in a car. Even if one takes the third way, past Sidney, Christ's
and Emmanuel, along St. Andrew's Street and Regent Street to the
Hills Road where the way is diversified, if not adorned, by Woolworth's,
Marks and Spencer's, and the John Lewis Partnership, the prospect is
not wholly disagreeable, though it is fair to say that here one might be
in Leicester or Derby or Nottingham were it not for the three colleges
on the left-hand. None of these thoroughfares has the death-dealing
traffic-horror of the High at Oxford; none, with the possible exception
of Sidney Street and its tributary, Market Street, on a Friday afternoon
or a Saturday morning, has the tunnelling throng of the Cornmarket;
none holds in store the awful prospect of a Cambridge Cowley. Even
now, and despite its City status, Cambridge remains a magnified
country town studded with colleges. As late as 1898 it was possible,
though already untrue, to say that 'if the University did not exist there
would be but little reason for the existence of the Town'. To-day, only
about six per cent of the population of more than 90,000 is employed
by the University and the colleges. However, the industrial growth of
Cambridge over the past hundred years has been in the main the
growth of light industries, and the typical marks of industrial development are scarcely visible, save in the region of the railway-station and
the gas-works. There is no need to go and search out the colleges in
the bowels of urban agglomeration. They stand forth. And where

---

[1] 'Unspeakably lovely, and no one speaks to you', a wit has said.
[2] Hobson's Conduit, that Jacobean jollity, originally stood in the Market Place, but
was removed to the junction of Brookside and Lensfield Road in 1856.

there are colleges there are trees and there is grass. Cambridge is still very noticeably a green place for most of the year.

It is also a place of many waters: not only of the threading rivers, but of the intrusive fens. A fenland town in its strange flat beauty and its muggy climate. There are little hills within sight all round: Madingley, Castle Hill, the distant rise to Newmarket Heath, and the wooded line of the Gogs beyond Cherry Hinton. But these are scarcely wind-blown heights: none rises much above three hundred feet, and none (except Castle Hill) crowd into the city itself. The result is a damp and bitter air in winter, bearing the ghosts of ancient agues and rheumatic spasms from the fenland plains, and of humid heats in summer. Not a healthy place at any time. A bronchial affliction for half the year, and a Turkish bath for the other. There are days and nights in winter when the chorus of coughs and sneezes shake the medieval pinnacles of King's and sets the towers and turrets of Tudor Cambridge rocking overhead. There are days (and nights) in summer when every shirt and blouse bears a half-moon at the armpit, when the brain contracts to a small sponge under a wet towel. Then the undergraduate lies in a punt in Grant-chester Meadows with a volume of the *Cambridge Modern History* or Gray's *Anatomy* on his knees and a gramophone whispering at his ear, and the don sighs for the hot dry airs of Provence and Tuscany. No one should live in Cambridge between the middle of June and the middle of September. It is really remarkable (as Gunning observed) that anyone lives there at any time. Which raises the question that everyone wants answered, some time or other: how comes it that the place is there at all? Why Cambridge, of all places? Why not Stamford, or Leicester, or York? Why (as they say) 'the middle of a fen'?

It was always an important place on the map. Geography saw to that. It is not, and it never was – for all the plaints of the rheumaticky – 'in the middle of a fen'. That is the whole point. Cambridge is on the *edge* of the fenland, that great amphibious tract of eastern England which for centuries divided the south-east from the north-east with a wilder-ness of swamp and marsh and sluggish rivers. Looking east and north from the tower of the University Library, or from the Castle Mound, this great plain – ditched and diked and made into rich agricultural territory by Vermuyden and his Dutchmen in the seventeenth century –

B

still stretches like a misty pancake away to the Wash and King's Lynn and the wolds of Lincolnshire, with the ghost-grey ship of Ely at anchor in the midst. Looking away over there, it is easy to believe what they teach in the Geography School, that there is no natural obstacle save water between you and the Ural mountains. Cambridge is, in several senses, a border town. It dominates the western frontier of the fens, and it marks the frontier between anicent Mercia (the modern Midlands) and the land of the East Angles (modern East Anglia). For long enough the Mercians and the East Angles glared at each other across the ford of the Cam below Magdalene College garden. The Mercians held that part of the town which rises up to the Castle Mound, north of the river, dominating the crossing-place, while the East Angles held the southern portion where the University was to grow up – where (apart from Magdalene in its transpontine solitude) the colleges still cluster along the southern shore[1]. Sometime in the ninth century, the ford gave way to a bridge, and 'Camford' became an impossibility. The Cam bridge is the only bridge in England to give its name to a county.

The river, winding through the fenland to join the Ouse, gave the town its wealth. Barges bore the merchandise of north-western Europe from the great port of King's Lynn not only to the shores of Mid-summer Common for the enormous annual mart of Stourbridge Fair but into the town itself where the hythes lined the river as far as Magdalene and St. John's and the Backs. Richard Bentley, the terrible Master of Trinity in the early eighteenth century, who was more responsible than any other man for giving to Cambridge its chief glory, 'The Backs', used to bring the produce of his rectory at Somersham to his private granary on the river bank behind Trinity. The bargees poled their barges along the Backs for pay where now the under-graduate poles his punt in play. Indeed, the two activities overlapped, as we can see from Walker's view of 'The Backs' in 1793, and no doubt there were collisions. The bargees were a familiar feature of Cambridge life long into the nineteenth century. Picking fights with the river-men was for long a favourite sport of the young gentlemen of the Univer-

[1] There is this much literal, and historical, meaning in the description of Cambridge as 'The University of East Anglia'.

sity. But Cambridge grew not only as a place of river debouchment for the merchandise of Lynn, but as the nodus of a whole system of land communications, too. Anyone, from a king with an army to a pedlar with his pack, wishful to skirt the fenland in his way from Essex and the south-east to Stamford, Newark and the north, would pass the river by the bridge beneath Magdalene. King John went that way from Castle Hedingham to Newark, and his death, in 1216. 'The Great Bridge' (now known as Magdalene Bridge, and rebuilt at least four times over the centuries) certainly carried all heavy traffic by land between the Eastern Counties and the Midlands. Ermine Street, from London to York, passes a little to the west. The Roman Road from Colchester to Chester, similarly skirted the town. The Peddars Way, from London to Brancaster across the fens, passed a little to the east; and Akerman Street, diverging from the Peddars Way, passes through the centre of the town and then dives south-west via Ampthill to Cirencester and Bath.

Gown

Thus the town, the borough, the city, needs little accounting for beyond the terms of topography, trade and travel. But – the University? How, and why, did it come to ensconce itself in the arms of this east Midland (or west Anglian) borough? Certainly not by invitation, nor in response to the calls of love. For centuries, town and gown fought each other, tooth and nail. In 'The Ages of Faith' it proved particularly hard for two communities in one town, one of clerks and the other of laymen, to live at peace. Quite apart from the bloody brawls among the clerks themselves (which often involved the townsmen, too), the heads of the two communities kept up a fierce border warfare over jurisdiction, privileges, police, rents, rates and market-prices. The most cursory account of the facts of life as they were experienced by the medieval clerks in the bear-garden beside the Cam would dispose at once of the fantasy that Cambridge began as the result of an exodus from Oxford, a migration of scholars who had picked up their gowns and their

manuscripts in flight from the tumult of 'another place' to find peace
in a fenland refuge from a naughty world. No one any longer takes
pleasure in what Maitland called that earliest form of inter-university
contest, a lying-match over the question of superior antiquity. That
there was an exodus from Oxford after the town and gown troubles
there in 1209 is certain. And it is likely enough that the migrants did
bring with them some sort of corporate life and organization. Twenty
years later there was another migration, this time from the University
of Paris. Soon after this, the scholars of Cambridge were recognized by
both King and Pope, but the formal recognition of the University as
a *studium generale* (which denoted that its masters had the privilege to
teach throughout Christendom) came at the hands of Pope John XXII
in 1318. Whether the present pontiff will signalize his adoption of the
name of John XXIII by anything in the nature of a friendly nod in the
direction of his predecessor's godchild remains to be seen.

Nobody can say for certain what it was that made Cambridge a seat
of learning. It can have been nobody's conscious decision. Perhaps it
had something to do with the town's proximity to the great abbeys of
the fenland. Barnwell Priory, whose remains may be seen beneath the
shadow of the gas-works, was on its doorstep. Croyland and Ramsey
were not far away. In the thirteenth century came the friars, and the
friars were notable teachers. You can still take your lunch at the Friar
House in Bene't Street where once stood the Augustinian Friary. The
Franciscans lived where Sidney Sussex College now stands, and traces
of their cellarage have recently been brought to light under the Master's
Lodge. Emmanuel College stands where the Dominicans came to
preach and teach. The Friars, and especially the Franciscans, brought
with them the attraction of good teaching in theology. Then, in 1284,
Hugh of Balsham endowed 'the scholars of the Bishop of Ely' with two
hostels outside the Trumpington Gate, together with the neighbouring
church of St. Peter. Thus was born the first college: St. Peter's, or Peterhouse. Another forty years were to pass before anything else of the
kind appeared. Then, in the middle of the fourteenth century, came
Michael House[1], Clare Hall, King's Hall, Pembroke Hall, Gonville

---

[1] The original form of Trinity College.

Gown! Gown! – Town! Town! – or The Battle of Peas Hill

Luggage and Gowns in Trumpington Street; a new Cambridge
term. In the background, the University Press

Proctor and Bulldogs

Hall, Trinity Hall and Bene't Hall:[1] the whole gamut between 1324 and 1352. This was the red-brick period of Cambridge, when halls of residence were being set up to house the floating population of scholars who came to sit at the feet of the doctors of a non-collegiate University, very much as students enter into hostels in order to attend the lectures at the Universities of Nottingham, Bristol and Hull in the twentieth century, or for that matter as they still do in order to attend professorial courses in the universities of Scotland and the Continent. At a later date most of them were to drop their earliest designation of 'hall' in favour of the later one What brought about the transformation of a congeries of 'halls' into a university of colleges was the great social and intellectual revolution that overtook England in the age of the Reformation. In the century and a half between the founding of King's in 1441 and the founding of Sidney Sussex in 1594, the community we know as the Cambridge college was well and truly born. No less than seven colleges were founded in the Tudor age alone.

These colleges resembled the medieval 'halls' only in the bare fact that they were buildings in which scholars lived while attending 'the University'. In all else – and the all else is all that matters – they were, and are (along with their sisters at Oxford), novel and unique in the world.[2] Paradoxically, the most impressive of them were built of red brick: Queens', Trinity, St. John's, Christ's, Magdalene and Jesus: and in their original aspect they must have looked very red-brick indeed, to judge from their somewhat raw-beef appearance after the scrubbings and scrapings that most of them have undergone in the present century. Their architecture was that of the half-fortified manor-house of their time, the Hampton Court style: entry through a turreted and crenellated gate-house; a series of cobbled courts; the great hall lying crosswise beyond the first court; chapel and Master's Lodge lying generally a little to one side. Indeed, they really were manor-houses set down in a country town, the crowning glory of the architecture of the great age of the rising gentry and the prosperous merchant and professional

[1] The original form of Corpus Christi College.
[2] Not quite true, though they like to think so. Colleges existed at Paris nearly a century before the first Cambridge college was founded, and there were more colleges in the Latin Quarter at the time of their suppression in 1764 than existed at Oxford and Cambridge together. (*See* Arthur Gray, *Cambridge University, an episodical history* (1912), Ch. 3.)

man which really dawned with the strong monarchy of the Tudors. To these handsome houses came not only the poor scholars who had once come to the medieval University, but the sons of an educated laity whose destiny it was to rule the land at Quarter Sessions and in the House of Commons. The poor clerks now came as sizars, second-class citizens, admitted at cut prices in return for certain menial duties. At the other end of the social scale – the top end – came the fellow-commoners, men of rank who wore gowns laced with gold and silver, and caps with gold and silver tassels. In between came the great mass of commoners or pensioners.[1] And in this social stratification within the college, the ancient University reflected, as ever, the changing social scene. The age of the individual, of the private household, of the entailed estate, of the peculiar sanctities of a protestant and propertied world, had produced its peculiar university.

It was in these new colleges of the Tudor age that was determined the character of 'Cambridge' as we still know it. The colleges, each with its Master, fellows, and scholars, its self-government under its own statutes, its tutors and lecturers, its deans and its chaplains, overshadowed the university. The colleges could, and did, supply by far the greater part of the teaching of their own little self-contained populations of undergraduates. Indeed, although the university was historically much older than the colleges, the time was at hand when the colleges might be said to have given the impression that they could get on perfectly well without it. Even to-day, when the world that produced the university of autonomous colleges is once more changing, when the university is coming more and more to overshadow the colleges, proctors in pursuit of an undergraduate have no authority to pursue him beyond the gates of his college. Nor would the city police think to set foot within college precincts save at the invitation of a tutor. The Englishman's home is his castle, and the courts of a Cambridge college are the college's kingdom.

---

[1] *Pensionarii*, those who pay for their board, lodging and instruction. The ordinary fee-paying undergraduates.

Getting In

Sometimes, on stormy nights in winter, when the wind howls up from the fen and great belches of smoke pour from the fire in the Senior Combination Room, one tutor will say to another:

"What was that?"

Then they listen, straining their ears to identify the noises of the night as the falling of a tree in the Fellows' garden or the crash of a chimney-pot from the roof of the college kitchen. Presently, one tutor says to the other:

"Just for a moment I thought it was some one trying to get into the College."

For this is the tutor's nightmare: some one trying to get into the College. A great deal of his time is employed in preventing it. Every year there are several thousand people trying to get into the College, and the tutors know that they will be lucky if they can admit many more than a hundred. It is, moreover, their duty to see that these hundred young creatures are of a suitable quality to benefit by what a Cambridge college can provide. The task of selection is almost exclusively in their hands. The tutors are men of power. Between them, for good or ill, they make the University.

It was not always thus. There was a time – only yesterday in some colleges – when the Master of the college looked after admissions. There is nothing in statute to prevent him doing so still, if he has the time or the inclination. A Master, determined to make the college in his own image, or (as it has been more delicately expressed) 'to lay upon the college the stamp of his own personality and ideals', might decide to take the whole business once more into his own hands, so that the tutors would only meet their new pupils on the first day of the Michaelmas term. Indeed, it is rumoured that where this last happened, the tutors were obliged to go round the staircases copying down the names of the freshmen and sorting them out among themselves. But this is nowadays no more than a residual tutorial nightmare, of which there are many. To-day, the Master of a college for the most part does little more in this matter of admissions than (perhaps) preside over the tutors when they meet to discuss and co-ordinate their respective 'lists'.

Since every young man on coming into residence is allocated to a tutor, it is proper enough that the tutors should have the biggest share in admitting their own pupils.

At Cambridge, a tutor does not necessarily teach his pupils, in the academic sense of 'teach'.[1] Out of a hundred young men for whose general welfare he may be responsible, it is likely that no more than a dozen or so will be reading his particular subject. In fact, a tutor takes general (perhaps one might say 'moral') charge of men reading a whole range of subjects which may, or may not, be akin to his own academic field. He will see them when they come up at the beginning of term, and when they go down at the end, and at any time in between when they may need his care or advice. He has his 'tutorial hours', when he is formally on hand for consultation. Indeed, in a sense, he is always on hand for his pupils. He may be summoned at any hour of the day or night to see them into hospital or out of the police-station. He is their ever-present help in time of trouble: money trouble, family trouble, girl trouble, anything and everything. He is not only a power. He is a proxy parent, by ancient description *in loco parentis*, and it is highly desirable that the number of his pupils shall be of a manageable size so that he may know them all personally. He has his pupils to lunch, or to tea, and his wife (if he has a wife, which he ought to have, generally speaking), tries to provide them with a home from home. The tutor gets an entertainment allowance to help him, here; for, considering all things, his stipend is small. He earns it. He needs the best qualities of a house-master and a family man, as well as a reputation for learning.

It is, or it should be, fairly easy to understand why 'getting into a college' is a particularly severe obstacle race, more especially in an age when public funds are available to swell the number of contestants. The college system, with its tutors and their personal relationship with their pupils, grew up in a different age, and a different society, when the number of potential undergraduates was small. How to retain all that is valuable in the collegiate and personal character of Cambridge life in an age of swelling numbers is the Cambridge headache. More colleges, more Fellows, and – thereby – more provision for more students? All these are under constant debate, and all raise more prob-

[1] *See* pp. 68 ff.

lems than they seem likely to solve.[1] Their advocates should at least be made aware that the system is already bursting at the seams, and that they can only have their way at the cost of changing its character. Nor should it ever be forgotten that the whole purpose of a university is not the education of young men and women. Its senior members are, or should be, no less concerned with promoting learning than with teaching undergraduates. Far too many of them to-day are fagging themselves beyond the capacity for original work by the deadly toil of trying to make silk purses out of sows' ears. For it is one of the great discoveries of academic life in the twentieth century that increased numbers have simply swelled the number of second-class men and women in the examination lists, and that the number of first-class candidates remains almost stationary however many candidates take the examinations.

So, 'getting in' is difficult, and rightly so.

Correspondence about admission should be addressed to the Senior Tutor, and should begin when a boy is sixteen years old.

Application for admission to the College should normally be made as soon as a boy has passed the General Certificate of Education at Ordinary Level: there is a registration-fee of one pound . . .

Some men choose their college. Most men are chosen by their college. The fortunate few who choose their college may do so on a number of grounds. Father, grandfather, elder brother, was there; and a college will take this into account, other things being equal, and very properly, just as a horse-keeper looks twice at a horse 'from the same stable'. It works the other way round, too. Certain colleges have long-standing connections with certain schools, and schoolmasters will advise their boys to apply to colleges they know well. Some colleges go out to cultivate schools, which may mean inviting headmasters to college feasts, or to conferences in college with tutors. It may mean cultivating the old schools of newly elected Fellows. It may mean a certain amount of commercial-travelling on the part of tutors, though this requires a

---

[1] These problems are discussed below – in the chapter on 'The Changing Don' (pp. 189 ff.) and in the final chapter.

brashness and a thickness of skin which are normally uncommon among learned men. But it is true that when an examiner, or a college tutor, asks a schoolboy candidate for admission why he wants, in the first place, to come to the college, the answer he gets nine times out of ten is: 'My headmaster advised me . . .'

There are many more crass answers, such as 'I am told that this is one of the cheaper colleges . . .' Down goes a gamma. There are no 'cheaper colleges', nor are there any colleges that are 'easier to get into'. Fees and living costs are fairly standardized. Of course, how much it will cost an undergraduate to keep up with the Joneses if he goes to what he calls a 'richer college' – a college whose undergraduates lead a more expensive social life – is his own affair. The only answer exceeding this one in crassness is that of Mr. Jones, who has religous objections to any choice which may involve his offspring in blasphemy. Mr. Jones senior is resolved that his son shall not be required to encourage the Second Person of the Holy Trinity from the touch-line or the tow-path.

"So", young Mr. Jones informs the tutor, "we crossed off all the colleges with religious names, like Jesus, Christ's, Emmanuel, Trinity, St. John's, Magdalene and Corpus Christi."

"I can see that you would not wish to announce to your friends that you were going to Jesus", says the tutor with becoming gravity, for the idea is by no means as new to him as young Mr. Jones appears to imagine. "And I can well understand that 'Come on, Christ's' would stick in your throat. But you could still have gone to St. John's. They call their Boat Club 'Lady Margaret', doubtless with the susceptibilities of people like yourself in mind. And after all, it is the Welshman's college."

"I'm not Welsh, sir," Mr. Jones objects.

"Even so," says the tutor, "you need not have sunk so low as Clare, Queens', Pembroke, Sidney and Downing."

In the end, Mr. Jones gets an omega and goes elsewhere.

For many months, college tutors have been shaping their final lists for the new academic year that will begin in October. At intervals they meet to compare notes and decide difficult cases. They have also to keep in mind a desirable balance of strength between the various subjects, and the total size of the college population as approved by the governing body, which decides all major problems of college policy. By the time the tutors hold their last meeting before dispersing for the Long Vacation, they can feel fairly confident of the shape of things to come.

"Altogether it looks like being a fairly typical freshman year," says the Master, presiding over the tutorial conclave at the round table in his study at the Lodge. "One hundred and twelve, not counting affiliated students, teachers in training, and various odds and sods."

"Too many, Master," says the Senior Tutor, a classical scholar who began life in what he modestly calls 'a minor public school', and has always leaned to the side of exclusiveness. "The thing gets more unmanageable every year. I foresee the time, not very far distant, when the whole business of admissions will be done by electrical computors."

"Come, come," says the Master, beaming and rubbing his hands, for he is a mathematician and secretly undismayed at the prospect of dispensing with tutors. "Come, come, the personal touch, what?"

"Precisely, Master," says the Senior Tutor. "My remark was intended to be elegiac rather than prophetic."

In fact, it was intended to annoy the second tutor, a doctor of science, whose passion is for doing everything by machines. He at once takes up the point, shifting the ground of argument from personality to political economy, for everyone knows that he is hand-in-glove with the bursar, and can always be depended upon to represent the bursarial point of view when that officer is absent – and often when he is present.

"We have to realize," he says now, "that this college lives on its undergraduates. We simply can't afford to be a small college. If we continue to admit less than something in the order of a hundred and fifty freshmen a year we shall be bankrupt inside five years."

"I seem to have heard you make that prophecy five years ago, my dear chap," says the Senior Tutor. "Or was it the bursar? At any rate, we have kept our annual intake down to between a hundred and a hundred and twelve for the last five years, and I am not aware that the bum-bailiffs are in the Lodge."

"Look here," the junior tutor intervenes, "I've got another thirty men at the bottom of my list who are at least as good as the ones I've admitted. I propose we admit the lot and save the college."

The junior tutor is a lawyer, a 'failed barrister' by his own admission (it is almost a boast). Very tall and thin and elegant, he speaks in a mocking, drawling voice and keeps his eyebrows permanently raised as if nothing can ever surprise him further, not even the fatuities of his fellow tutors.

"You know that is quite impossible," says the Master. "It would upset the balance between subjects."

"Moreover, it would fill the college with third-rate lawyers," says the Senior Tutor. "We have more than enough already . . . Though I will admit," he adds as an afterthought, "that the prospect alarms me considerably less than the present policy of filling the college with third-rate scientists."

"It would present insoluble problems in the matter of food and accommodation," says the second tutor. "The bursar and the steward are at their wits' end already."

"All right," says the junior tutor, shrugging his lean shoulders. "It was only a suggestion. I thought we needed the money."

"So we do," the second tutor snaps. "But we can't pick up money by letting in riff-raff at a moment's notice like a cinema proprietor. We all know that any increase in numbers requires the sanction of the Governing Body. We are tied to something in the order of one hundred and twelve at present. My point was that the Governing Body should reconsider the whole question of numbers in the context of general college policy."

"I couldn't agree more," says the Senior Tutor. "And if it does, I shall recommend an annual intake of round about – forgive me, I should have said of the order of – seventy."

"In that case we shall have to double tuition-fees and the cost of rooms and meals," retorts the second tutor.

"Which is absurd," says the Master, clipping his papers together. "Going at 112, going at 112 – gone at 112. And now, gentlemen, let me offer you some coffee."

The potential freshman in Leicester, Leeds and Wimbledon mercifully knows nothing of all this. He only knows that he has received a typewritten letter containing the magic phrases: 'I am pleased to be able to offer you a place at the college in October next to read . . . Kindly notify me as soon as possible of your acceptance . . . I am

returning your birth-certificate . . . You will shortly receive the necessary information about caution money, etc. . . . May I offer you my
best wishes for a happy and successful career at the college . . .?'

Letter after letter; examination after examination; interview after
interview; college registration fee; college admission fee; caution
money (a deposit of anything between £25 and £70, against the payment of college bills, and returnable when the student goes out of
residence); and then, after several years of the mountains in labour,
you are 'in'. You are 'going up'.

"I wonder," says the New Zealand farmer, being shown round the
colleges, "I wonder whether these young men realize what a privilege
it is . . ."

A question that no don cares to try to answer.

Going Up

Three times in every year, some seven thousand young men and
women converge upon the town of the twenty[1] colleges in order to
'keep' fifty-nine nights of residence there by way of part-fulfilment of
the statutory requirements for the acquisition of the degree of Bachelor
of Arts. They don't talk of converging. They talk of 'going up'. Men
and women always talk of 'going up to high and holy places', like
London or the older universities. Similarly, they 'keep' there, which is
their way of saying 'reside'. They 'keep' their fifty-nine nights, very
much as budding barristers 'eat their dinners' at the Inns of Court.
When they have kept their nights, which compose the term, they 'go
down'. To 'keep' literally means to sleep, or otherwise to spend the
hours between midnight and six a.m., within statutory distance of
Great St. Mary's, the University Church, the ancient centre of Cambridge.[2] In order to supplicate the Vice-Chancellor for the degree of
Bachelor of Arts, it is necessary to produce unimpeachable evidence
that nine terms of fifty-nine nights have been 'kept', and normally in

[1] Twenty for convenience and a round number. There is also Churchill College,
founded but not yet (1960) built. In addition there is Fitzwilliam House, at present the
home of non-collegiate students but now designed for college status, and New Hall, a
'third foundation' for women, opened in 1954, as yet a college in embryo.

[2] Absence from Cambridge (with Tutorial permission) after midnight does not mean
losing a night, providing one is back before 6 a.m.

succession. Then, having passed the necessary 'Tripos' examinations,[1] or, failing these, having been allowed to proceed to an 'ordinary'[2], as distinct from an honours degree, and having afforded your college sufficient evidence to assure the Vice-Chancellor that you are sound in both mind and morals, you will acquire the privilege of wearing a hood trimmed with something passably like the fur of a white rabbit and of writing the letters 'B.A.' after your name. It is as simple, or as complicated, as that. Whether, during your nine terms of fifty-nine nights of residence, you have attended any lectures is your own affair, though your elders and betters will have seen to it that you have read some books, and written some essays, and engaged in some weekly conversation of a more or less intellectual character with a person known as a 'supervisor'. Of course, you will have done a great many more things having little or no ostensible connection with academic studies: debating, singing, acting, sport and talking until three in the morning about everything under the sun. But, by and large, the fulfilment of strictly academic requirements for the award of your bachelor's degree amounts to little more than keeping your terms, passing your examinations, and maintaining a mediocre reputation for virtue and sober living.

And is this why the seven thousand come? Is the university first and foremost a degree-factory? More than six thousand of them would tell you so if you asked them. Another thousand will murmur something about 'liberal education', or 'learning to think', or 'a sense of values'. They have been reading some elderly person's book on *Culture and the University*, or mugging up Newman's *Idea of a University* for an examination. Regard them not. The six thousand know they are right. To them the university is the place to which young men and women, in a highly competitive world, come to get a good degree, and thereby to get a good job. The fact that they are honest enough to say so is the

---

[1] *See* pp. 219-21.

[2] No longer will colleges allow men to come into residence to read for an ordinary, or pass, degree, *ab initio*. The ordinary degree has become a kind of consolation prize for the failed honours candidate, of whom there are nowadays very few. Which is a pity, though perhaps inevitable with the vastly increased pressure of numbers of what are generally called 'serious' students. The old pass degree enabled many men whose interests were not catered for by tripos courses, as well as mere socialites and idlers, to spend three years in a suitable place for general cultivation of mind and body, and perhaps to contribute something valuable to the life of the place. Many a man of all-round distinction once 'passed out in the poll' – a term somewhat invidiously derived from *hoi polloi*.

best tribute they could pay to the university as a patron of clear-thinking and plain-speaking. Nor need this imply that they are any more barbarous than their thousand thousand predecessors of more leisurely generations. The fact is that they have had the devil's own job 'getting in', and they are not to be blamed for making the most of it, in very practical terms indeed, once they have succeeded. Besides, although they are too decent to talk about it, they know perfectly well that they get a good deal more by their stay at the university than could ever be expressed in terms of spurious rabbit's fur or diplomas. Perhaps it is just as well that no one but the more solemn dons ever try to say exactly what it is that they get, or ought to get.

Nor, in the unlikely case of any one of the seven thousand arriving at the railway-station or at the city boundary's asking the way to the university, would anyone find it very easy to answer the question. The literal-minded might point the way to the University Registrary at the Old Schools, where most of the administrative work of the university is done. The visually-minded might propose chartering a 'plane at Marshall's airfield in order to circle around the place for an hour. The sensible guide would probably quote the epitaph of Sir Christopher Wren: *Circumspice*. He might equally well refer his questioner to page 1 of the *Student's Handbook* (a volume that singularly few students ever look at), where he will find the statement: 'The relationship of the University and the Colleges is so close, and is manifested in so many different ways, that it is impossible to think of the one without the other; they form a closely integrated whole which is the result of some seven hundred years of natural growth.' The undergraduate may say he is 'going to the university', but he really means that he is going to Peterhouse, or Jesus, or John's, or Trinity. Only by going up to a college does he go up to the university. For good or ill, the under-graduate entry to the university is wholly in the hands of the colleges.[1] The colleges admit the undergraduates, and the university takes what the colleges give it. The sole qualification to this statement consists in the fact that no one can come into residence unless he has passed the University Entrance Examination – the Previous (better known, hither-to, as the 'Little-go'), or secured exemption from it by passing in

[1] *See* pp. 23-6.

certain subjects at a certain level in the G.C.E. examination while at school. The life of the undergraduate, once he is up at Cambridge, is in the first place a collegiate life. He will live in his college for at least one year out of three. He will take most of his meals in his college hall. He will be taught by college supervisors (either in his own college or some other).[1] His college will send him to lectures laid on by the university, in university lecture-rooms or laboratories, enter him for university examinations, and supplicate the university for his bachelor's degree at the end of his three years. Yet he will come upon that somewhat unlocated entity, 'the university', at every turn, whether by going to university sermons at Great St. Mary's (the University Church), or by encountering the university proctors (or police) in the streets after dark. Quite a large proportion of his fees will be paid (through his college) to the university. But his home, his hearth, his family is the college. He will, if he ever learns it at all, learn his membership of the university through membership of his college. The college, like home, in Mr. Eliot's poem, is 'where we start from'. Some of us end there, too. But the natural thing is to advance from home and hearth to the greater world which embraces hearth and home in the larger unity. The college is the perfect example of Burke's 'little platoon'.

To be attached to the subdivision, to love the little platoon we belong to in society, is the first principle (the germ, as it were) of public affections. It is the first link in the series by which we proceed towards a love to our country, and to mankind.

True, there is the breed generally known as 'the good college man', who is never good for anything else; the parish-pump patriot; the zealous counter of college 'firsts' and 'blues'; the product of college in-breeding. This man has generally missed the university bus. Most colleges have at least one among their senior members. But every pack has its joker, as every work of art has its parody.

Because he comes up to a college in order to be a member of the university, and not the other way round, the undergraduate is untroubled by the complexities of university-college relationships which

[1] Although an increasing number of undergraduates are now taught by men and women unaffiliated to colleges. *See* pp. 288-9.

bother the casual visitor or the foreigner. And anyway, out of the seven
thousand who come up and go down thrice in the academic year, there
are few – even among the freshmen – to whom the place is *terra incognita*.
The freshman (even if he is the son of an old college man) has already
come up from school either to be interviewed by a tutor, and/or to
take a college entrance examination, and/or as an incipient undergraduate to live in a college while competing in the open scholarship
examinations. He has felt his way into the place, for a day or two, or
for a whole week,[1] long before he comes into residence to keep his
terms.

Consequently, the Pisgah-sight of his Alma Mater from Madingley
Hill, or Castle Hill, or the Newmarket Road by the arriving undergraduate is almost entirely a novelist's fiction. There is little or no
likelihood of John Freshman mounting silent to a peak in Darien some
few miles this side of Bedford, Huntingdon, Newmarket or Royston,
in order to indulge in a wild surmise as a new world swims into his
ken. It will not be new. But it may still be exciting. Especially if he
comes the Madingley road from the Midlands, or the Newmarket road
from East Anglia. There are few distant prospects more beautiful than
the first glimpse of Cambridge from the St. Neots road above
Madingley, when the trees and turrets, the blunt tower of the University Library and the long low line of King's Chapel first show themselves above the autumn trees below the hill. The first view from the
Newmarket approach is more distant and more mysterious, specially
on a grey October afternoon when the sun flings cascades of silvery
light upon the plain, and the eye strains to pick out the tiny furniture
of crockets and turrets between the foot of the Gogs and the fen. The
Londoner, or the southerner in general, coming from the Royston
road through Trumpington, enjoys no such distant prospect. He enters
by the only avenue which bears inspection at close quarters. Only the
Newmarket entry into Norwich, or the southern entry into Stamford,
can rival this approach to an ancient English town for tree-lined beauty
and comely buildings. And before he knows, he is in Trumpington
Street, riding down to the pale splendours of King's Chapel and the
Senate House and the mock-château of Waterhouse's Caius.

[1] *See* pp. 119-20.

C

The Social Realist, with a mistrust for fine buildings, or even for fine trees, makes a point of arriving by train. The front of the railway-station is worth study. Like the front of King's Cross, it is an impressive example of what the Victorians could do when, forgetting Gothic cathedrals and French châteaux, they submitted to the plain, and not inelegant, common-sense of an industrial age. But, of course, you only notice the face of the railway-station when you are going away, and on such occasions you will be in a hurry. Coming into Cambridge by railway, you might imagine that you are approaching Sheffield. The horrid mess of old iron, smoke-blackened sheds and stunted chimney-stacks is rivalled only by the approach to the station at Oxford. The train crawls through mounds of scrap-metal, generally stopping for severa minutes in the midst of the wilderness in order to afford the expectant traveller an opportunity to inspect the gas-works, the filthy Mill Road bridge, and the grimy back streets of Romsey Town. Only when he arrives at Cambridge station will he understand the true, and almost unbelievable, reason for this delay. It is, that main-line trains from either direction have to share a single enormously long platform. Unless you travel in the front of the train, you will have to do no inconsiderable part of your journey to Cambridge on foot.

The old joke about the American visitor who comes to Cambridge only in order to see its phenomenally long railway platform, has been handed down from generation to generation of undergraduates for more than a century. It certainly is a platform for the connoisseur, the Southend Pier of the railway world.

What a surprise! I had no idea of such a length of building, all covered over and comfortable: it cannot be much less than 400 feet! This is really one of the best stations I have seen for many a day. *Pictorial Guide to Cambridge, 1867.*

A second joke, of no less antiquity, and no less dear to all freshmen's hearts, concerns the Vice-Chancellor who originally protested that to bring the railway into the precincts of the university would be not only offensive to Almighty God but displeasing to the Vice-Chancellor.[1]

---

[1] More accurately, he said 'as distasteful to the University authorities as they must be offensive to Almighty God and to all right-minded Christians,' and he was talking of Sunday excursions.

MICHAELMAS TERM

Swallows and Daffodils

Like the swallows in May, so the undergraduates in October. One day they are not. Another day – and they are. Skimming in from all points of the compass, they are suddenly revealed as starlings rather than swallows, as they alight and strut and chatter over the pavements. Taxis whiz up and down Regent Street and Station Road; bus-loads, with luggage piled under the stairs, labour down to Woolworth's and the Round Church and Chesterton Lane; motor-cars of every vintage crowd in from the Trumpington Road, the Newmarket Road, and the Huntingdon link with the Great North Road. In three thronging traffic-jammed afternoons, pretty well the whole invasion is completed, and the old town is alive again after its familiar pattern.

To hear them, you might imagine that the university has been awaiting their arrival all summer. They are not to know that the old grey cat in the fen has scarcely had a wink of sleep since Degree Day. All that happened when the university 'went down' at the end of June was a change of pattern. Instead of undergraduates, the place filled up with wave after wave of 'conferees'. The Institute of Meat, United Steel, the Eastern Region Electricity Authority, the Institute of Chartered Accountants, the Society for the Preservation of Ancient Churches, all have been here in pin-stripe parody. College bursars and stewards welcome these profitable guests. Kitchen staffs, no longer dispersed to East Coast seaside resorts on board-wages, can now be employed at a profit while some hundreds of useful citizens enjoy a fleeting experience of living in a college. The dons[1] are not implicated, though the un-married Fellow who lives in college all the year round may grow

---

[1] Don, or dons. *Verbum satis sapienti*. The term has already been used several times, and perhaps some attempt should be made to define it. 'Don' derives from a Spanish title for a man of high rank, a distinguished person. By a mysterious process of transference, it has come to be used, since the seventeenth century, for heads, fellows and tutors of colleges at the older universities. Thus Dryden: 'The great dons of wit. . . .' Undergraduates apply it to any senior person whatever. It is conveniently vague, and covers a multitude of sinners.

37

about 'Captains of Industry' who drive up in the kind of cars that Fellows of colleges can't afford and walk about on the grass where only Fellows are normally allowed to walk. What with conferences and sight-seeing crowds, pin-stripes and jeans, horse-tails and jumpers, the bachelor don is inclined to think that his college pays a high price for being a profitable showplace. 'Oh dear, oh dear,' Lowes Dickinson used to sigh, as he looked out of his window in Gibbs Building at King's, to see the spinsters imbibing culture *via* medieval architecture on hot summer afternoons; 'oh dear, what is to happen to them? I don't know, and they don't know . . .' and then, suddenly, inspired: 'oh dear, what they want is a husband.' Yes, indeed, the old grey cat is kept pretty well awake until early September.

It is then, when the University Library closes, and even the don who is writing a book thinks he might as well snatch a fortnight in Austria, there is at last a hush of deep repose. 'Days die in September . . .' though transatlantic voices still murmur in the Cury and along K.P. . . . By the end of the month, when the trees along the Backs are turning to crimson and gold, the old cat stirs once more in her sleep and winks a somnolent eye as she flutters the pages of her Cambridge Pocket Diary. The pages are beginning to fill up, now, with grim appointments at the Examination Schools: qualifying examinations in medicine and mechanical sciences. Many of these are for 'hang-overs' – men who failed in June and are being allowed another try in order to be permitted to resume their residence. Some, on the other hand, are routine examinations for budding M.B.s, hairy-looking young men up from hospital, perhaps for the fifth or sixth time, because they can't 'make it' in anatomy or pharmacology. Within about three days the medics and the engineers are gone again, and suddenly the year is at its prime – prime in the proper sense of beginning.

   1 October. Michaelmas Term begins.
            Vice-Chancellor enters upon office.

And then, on the sixth day of October: 'Full Term begins'.

'Full Term' means, as so often happens at Cambridge, the exact opposite of what the words would mean anywhere else (except at Oxford). 'Full' term is about three weeks shorter than 'term'. The dates marked 'Full Term' in the diary mark the beginning and end of that period of fifty-nine nights which an undergraduate normally 'keeps' in order to count that term of residence towards his degree. He needs nine of these periods of fifty-nine nights, or a total of some five hundred and thirty days spread over three years (or slightly less). The rest of the time consists of 'vacations', of which the summer vacation or 'the Long Vac.', is the longest – about four months on end. Vacations are not holidays. They are periods when the young are supposed to vacate Cambridge in order to work somewhere else, and in order to give their elders and betters time to get on with their own work, which is (contrary to undergraduate imaginings) nothing to do with teaching undergraduates.

On the whole, the young in these days don't like vacating Cambridge. They come up as early as they can and go down as late as they can. Crowded home conditions account for some of this clinging to Cambridge. Weary dons, gazing out of college windows, watch these perennial figures drifting across the courts, and mutter strange imprecations upon 'men who never seem to go down'. Residence in Cambridge outside the limits of full term requires tutorial permission, and tutors grant it reluctantly. There are, however, a certain number of good college reasons for permitting men to come up early. It gives overburdened tutors more time to interview their over-long lists of pupils before teaching gets into its stride. It also allows rowing men, and other athletic persons, extra and preliminary time to get their muscles into action. But, on the whole, the harassed don does not regard these academic daffodils, who come before the swallow dares, as taking the winds of March (or October) with beauty. To donnish ears there is always something ominous about the noise of the piping vanguard which declares its presence ahead of the main army in Trinity Street or the Cury towards the end of September or the first days of October.

"Hi, John, Good vac?"

"Not bad, Peter. And you?"

"A month in Spain. Portering at Liverpool Street ever since to pay for it."

"Tips good, I trust?"

"So-so. Where did you get to?"

"Skegness. Holiday camp. Waiting and washing-up."

"Poor old so-and-so. I trust you skinned them?"

"Not a hope. Three quid a week, all in."

"Get any work done?"

"Not a stroke. Did you?"

"Work? In Spain? *Mañana*, old boy."

"Be seeing you."

These, in the terminology of Mr. Stock, the Senior Tutor, are the 'daffs'. Mr. Stock watches for them from his window, or rather they impinge upon his inward eye as he hugs the departing bliss of solitude. He knows very well that within a few days he will meet them on his hearth-rug and pretend to be interested in their lamentable and un-intellectual vacation work. He also knows that he will not be able to blame them for their portering and waiting, since their fathers are railwaymen, clerks, civil servants and schoolmasters who can't be expected to keep hungry young men at home for sixteen weeks at a time without contribution to the family exchequer; and even if they could, Mr. Stock is prepared to admit, they shouldn't. He has held converse with these hard-working fathers of families at Degree Day garden-parties, and elsewhere, and he knows that even if they went down on their bended knees to their undergraduate offspring to accept free board and lodging at home throughout the Long Vacation, the said offspring would still go and get jobs.

It is, in part, these thoughts that make Mr. Stock the savage beast he knows himself to be at the beginning of the Michaelmas Term. But it is something more. It is a deep-seated and healthy hatred of young men. This hatred makes him the good tutor that everyone (except the said young men) knows him to be. It is the tremendous effort that he has to make, as each October comes round, to master this hatred, that keeps him on his toes. If he loved the young men he would be quite useless to them. Worse than useless. A positive menace. So, with infinite and diabolical care, he sets up a machine-gun at the top of his staircase, sighting it to cover the whole arc of approach to his door, and fixes a long trigger-string through the letter-box so that he can sit at his desk (with his back to the door) and pull it the moment he hears the first returning footstep on the stairs. The approaching undergraduate never sees this lethal apparatus. Nor does Mr. Stock ever move his finger to pull the string. He simply takes a firmer grip on his fountain-pen and goes on writing with invisible ink until the second knock on the door-panel, when he lets out a moaning roar.

"Come in."

For another five seconds, counted very slowly, he remains seated, and seemingly writing, after which he turns slowly in his chair, surveys the fresh but familiar face with slow-dawning recognition, and says:

"Hello, Peter. Come and sit you down. Had a good vac?"

"Splendid, sir. And you?"

"Dons don't have vacs . . ."

This is known in the college as 'a stock response'.

"Sherry?" says Mr. Stock.

"Oh, thank you, sir."

And this, Mr. Stock reflects as he pours out, this is the Peter Plummer who had called himself 'Mister Plummer' when he came up from Norwich as a freshman two years ago. Funny how the sons of the working-class hang on to their 'Misters', like the new dispensation in college servants. It takes several weeks, Mr. Stock has found, to get them to admit to their unadorned surnames. And now, this one answers to 'Peter' without turning a hair. Mr. Stock always calls them by Christian names in their third year. Peter is smiling, now, with well-mannered matiness over his sherry, quite a passable image of the third-year man who has fallen into the frank give-and-take of tutor and pupil relationship. It is, after all, rather nice to see his pleasant young phiz again.

Mr. Stock has long passed the age when the young don sighs: 'Cambridge would be quite a nice place if it were not for the under-graduates.' Nor is he sufficiently senile to sigh: 'Cambridge is the city of eternal youth – God bless 'em.' He knows that neither position is quite true. He is prepared to agree, as a minimum concession, that Cambridge would be an odd and barren place without them. A thousand times in every term crabbed middle-age wishes them away. But if, in some mute and unthinkable October, they failed to arrive, it would be like spring without the swallows or beef without mustard. Cambridge would be flat, stale and unprofitable, a sterile promontory.

Dons would be reduced to taking in each other's washing. They would die of progressive hardening of the intellectual arteries. The breed of dons would, in fact, dry up and die out. And, although in his more despondent moods Mr. Stock feels that he could face this prospect with equanimity he is on the whole in favour of the survival of the species to which he belongs. Whatever may be said against undergraduates, and Mr. Stock has said it all in his time with deadly hatred, they are a source of perennial refreshment to their elders and betters, if only because they compel their elders and betters to make themselves intelligible. Like most dons, Mr. Stock hates dons more than he hates undergraduates.

'The University is a body of over sixty-five thousand members, all but about seven thousand of whom are graduates.'

Occasionally, when confronted with some returning pupil whose smug young countenance positively exudes a misplaced conviction that the university has been sighing for his arrival ever since the beginning of the summer vacation, Mr. Stock takes up his copy of *The Student's Handbook* and reads aloud to him this, its opening, and (Mr. Stock hopes) chastening sentence. Nine times out of ten the smug face expresses a momentary incredulity. 'Where on earth,' it seems to say, 'are the other fifty-eight thousand?' Of course, Mr. Stock would never dream of attempting to throw light upon this perplexing problem. He gently steers the young man out of the room and leaves him to think it out for himself. Then, gazing out of the window at the roofs and spires and towers and turrets of the hive which is Cambridge, the answer to the young man's unspoken question dawns for the thousandth time upon his inward eye. Several hundred are doing the washing-up and frenziedly trying to write lectures in the sprawling donneries of Grange Road, Barton Road, Madingley Road and Storey's Way. Several hundred more are crouching in laboratories off Free School Lane or on the Downing site, watching bits of apparatus do odd things that undergraduates will never understand. A few score are in the University Library snatching the last crumbs of liberty in order to check up on references for the footnotes of the latest book. Hordes of them are sitting on Boards and Committees: Council of the Senate, General Board, Faculty Boards, College Councils, Tutorial Commit-

tees, Press Syndicate, and a dozen more fool-proof time-wasters. More
than sixty thousand non-resident members are well beyond sight and
sound of Alma Mater, ruling Church and State and what remains of
the Empire; running the armed services, the law courts, the hospitals
and the schools; prescribing medicines, reading briefs, writing sermons
in chilly rectories while their wives darn their socks. All these, and
many, many more, are 'the University'. The thing is as ubiquitous
as sin.

Mr. Stock turns from the window at a discreet knock on the door:
a freshman's knock.

"Come in," Mr. Stock howls mournfully.

For several seconds he keeps his back turned to the door, wondering
whether he can face it. For this, he knows, is the future of 'the
University'.

Mr. Stock faces it. The fresh young man smiles shyly.

"You are . . .?" begins Mr. Stock.

"Hughes-Browne, sir."

"Of course," he smiles. "I remember your father . . ."

The Old B and the Trog

Philip Hughes-Browne is wholly a product of the Home Counties,
and no trouble to anyone, least of all to examiners who will give him
an average second class whatever he does. He is what Mr. Stock calls
one of his penny-a-week men: a pupil who costs him exactly that
amount in terms of anxiety or effort as a tutor. Philip's male ancestors
on both sides have been coming up to the college for several centuries
as a vestibule to the Army, the Church and the Civil Service. He has
always known that he would be 'going up' in God's good time, just as
his uncle, the Bishop, has always known he will be going to heaven
by the same divine disposition. His college has been waiting for him
as naturally and uncontroversially as the stag-beetle's chrysalis awaits
the extended horn of the incipient larva. It is not that anyone ever
brought any influence to bear on his behalf. It is just that the name

Hughes-Browne belongs to the college as simply and unquestionably as the college flag or the college porter. No one minds Philip Hughes-Browne coming up, and anyone who does has not yet found a foolproof way of keeping him out. He has an adequate intelligence, nice manners, and hardly any money. His family have been recently impoverished (as they would call it) by one-sided social legislation (as they would call it), so that Hughes-Browne senior has had lately to resign from two of his five clubs, to give up one of his two cars, and to buy his suits off-the-peg. And Philip will benefit enormously from Cambridge, little though he may seem outwardly to take any particular notice of the place. For one thing, he will get to know what the Trogs are really like. He could have got to know this in the Army, if National Service hadn't been discontinued, for National Service in its time practically solved the problem of 'the Two Nations'. The Trogs, to Philip Hughes-Browne and his kind, are the Grammar School boys, and anything lower that may raise its ugly head above the anonymity of democracy.

There was a Trog in the train, coming up from Town. Half a dozen Old Balmorallians, Philip among the rest, had crowded into the compartment, sticking together as Old Balmorallians always do stick together. And there was this Trog, hunched up in a corner, eating sausage-rolls out of a paper-bag. When he had finished, the Trog threw the bag out of the window and started to smoke a very new pipe filled with very foul tobacco. You could tell he was a Trog not only by these troglodytic habits, but by the way he grinned at the Old B's, as if he expected them to speak to him, to share the fascinating experience of going up to Cambridge. They didn't take the least notice of him, except to cough at his tobacco-smoke and open the windows so wide that he had to put his collar up. Philip had insisted on drawing up the window half-way after this. He even apologized to the Trog for the lack of consideration shown by his friends, although he didn't put it like that. The Trog grinned again, said it didn't matter, and what college was he going to? Philip told him.

"So am I," said the Trog, and held out his hand.

Philip shook it briefly and was glad to observe that the other five Old B's were one and all resolutely hidden from sight by their widely extended copies of *The Times*, the *Telegraph*, and the *Mail*. At Cambridge, the Trog got out first, mainly because the Old B's waited for him to go. In any case, they did not care to exhibit any undue haste in descending at so familiar a destination. Thereafter, they shared a couple of taxis, peeling off at various colleges without the slightest interest in possible reunions. The Trog, Philip noticed, had waited for a bus.

When a young man like Philip Hughes-Browne sets foot over the threshold of his ancestral college, it might be expected that porters would flock to his side with bare heads and eager hands. Not a bit of it. A college is a republic where all men, especially freshmen, are equal in the sight of the head porter. So the magnificent Alfred merely takes a long appraising look at young Mr. Hughes-Browne, pushes his bowler-hat to the back of his head, and points a thick finger at the open page of the Redit book.

"Just sign your name here, sir, if *you* please," he says. "Father quite well, I hope? We've put you in his old rooms at B.5, Old Court. Only one room in these days, sir, I'm afraid. The days of sets is past, you'll understand. But you'll find it quite a nice place, all the same."

"Any chance of Old Joe to look after me?" Mr. Hughes-Browne inquires.

Old Joe was his father's gyp, and young Mr. Hughes-Browne has heard all about his faithful services for as long as he can remember.

" 'Fraid not, sir. Old Joe passed away at midsummer." (College servants, like parents, never die, they only 'pass away'). "But you'll find Mr. Swetman is willing. Not like Old Joe, of course. They don't train 'em up like Old Joe in these days, sir, what with this here full employment. . . . There'll be a barrow for your trunk, sir, if you can hang on a minute. . . ." Then, his gaze travelling over young Mr. Hughes-Browne's shoulder: "And you, sir? What name?"

"Evans, Daffyd Evans."

Mr. Hughes-Browne finds the face of the Trog just behind him. He steps aside, and out of the lodge, while the head porter continues his ritual chant: "Just sign your name here, sir, if you please . . . You'll be at B.6, Old Court . . . There'll be a barrow. . ."

Mr. Hughes-Browne decides against waiting for the barrow, and picks up his trunk with a strong-armed pretence that he could carry a hundredweight-and-a-half for a mile without so much as lowering a shoulder.

"Here, let me give you a hand," The Trog is beside him, reaching out for a handle. "We're going the same way, and I've only got a grip."

The sheer generous strength of the lift at the other end of the trunk defeats all resistance.

"Thanks very much. Absurd that one can't drive a taxi through these college entrances."

"Indeed, no. A place like this was built before anyone thought about motor-cars, thank goodness."

The lilt of the fellow's voice lifts the sentiment above sententiousness. Philip Hughes-Browne looks across the barrier of the cabin-trunk, with the bulging grip perched thereon, and thinks he likes the chap. He is smiling beatifically at the opening vista of Great Court as if his feet are set upon the summit of Mount Pisgah. The sight of his joyful countenance, long, thin, dark, with bushy brows and a stand-up double quiff of black hair, lights a little spark of enjoyment in the bosom of the Old Balmorallian.

"I tell you, man, this is a great moment in my life. Do you not feel your heart knocking at your seated ribs at this moment?"

"I can't say that I do," lies the old B. "I say, take it easy."

They set down the trunk at the entrance to B. staircase and take a breather before ascending the stairs. Daffyd Evans still smiles ecstatically, his face turned to the vast perspectives of rose-red Tudor bricks, the grey-green cobbled ranges of the courtyard, the four green rectangles of close-shaven grass, the domed and pinnacled fountain making music in the midst, all under the high, pale Cambridge sky of an October afternoon.

"Indeed," says the Welsh Trog, "this is a beautiful world we have come to."

Oh dear, thinks the English gentleman, have I got to live next door to this? But all he says, when they have humped their goods up the deeply-hollowed stone stairs and deposited them on the little landing space which separates the doors leading into B.5 and B.6, is:

"See you in hall, I expect."

They do not see each other in hall. Daffyd Evans dines alone, eyeing his neighbours (all of whom seem to have known each other from birth, with their Charles this and Roger that and Peter the other) with quiet and amiable interest. For all the scope afforded by dinner in hall for his prolific Welsh powers of conversation, he might as well have dined alone in his room. He sees his neighbour of B.5 at an adjoining table, deep in unanimated conversation with a company of Charles's, Rogers and Peters. He does not catch his eye, nor does he try to. Not until the following evening, towards midnight, do the near neighbours meet again. The initiative is taken by the Old B.

"Come and have some beer," he proposes, putting his head round the door of B.6, where Daffyd Evans is discovered, sprawling in a basket-chair, reading a Penguin, with a bottle of pale ale at his elbow.

"Have some of mine," Daffyd Evans suggests.

Philip accepts reluctantly: not that he would evade the chap's company, but he has felt for the past twenty-four hours that he owes his neighbour several drinks for his help with the trunk. Daffyd seems to have forgotten this. He produces several bottles and two clean glasses, offers his tobacco-pouch, and fixes a second basket-chair by the roaring gas-fire.

"Sorry I've neglected you up to now," Philip apologizes, nodding a greeting over his glass. "So many people to see, you know. Old B's all over the place. . . . Many of *your* crowd up?"

"I," says Daffyd proudly, "I am the first from Llantovery Grammar School ever to put in an appearance at Cambridge."

"Good for you." He doesn't like to enquire whether Daffyd Evans won a scholarship; and anyway, he feels sure he will be told about this quite soon. "What are you reading?"

Daffyd picks up the discarded Penguin: *Swann's Way*, by Marcel Proust.

"Good God," says Philip. "A bit highbrow!"

"You think so? If I were, I'd be reading it in French. My subject is English. My French is shocking."

"So is mine. English, too. I'm reading History. Anyone can get through in History, I'm told. I hope it's true. I wanted to read English, but they wouldn't let me, at school. They say it isn't really a subject. Comes natural, and all that."

"I know exactly what they mean," Daffyd nods wisely. "But it's different for me. You see, I'm not English. I didn't know a word of English until I was fifteen. English, to me, is a foreign language."

"You're a Welshman? The Welsh believe in education, don't they?"

"We do, indeed. Don't you?"

"Not particularly."

"You have the advantages of a conquering race. In Wales we prize these things because we have had to fight for them."

"That sounds a bit solemn. I say, how do you like this place, now you are here?"

"There again, I like it all very much, probably more than you do, and for the same reason."

"You mean – because you've had to fight for it?"

Daffyd nods, unashamed of his solemnity.

"D'you know, this is the first time I've had a room of my own, somewhere that I can read, or write, or just fool around. You wouldn't understand what this means. I dare say the whole set-up is just another stage of what you've been used to, at home, and at school. . . . Ah, you public school chaps are beastly unlucky, after all. Cambridge can never mean to you what it means to chaps like me."

"All the same," Philip protests, "we manage to bear up."

They both laugh then, and Daffyd offers something like an apology.

"I dare say I shall get used to it," he says. "Forgive me if I seem superior, and all that. Inverted snobbery, you know."

There is only one thing that Daffyd Evans declares that he will never get used to. Mr. Swetman.

"Oh, Swetman's all right," says Philip loftily. "Not as good as Old Joe, who gypped my father. But he's willing."

It appears that 'Mr. Swetman' had come in before Daffyd Evans was awake, on that first morning, and walked off with his clothes and his shoes. Daffyd, awakened just as he was leaving the room, had leapt out of bed and collared him.

"I thought it was one of those undergraduate jokes that one reads about in novels. I was half-expecting to have practical jokes played on me, as a freshman."

"Oh, no," Philip protests. "We don't have that kind of thing at Cambridge."

Anyway, it had been appalling to have to listen to 'Mr. Swetman's' apologetic explanations.

"Just as if he was to blame rather than me," Daffyd groaned. "And the man expects me to call him Swetman, just like that. Why, he's old enough to be my father. He *is* my father, if you gather what I mean. My father is a railway porter. He talks like Mr. Swetman, and thinks like him, and wears the same kind of clothes, and everything, God bless him. I'm damned if I'll call him Swetman."

"He'll be mortally offended if you don't. Only the servants call each other 'Mister'."

"But why should he wait on me, and call me 'sir', and touch his hat every time I look at him? It's disgusting."

"Bear up, Daffyd. You'll get used to it."

"Never."

They are destined to sit up into the small hours over their analysis of social relationships. Philip Hughes-Browne finds himself defending the principle of the division of labour, the validity of master-servant relationships in terms of forms of address, the priority of intellectual over manual labour. . . . Daffyd Evans finds himself expounding the Socialism of the South Wales coal-field. . . . They both learn a great deal, thus vindicating the great tutorial alibi: 'We don't educate them. They educate each other.' More important still, they become friends.

The College Dines

Surveying the ranks of undergraduates at dinner in Hall on the first night of full term, Mr. Stock, the Senior Tutor says to himself, with a purr of satisfaction: "Ah, it's beginning . . ." by 'it' he means that process of mutual education of the young by the young which is the acknowledged salvation of donnery.

D

High Table, where the dons dine, is in nearly every Cambridge college set on a dais some six inches above the general floor level of the Hall. Colleges being descended from late medieval, or Tudor, manor-houses in their domestic architecture, High Table on its dais represents the pre-eminence of lordship. Here Master and Fellows dine within sight of the ranks of lesser men. It enables lesser men to see, if they care to take note, who their masters are. It also allows Masters to keep a watchful eye on their men. Not that they betray any sign of interest in the gobbling, chattering rank and file of the underworld, at least in well-conducted colleges. Half of them sit with their backs to the *hoi polloi* anyway, although it is sometimes to be observed that the tutors sit with their faces turned to the general throng, and even (where tutorship is taken with professional, not to say obsessional, zeal) side by side. But it is the business of the undergraduates themselves to take care of decorum at the undergraduate tables. Some colleges have a president of the undergraduate tables, generally the President of the College Amalgamated Clubs. How great is his authority, or his power to exercise it, varies from college to college. There are colleges (generally the oldest and least self-conscious in their manners and customs) where the undergraduates drift in and take their food and drift out again with the easy casualness of guests at a family hotel. They even take short-cuts by walking over the tables. There are others where 'the unwritten rules of Hall' require the undergraduates to be assembled before the dons arrive, and to remain seated until the president of the undergraduate tables decides to make a move. There is at least one college where the president has traditional authority to 'sconce' a late-arriving undergraduate. This involves ordering a 'sconce-cup' containing several pints of ale, which the offender must drink without setting down the cup. If he fails, he must pass it round the table – and pay for it. This barbarous custom is thought to descend from our rude fore-fathers of Saxon times.

Grace is read, in Latin, either by a Fellow or by the senior scholar among the undergradates. Where the undergraduates say Grace, accord-ing to a rota, a good deal of betting goes on at the lower tables on the time it will take the grace-reader of the evening to get through it. Readers have been known to indulge in 'pulling', in order to oblige punters among their friends. There is also a certain amount of mumbled comment, applausive or otherwise, on the reader's Latin quantities, although this is in fact dying out with the decline of Latinity. Hissing a grace-reader's performance is indulged in only by intellectual Trogs. On the whole, better sport is to be had from betting on the appearance, or the non-appearance, of certain members of the High Table. Since, in most colleges, the dons enter Hall in procession through the door of the Senior Combination Room behind their dais, this form of betting has a certain dramatic value. Many a don, arriving in Hall after an absence of several nights, has been surprised, and flattered, to detect a murmur of applause (or dismay) at his entry. The spoil-sport in this form of punting is the Master of the college who elects to dine on certain pre-arranged nights. A good Master dines according to no set pattern. This not only encourages the sport. It enables him to meet a more varied selection of diners. This is the good Master's chief concern, and it meets with much wider approval than he knows.

Dinner in Hall is the ancient symbol of collegiate life. It is descended from the monastic ideal of community living. It is the one time of day when everyone (ideally, at least) sees everyone else. Dons and undergraduates whose day-long avocations in labs and libraries and lecture-rooms keep them far apart from each other, now assemble beneath one roof and (ideally, again) warm each other's minds and souls by communion at the common meal. So tenacious is this idea, or ideal, of community living, that some colleges for long cherished the hope of keeping their numbers limited to the capacity of the dining-hall, so that all might sit down together. In fact, however, two successive sessions are the general rule. College halls were built to house small societies. Nowadays, even a middle-sized college has a population of about three hundred and fifty. There is always a certain number of undergraduates who secure permission of their tutors to 'contract-out', the vegetarian, the dyspeptic, the occasional married man, the dweller in digs two or three miles away from Cambridge. There is also the solitary bird who secretly believes that he can find a better and cheaper worm at café or restaurant in the purlieus of the town. Tutors are always reluctant to appease these characters. Imbued to the core of their being with the cult of 'The College' as the essence of a Cambridge education (for, after all, the cobbler will always swear there is nothing like leather), they dream of the distant day when there will be a place for every undergraduate within the college domus, and town digs, more especially 'out-of-town' digs, will be a thing of the past.

A college at dinner (even if, as in these days, it is only half the college) must be an inspiring spectacle. Few people, however, have ever seen it. Those who are intimately involved, like those who fight in a battle, can scarcely be aware of more than the small group of their nearest neighbours. They are much too deeply engaged in the hurly-burly to enjoy a view of the thing as a whole. This applies equally to the persons whom the late Sir Henry Newbolt rather unwisely called 'the dons on the dais serene', for the average don is almost entirely pre-occupied in lip-reading the high intellectual utterances of the don opposite, against the uproar and clatter from the undergraduate tables, or thinking of suitably high intellectual utterances in reply. The butler and his staff of waiters who spend the whole time on foot, and the dead dignitaries whose more or less distinguished faces look down from the portraits on the walls, are the only eyes ever to see a college at dinner in a single *coup d'œil*. What they think of the spectacle they either will not, or cannot, say. Only a speechless member of the High Table, despairing of making himself heard above the din, and prepared to risk the charge of being thought unsociable, would be in a position to get some idea of it. As for the freshman undergraduate, he is likely to feel a little overwhelmed. He finds himself an insignificant item in the multitudinous ranks of young men, all looking a great deal older, more experienced, more sophisticated, than himself; people upon whom he must, for good or ill, try to model himself, even though he is at present quite resolved to remain different in his inmost being. He sees a good deal of nourishing, if not particularly interesting, food and drink, which appears and vanishes from under his nose with remarkable speed. He sees a double row of tufted heads at High Table, a little above and apart from the throng; heads and faces as yet unfamiliar, yet assumed for the nonce to be the heads and faces of distinguished men, and there-fore, he assumes (rightly), eating more distinguished food. He will learn more about them quite soon. He will learn that they are the Fellows as distinct from the Chaps, and that the justification for their superior diet is hard to seek. He may wonder – or perhaps he will not – about the faces in the oil-paintings on the walls. They, he will suppose, are 'history', as is the well-scrubbed table before him, the hollowed stone floor beneath his feet, the black-beamed rafters above his head. History, indeed, is in the air. You can smell it in stone and timber and the ghosts of ten thousand departed meals.

All this is very good for him, since it will gradually sink into his consciousness, if he possesses the slightest sensibility of heart and mind (and at nineteen one possesses a good deal), that he now belongs to something bigger and older and more inspiring than himself; something that he did not make, and yet something in which he has a share; something that has been going on for many generations before he came here, and that will go on for many generations after he has departed hence; something that may be said to resemble Denis Diderot's concept of living nature: *un ordre momentané*. This, at any rate, is among the things that Mr. Stock, the Senior Tutor, likes to think is 'beginning' among the ranks of fresh young faces down there, as he sits at High Table at the opening of the new term. He doesn't think about it at all consciously. His immediate concern is to try to remember which name goes with which face, for, although Mr. Stock has often been heard in Senior Combination room to declare that all undergraduates are exactly alike, he would resign his Fellowship on the spot if he ever gave the wrong name to a single face among his ninety-seven pupils. Dining at High Table, at a point of vantage above the throng, affords a tutor the best possible practice in face-and-name spotting, and guests who imagine that a tutor is not really attending to their conversation as closely as they could wish would do well to remember this. Nor is Mr. Stock wholly concerned with names-and-faces. He also likes to observe who is making friends with whom. He hates to see a freshman sitting lonely and forlorn, trifling with his food, with downcast eyes or circumambient glances, rising up alone as he sat down, to return in solitude to his rooms.

So I sit down to dinner in the Hall in silence, except for the noise of suction which accompanies my eating, and rise up ditto . . .

That was the account given of his first session in Hall by that voluble young freshman, Coleridge of Jesus, in the Michaelmas Term of 1791. So it might have been the account of the young Daffyd Evans, the freshman from Llantovery in the Michaelmas Term of 1959. But no. Mr. Stock is gratified to observe the man from Llantovery deep in vivacious talk with a young man from New Zealand. Trust a Welsh-man, Mr. Stock reflects, and would very much like to know what he is talking about.

Silas Stock thinks he can generally tell when his pupils are talking about him. There is something about the way they put their heads together over the roast beef and spinach or the gooseberry tart. . . . Young Mr. Evans and the New Zealander (whose name Silas Stock is racking his memory to recall) are not doing that kind of thing. Of this he feels sure. But, a little farther down the table, he can see Peter Plummer, the newly-fledged third year man, smiling coolly in his direction as a second-year Moral Philosopher, whose name always eludes him (perhaps because he despises Tompion, the college Philo-sophy don and discourages his pupils from reading the subject) whispers in his ear.

What Silas Stock does not hear is this:

"I was drinking your sherry this morning, Peter."

"How come? I haven't seen you all day."

"Silas thought I was you."

"Impossible. . . . Oh well, I dare say I shall be drinking yours when I go to see him to-morrow."

"Think he'll remember he's seen you already?"

"I doubt it."

"Don't tell him, anyway."

"I won't. When you get to old Silas's age, anything might happen."

For dons, and more especially tutors, are ancient men by definition. They have been losing the full use of their faculties for years. It is, taking all things into consideration, remarkable that they do as well as they do.

The conversation continues:

"How much do you suppose old Silas gets p.a. for his tutoring?"

"God knows. According to my college bill, someone gets £15 per term tuition fee."

"That's not Silas. That's your supervisor. Silas gets a stipend as a tutor. Say £1,200 p.a."

"He gets a Fellowship dividend, too. Say another £350."

"And he supervises about fifty hours a week. That's another £500 at least."

"About £2,000 p.a. all told?"

"Don't forget perks. Free dinners, free rooms, heating service, and all that."

"One way and another, round about £2,500. . . . I say, how does one get in on this racket?"

"Work hard, laddy, and you'll learn."

"Oh, but think of having to face Peter and John and me. . . . Several times a term. . . . I wouldn't take it if it was offered."

"It won't be, laddy, never fear."

Undergraduate financial estimates are notoriously unsound. Where dons' pay is concerned, they are fantastic. Only one thing is certain. No don is ever overpaid.

The conversation concludes:

"What do you suppose dons do when we're not here?"

"When we're not here they don't exist. Like that tree in the quad when no one is looking at it."

"Pray remember, laddy, that the tree still exists in the mind of God."

"You're not trying to suggest that dons exist in the mind of God?"

"Why not? God must be used to some pretty rum things existing in His mind."

"Not as rum as all that, I'd say. . . ."

For dons are undoubtedly rum. They think so themselves. At least, every don thinks every other don is rum. He knows that he should never have been a don himself, that he is really a fish out of water, a novelist *manqué*, a Marshall Hall who didn't quite make it, a Harley Street specialist who was too honest to be a quack, a big business man who was not quite vulgar enough for big business. In his heart of hearts he knows that Bernard Shaw was right: 'Those who can, do. Those who can't, teach.' This knowledge makes him a neurotic, for all dons are neurotic, though some dons are more neurotic than others. It also makes him a good don. It imparts just that flavour of sour grapes which gives an edge to his mind. The young benefit enormously from regular contact with that edge. Only the don who tries to inspire his pupils – the don with disciples – is really dangerous.

Footnote to a conversation:

"What I find most beastly about dons is their incredible self-esteem. Anyone would think the university belonged to them."

"It does. Before God was, I am. If you read Moral Philosophy you'd soon discover that Nietzsche was right."

"I prefer Berkeley. I still think they only exist when I'm looking at them."

This is the kind of conversation for which Cambridge has been waiting all the summer. People often imagine, from reading novels by dons' wives about university life, that such conversation goes on only between those tufted heads gobbling at High Table, or round the fire in Senior Combination Room. Some people also wonder why dons dine on a dais, and at a distance of some ten feet from the nearest undergraduate table. At this very moment, Dr. Skinner, the second tutor, is saying to his friend and ally, the bursar: "Must we always stick to gilt-edged? What's wrong with equities, anyway?" and the bursar is trying to think of a sentence he read in the *Financial Times* that morning as a suitable retort to amateur stock-jobbers like the second tutor.

'They are in the right, sir,' said Dr. Johnson, when he was told that dons at Oxford excluded undergraduates from their company, 'for there can be no real conversation, no fair exertion of mind amongst them, if the young men are by; for a man who has a character does not choose to stake it in their presence.'

Freshmen

Michaelmas Term is the freshmen's term, when Cambridge is alive with newcomers trying to look like oldest inhabitants. The freshness of freshmen is betrayed, however, by certain unmistakable characteristics. For one thing, freshmen wear their gowns in public places on all possible occasions. Mostly they wear them rakishly, off the shoulder, or low-slung from crooked elbows. Trailing their coats, one might say. University regulations require a gown to be worn by all persons *in statu pupillari* (which means everyone below the standing of Master of Arts) in the town after dusk, and at all times to academic appointments, such as calling upon those in authority (tutors, directors of studies, supervisors, etc.), and when attending lectures (though not in laboratories), libraries, chapel, and so on.[1] The ancient cap, or 'square' (known elsewhere than in Cambridge as a 'mortar-board') went out of obligatory use during the Second World War, when it became almost as rare as a fresh egg. An attempt to revive it as a compulsory part of undergraduate academic dress, after the war, met with failure, much to the regret of certain gentlemen's outfitters and a large number of maiden aunts of both sexes; although a photographer will generally supply one for the occasion if the sitter insists on it.

In some ways, the disappearance of the 'square' is a matter for genuine regret. That ancient black skull-cap, surmounted by its black square and short tassel, had important ceremonial uses. It gave the young man something to doff when he met his superiors. It had other uses, too. It made a useful begging-bowl on Poppy Day. It afforded endless opportunities for sartorial inventiveness. The corners could be turned up to meet at a point, when it become a reminder of its historic kinship with the biretta. They could also be turned down to form ear-flaps. Collapsible squares (i.e. with the cardboard removed from the skull-cap) could be skimmed up at windows. Foldable squares (i.e. with the cardboard of the square itself cracked down the middle) could be stuffed into pockets and used as a cosh on suitable occasions. The thing could even be used as a form of head-wear in wet weather. Its disappearance has helped the umbrella trade, and fashion too, for it is strictly forbidden to wear any other form of headgear with a gown, although women undergraduates are permitted to wear scarves or hoods.

The really fresh freshman buys his gown from a tailor, or 'university outfitter'. The knowing ones buy them from college porters who inherit cast-offs. Some undergraduates, on going down with a bachelor's

[1] There is a proctorial fine for failing to do so. *See* note on p. 101.

gown, see fit to reward faithful service at the porters' lodge with a parting gift which can be sold at a profit. Not any old gown will do, however, for different colleges have their own models in slightly distinctive styles: different buttons, or braided strips at the arm-holes, or even different colours within the range of black and blue. Occasionally a college will make a dead set at its undergraduates' habit of wearing gowns acquired from members of other colleges. Donnish appeals are made to that celebrated 'college spirit' which, it is hoped, should preserve the undergraduate against willing contamination from 'foreign' gowns and quicken his pride in wearing the traditional dress of his college. For a short time, the undergraduate resumes something like the standard black cord (closely resembling 'black-out material') of his clan. No one and nothing, however, is capable of making more than a transient impression on the undergraduate's indifference to the glory of a uniform. So long as he has what he (accurately) calls a 'rag' to cover his academic nakedness, and to pass the proctors, he couldn't care less, once he has got over his freshman's pride. Then, indeed, it becomes a matter of pride to wear a genuine 'rag', something that will only just survive scrutiny by those in authority over him. Like freshman jokes about alcoholic dons and the running water in Trumpington Street, the tattered gown belongs to immemorial tradition.

The Master of Jesus: When will you leave off wearing that disgraceful gown, Mr. Coleridge?

Mr. Coleridge: Why sir, I believe I have left off the greater part of it already.

Another symptom of freshmanship is the bearing of parcels. It takes a little time to discover that shopkeepers are ready, and even willing, to deliver goods, and that they are permitted to allow credit up to £20. However, most things that a freshman needs can be bought at Woolworth's or Marks and Spencer's, and so one sees youthful figures staggering through college gateways with bulky and oddly-shaped parcels containing kettles, lamp-shades, coat-hangers, pictures, coffee-making apparatus, cups and jugs and stationery. The days when the freshman brought with him a crate of china and kitchenware, a canteen of cutlery, and a vast array of cooking utensils, not to mention his blankets and curtains, have long passed away. Mother's headaches over her freshman son's domestic furnishings are relieved by the regulations, which apply in most colleges, forbidding cooking in undergraduate rooms (beyond the boiling of an egg and the brewing of beverages), and by the provision in most colleges of decently standardized furniture, blankets and curtains. But, of course, there are still many things that the young man setting up house in college finds indispensable, things that he prefers to acquire for himself if only to display some evidence of his personal tastes. He will take all his meals, except tea and after-dinner drinks, in hall, if he lives in college during his first year. And colleges are increasingly anxious to put freshmen into college rooms for a year in the interests of sociability and the early acquisition of the cherished 'college spirit'. The lonely freshman living in digs at the far end of Mill Road, or in the distant purlieus of Cherry Hinton or Chesterton, is far rarer than he once was. The fact that some under-graduates prefer the bliss of solitude is resolutely ignored by those who arrange these matters. They ought not to prefer it. There is a premium, in these days, on the Edward Fitzgeralds.

Another symptom of freshmanship is lighted windows. It takes the average freshman several days to get used to the idea that he can stay out until midnight, if he cares to, without anyone asking him why or where. College gates are mostly closed at eleven. Only after that hour, if at all, are gate-fines imposed. 'Keeping an eleven' is, generally speaking, financially worthwhile. Seven sixpenny fines a week come to a pound a term, and will also involve tutorial enquiry. 'Keeping a twelve' is essential, unless one has a late-leave. Failure here will normally mean a ten-shilling fine and certain words with the Dean. The rule is not unreasonable, since tutors stand *in loco parentis*, and if they are to be responsible for the young men under their charge it is fair enough that they should know what the young men are up to. Putting the thing at its purely utilitarian level, the tutor will have to certify, sooner or later, that the young man has 'kept' his fifty-nine nights to qualify for his degree by residence. But it takes the freshman a little time to get used to these things, and mostly he will tend to keep rather nervously on the safe side of the law at first.

Anyway, new friends are gathering around. To sit in each other's rooms after hall, dispensing or accepting coffee or beer, may still be a novelty. Nearly everything that a freshman learns, in his earliest days, he learns from the endless talk that goes on in college bed-sitters after hall or from the casual gossip that goes on in the Junior Combination Room, or the Junior Parlour, or whatsoever the college provides by way of a meeting-place for its undergraduate members. The J.C.R. or J.P. is not, as a rule, a 'club-room', replete with piano and billiard-table. Rather it is a lounge, replete with armchairs and newspapers. It may have a bar – a hole in the wall which appears for about two hours before hall and vanishes behind a shutter thereafter. People drift in and out at all hours, but mainly in the half-hour before or after a meal in hall, or when coming in to collect mail from the letter-racks in the vestibule. Here it is that the 'Amal. Clubs' hold their sessions at intervals throughout term: a shorthand expression for 'The College Amalgamated Clubs'. Everyone of junior status belongs to the Amal. Club by virtue of the membership fee which is included in one's terminal college bill and entitling one to membership of all college clubs, sporting or otherwise, without further subscription.[1] Possibly, but improbably, the president of the Amal. Club will hand out advice to freshmen at a special meeting at the beginning of Michaelmas Term. Possibly, and less improbably, the Master or one of the tutors will call the newcomers together for a similar purpose. Most of what is said, and in some particulars a good deal more, could equally well be gleaned from certain small, cheap publications on sale at the bookshops, notably the excellent *Varsity Handbook*, published annually by the proprietors of the undergraduate weekly. *Varsity* itself comes out on Saturdays. The newly-fledged undergraduate, buying his first *Varsity* on his first Saturday morning in Cambridge, feels that he has at last got hold of something that belongs to him, and to him alone. The simple truth is that the freshman learns his Cambridge as D. H. Lawrence recommended men and women to learn life itself – by 'proving it on the pulses'.

Silas Stock, the Senior Tutor, with his notoriously ambivalent attitude to the young, has his own ideas.

---

[1] There is generally a small additional fee for membership of the Boat Club, for rowing is an expensive pastime in terms of equipment.

"Chuck 'em in," he says. "They'll either sink or swim. It wouldn't be any great loss to the college if quite a few of them sank."

Silas Stock generally says this kind of thing in the presence of the second tutor, Dr. Skinner, who is a great believer in formal instruction. This, however, is only one of Dr. Skinner's undesirable characteristics in the eyes of the Senior Tutor. Another, to which Silas Stock refers several times a day, is Dr. Skinner's predilection for 'filling up the college with second-rate scientists'. Everyone knows, as Silas Stock never hesitates to point out, that a First Class can be gained in the Natural Sciences more easily than in anything else. That, he insists, is why Alan Skinner does it. Alan Skinner admits it. He is perfectly open about his fanatical devotion to what he calls 'the good of the college'. His contempt for the cheerful cynicism of the Senior Tutor, a classical scholar whose long term of tutorial duties has (he maintains) precluded him from reaching the heights of classical scholarship, is both profound and thinly disguised. He believes that the Senior Tutor should have retired long since in order to make way for an efficient successor. In any case, he holds, it is the plain duty of the Senior Tutor in what he calls 'these competitive times' to imbue the young, and more especially the freshman, with an ardent college spirit. At the opening of each Michaelmas Term, Dr. Skinner tries to goad the Senior Tutor into addressing the freshmen on the glories of the college and the vital necessity for every man Jack of them to get either a First or a Blue. 'To get *us* a First or a Blue . . .' is the way he puts it. It is Mr. Stock's private opinion that before very long Dr. Skinner will post a large portrait of himself on the college gates with the inscription: LET ME BE YOUR TUTOR, followed by a statistical table of RESULTS in terms of FIRSTS and BLUES for the past ten years.

"Someone's got to do it," Alan Skinner remarks as he leaves the Senior Combination Room after dinner on the first night of term. "I really don't know why it should always be me."

"The answer is simple, my dear Alan," says Silas Stock, sipping his second glass of port. "It is, as everyone knows, because you have the interests of the college at heart. God be with you, my dear fellow."

Dr. Skinner glances at his wrist-watch, wraps his Doctor's gown about his shoulders, and opens the door leading into hall. A loud hum of undergraduate chatter is audible for a moment. Then it is cut off. There is a profound silence. Presently, the voice of the second tutor is heard distantly as he enters upon his annual harangue.

"Oh dear," sighs Mr. Stock. "I do hope they will benefit."

A little after ten o'clock, when Dr. Skinner's initiatory address is over, two or three of his hearers are to be found crouching behind locked doors at the top of K. Staircase. These are, for the most part, genuine backwoodsmen from Bokhara, 'Bwango-'bwango, or Bootle, regions where Dean Farrar and Talbot Baines Reed are still held in reverence.

"I know these English boys," says Mr. Shalimar, a Hindu gentleman. "They play tricks. They are full of good feeling. But one should be prepared for them."

"What kind of tricks?" enquires a gentleman from Africa who is already known as 'Albert' because his name sounds like that, "I would like to know, please."

Mr. Zogropolous, from the neighbourhood of Athens, points to a revolver which he has placed in the middle of the table. It is in Mr. Zogropolous' rooms that they are met for safety, and Mr. Zogropolous' excessive preparations to meet invasion have already created a disposition to take the situation light-heartedly in the bosoms of his companions. Mr. Zogropolous contents himself with pointing to the revolver. He speaks little at any time. This is mainly because he knows little English. If he knew Latin, which he doesn't (being a Greek), he would doubtless have had the maxim *ultima ratio* engraved about the muzzle of his revolver.

"None of that, chum," says little Mr. Thwaites, the red-headed freshman from Lancashire who finds himself a member of this miniature league of nations mainly because his rooms are on the same staircase, but who is enjoying himself enormously because he feels that the university is fulfilling the predictions of his form-master who taught him to expect to consort there with all sorts and conditions of men as brothers. "Some of us have seen enough of fire-arms in the Forces. . . . By the way, is the blasted thing loaded?"

"Yes," says Mr. Zogropolous. "I do not play games of bluff."

Albert from Africa rolls his eyes. Their whites look like the whites of a couple of fried eggs. Mr. Shalimar's tiny black pupils almost disappear among rolls of coffee-coloured fat. Mr. Thwaites takes action. He breaks the gun, empties the cartridges into the palm of his hand, and drops them into his pocket.

"Ought to be blasted well ashamed of yourself," he tells Mr. Zogropolous, tossing the empty revolver on to the bed. "Where do you think you are? Cyprus?"

"Do you seek to offend me?" Mr. Zogropolous enquires.

"Not in the least," Mr. Thwaites assures him. "I'm protecting you. If the Stinker knew about this, he'd have you sent down on the spot. And blasted well serve you right."

"You refer to Dr. Skinner?"

"Stinker, to his friends."

"He is no friend of mine. My tutor is Mr. Stock. I like Mr. Stock. He spoke to me in modern Greek when I went to see him. It was so bad that I apologized to him. I thought he was reprimanding me, whereas he was kindly enquiring after the state of my health."

This is a long speech for Mr. Zogropolous, and when it is over he sinks into sulky silence for the remainder of the evening. Mr. Shalimar, however, is beaming with satisfaction. He beams with special satisfaction upon little Thwaites, whom he will describe for the rest of his life as 'the bravest English boy I have ever known, the English boy who disarmed a Greek bandit with his bare hands . . .' He is sure that Mr. Thwaites is not only as brave as a lion, but an academic genius.

"You are a Scholar of the college, yes?" he asks Mr. Thwaites. "Oh yes, I know you are modest. But one can see that you have a brilliant future before you."

"Balls," says Mr. Thwaites. "Don't talk such blasted rot. . . . And, by the way, how did *you* get in?"

"I took a taxi from the station."

"Simply told the chap to drive to the nearest college, I suppose?"

"The *best* college," Mr. Shalimar corrects him, beaming fit to burst. "Not too big, I told him. A nice middle-sized college where one may make friends."

"That's one way of doing it," says Mr. Thwaites. "Never thought of it, myself."

Mr. Shalimar's account of his admission is true. The college of his choice – or rather of the taxi-driver's choice – having been built directly opposite one of the best hotels in Cambridge – at least, that is how the disrespectful put it – Mr. Shalimar had put up there for the night and proceeded to lay siege to the college next day. The junior tutor, to whose presence he secured admission by going into the first staircase he came to and knocking on the first door, was about to depart for the United States on a term's leave of absence (after his habit in alternate years). He entertained Mr. Shalimar to sherry, listened sympathetically to his eulogy of the college and his enthusiastic preference for the Law tripos (which was the junior tutor's tripos), and dismissed him with vague promises. Two days later, the chief clerk of the tutorial office rang up the junior tutor to enquire what to do about the tentative applicants at the tail of the junior tutor's admissions list.

"Admit the lot," the junior tutor ordered.

An hour later he was on his way to London air-port, and Mr. Shalimar, along with some half dozen other young gentlemen, found themselves 'in', much to their joyful amazement.

Of course, this story took some swallowing on the part of those whose admissions had been negotiated by mountainous labours extending over two or three years. No one lived to regret its outcome, however, for Mr. Shalimar was to take a respectable second class in both parts of the Law tripos, Mr. Thwaites was to become cox of the college first boat, Albert of Africa was to prove a tower of strength to the college table-tennis team, while Mr. Zogropolous was to surprise everyone by getting a third class in Geography. Only the Senior Tutor, at the time of their admission, gave way to signs of alarm and despondency.

"I really don't know how we come to admit some of these young thugs." He sighs deeply as he gazes out at the court from his high window. "I suppose they were all wished on us by young Alistair before he left us for his spiritual home."

"To which young thugs in particular do you refer, my dear Silas?" asks the chaplain, who is carrying out Alistair Wynne's tutorial duties

during his absence in America. "I find my pupils an unusually rewarding crowd, I must say."

"Well, there's that nigger-boy they call Albert. He looks like a
junior Paul Robeson."

"An excellent person," says the chaplain. "He is already proving a
pillar of the Chapel. He sings like an angel. I am thinking of recruiting
him as sacristan next term."

"I wish you joy of him," says the Senior Tutor. "And, look, there's
that Hindu scoundrel with cheeks like tanned pincushions and eyeballs
like black-currants. He's sure to be reading Law. God help the poor
Indians."

"Shalimar? He is not, as you will have gathered, a chapel-
worshipper, but he is settling down very well. People like him."

"Pale hands I love beside the Shalimar," warbles Mr. Stock. "But
look, who comes here? Calls himself a Greek and doesn't understand
his own language. I am prepared to bet the fellow's a Turk."

"He is not one of mine," says the chaplain, secretly wondering
whether Silas Stock knows that the fellow is one of his own. "I
gather he has been given rooms next to that nice little Lancashire man,
Thwaites – one of Skinner's people. They will do each other a power
of good."

"Poor little Thwaites," Mr. Stock commiserates. "I must say he
looks decent enough."

"Lancashire to the back-bone," the chaplain laughs. "Pity he's a
Roman Catholic."

"Haven't we got any honest-to-God Englishmen this year?"

Proved on the Pulses

The nearest thing to Mr. Stock's ideal of an honest-to-God Englishman is Philip Hughes-Browne, but he has yet to meet young Duncan
Macleod, a Scot from New Zealand.

E

Duncan Macleod has come from the uttermost ends of the earth with this moment shining in his mind like a window at the far end of a tunnel. Yesterday he went round the colleges with his father. The pair of them, Duncan was proud to think, had looked very much what they were: a New Zealand farmer and his son, honest and healthy outdoor types, fresh from the sheep-farms of Wangarai, striding boldly but respectfully over the cobbled courts of the ancient civilization which had bred their ancestors. True, the younger Macleod had been a trifle embarrassed by the older Macleod's reiterated question: whether these young men dodging in and out of staircases, crowding the pavements, and talking as loudly and intimately as if the town were their private parlour – whether they really 'appreciated' what a privilege it was to be 'students' within these ancient and honourable precincts . . . ? The younger Macleod appreciated it all right, though he privately thought it a pity to make a fuss about it. . . . And now, the older Macleod had returned to London to spend a few weeks looking up his wool-dealing acquaintances *en route* for Wangarai, and the freshman from the antipodes has washed and shaved and brushed his hair with enormous care, and dressed himself in a brand-new gown, and tucked a brand-new note-book under his arm, and enquired of the porter the way to H. Staircase, where he imagines that his tutor awaits him, if not with excited anticipation, at least with interest.

Now, five minutes after entering the tutorial sanctum, he is out in the court again. Somewhere close at hand a clock sweetly chimes eleven. He looks at his watch. Half an hour ago he had climbed those boarded stairs to keep his appointment with Mr. Stock. Twenty-five of those thirty minutes had passed in a crowded cubby-hole with a queue of young men who all looked about as fresh as himself, but all of whom seemed to have known each other from their cradles. The remaining five had been spent in the presence of the rather harassed and untidy gentleman who kept howling 'Come in' at regular intervals from the inner room. He had the memory of a hurried handshake, a cursory but not unfriendly scrutiny, a couple of questions about 'reading' and a parting admonition to come again if and when any problems should arise. With wandering steps and slow, the young man from the antipodes takes his solitary way across Great Court and up the stairs to the oaken double-door with the name D. MACLEOD freshly inscribed in white paint over the lintel.

As he goes in, another door on the opposite side of the landing opens and a face looks out at him from beneath the by-no-means freshly-painted inscription P. PLUMMER. The face that goes with P. PLUMMER has intrigued D. MACLEOD since he was awakened by sounds of song and dance coming from the room across the landing at two o'clock in the morning.

"Come in and have some coffee," says P. PLUMMER.

"Thanks," says D. MACLEOD, and goes in, shedding his gown.

It is a very untidy room, quite unlike the bare and virgin lodging where the freshman has spent his first night in college. There are brightly coloured railway posters on the walls: they depict the allurements of Norwich, Edinburgh (complete with pipe-band), Southend-on-Sea and the Isle of Wight. Hanging from the cornice above the mantel-piece are several public notices ordering people to KEEP OFF THE GRASS, indicating GENTS, and LADIES, and prohibiting HAWKERS AND SOLICITORS. On the table, among stacks of books and papers, a coffee percolator like an alchemist's retort distils a ropy black fluid, drop by drop.

"You're fresh," says P. PLUMMER. "Anyone can see that. S'pose I shouldn't be talking to you for another twelve months at least. But to hell with this snob-show."

"It's jolly decent of you," says D. MACLEOD.

"None of that." P. PLUMMER stares at D. MACLEOD over his coffee-cup. "Anyone can see you're no beardless boy from school. Older than I am, I shouldn't wonder. . . . I say, you're not an American?"

"God forbid."

Explanations follow rapidly and easily. Peter Plummer reveals himself proudly as the son of a Post Office clerk. Norwich Grammar School, Open Scholarship and State Scholarship, reading Classics. Third year. Lucky Jim in the egg. Except that 'this place' is devoted to making every lucky Jim into a Fortunate James, that being what they pay Silas Stock three thousand a year for. By the way, what *about* Silas? Has he done his stuff?

"I wouldn't know," says the baffled freshman. "I only saw him for five minutes."

"You're specially favoured. It generally comes to two and a half. Three at the outside."

"I always imagined a tutor's job was to tute."

"We all come up with the notion that our tutor tutes us. One of the first things you have to learn is the difference between a tutor and a supervisor."

"Tell me . . . I had a notion that a supervisor was that woman who helps you when you go wrong in a call-box."

"No, that's a tutor. And not in a call-box simply."

It takes a long time to clarify these things, and Duncan Macleod will only get things right by personal experience. Nor does he find himself much nearer enlightenment when summoned to call on the second person of the academic trinity, his director of studies. Dr. Smart, director of studies in History, has had a considerable number of overseas undergraduates to direct in the past, and flatters himself that he can make the Cambridge academic system clear to a person of the meanest intelligence (a category to which he privately consigns all visitors from overseas, British, American or merely foreign) inside ten minutes.

"You have seen your tutor, Mr. Macleod?" says Dr. Smart.

"I saw him this morning, sir." Mr. Macleod wants to add 'just about', but he refrains, for Dr. Smart with his rimless glasses and his thin pointed face looks far from matey. "I gather that he doesn't want to teach me himself."

"He couldn't," says Dr. Smart. "You may take it from me. Quite beyond his powers, I assure you."

"I wouldn't call myself an advanced student," Mr. Macleod protests modestly.

"We don't have students at Cambridge, in any case," says Dr. Smart with a cold smile.

"Pardon me," says Mr. Macleod, suspecting that he has been trapped into an Americanism, a thing which he detests. "What *do* you have, sir?"

"We have men. . . . Merely a matter of vocabulary, my dear sir. You will become accustomed to our odd little locutions in time. No, they have students in the more modern universities, and – I understand – overseas. Here we only have – men."

"Thank you, sir. Well, I wouldn't call myself an advanced man."

"Nor would I." Dr. Smart has picked up a copy of Mr. Macleod's 'record', all the way from the Queen's College, Wangarai, North Island. "I see that you took quite a good pass in History at – er – Wangarai. However, I ought to warn you that over here that means little more than advanced level G.C.E. That is to say, you will start your university studies at about the same level as an English boy leaving school after two years in the sixth form."

"As you say, sir, of course. But I thought . . ."

"I shall send you to Mr. Parker," says the director of studies, sweeping aside whatever it was that Mr. Macleod thought. "Mr. Parker takes our first year commoners reading History. He lives at C Staircase, Old Court. You are sure to find him in if you call on him before hall this evening."

Armed with a lecture list with certain courses underlined, and a reading list with certain titles marked off for immediate attention, Mr. Macleod wends his way at five o'clock that same evening in the direction of C Staircase, Old Court.

Peeling an onion, he tells himself. Or is it Chinese boxes? Anyway, as soon as he gets inside Mr. Parker's rooms he feels that he has reached the heart of the matter. This man with the ginger moustache and the striped pullover, who grins at him over a curly-stemmed pipe and bids him 'squat down somewhere . . . shove those papers off the settee . . . have a cigarette. . . .' Yes, this man is the heart of the matter.

In which, Duncan Macleod is perfectly right. The supervisor – who may vary in technique between an inquisitor and a crammer – he is, as Bismarck said of Lord Beaconsfield, 'the Man'. Tutors may (or may not) tute; directors may (or may not) direct; supervisors are simply compelled to supervise. For something like an hour every week, every term, the supervisor is shut up in a room with his pupil and his pupil's 'essay'. What takes place during that hour is nobody's business but their own. But there they are, locked together in friendly or antagonistic embrace, with the dead body of the weekly essay, or other 'piece of work', to show for it at the end of the hour. If the supervisee gets nothing out of the contest, that is because he has put nothing into it, or because the supervisor has thought of some other way of passing away the time than in intellectual labour – such as discussing the match at Fenner's, or cleaning his nails, or standing on his head in a corner. It is entirely up to the pair of them. It is quite certain that with his supervisor the undergraduate is as near as he will ever get to the heart of the 'Cambridge system'.

Mr. Parker takes young Mr. Macleod's lecture list from him, grins or scowls over the lectures that Dr. Smart has indicated as worth attending, crosses out some and adds others, and concludes with the generalization that lectures are pretty pointless anyway. 'As soon as you find out what book they are coming from – which is fairly easy, because you will find it is the only book that the lecturer will refrain from mentioning – go and read the book.' Mr. Macleod suggests mildly that there doesn't seem much point in having lectures if one doesn't go to them. Mr. Parker agrees. Lectures, he declares, are simply one among many pieces of evidence that the older universities have not yet heard of the invention of printing. He goes on to quote Dr. Johnson, a habit which young Mr. Macleod has already discovered to be endemic among Cambridge dons. Mr. Parker actually has his Boswell at his elbow, on his desk, day and night. He pushes over the volume, with the relevant passage marked, for Mr. Macleod to read, while he explores the spare hours in his time-table. Mr. Macleod reads:

People have now-a-days (said he) got a strange opinion that everything should be taught by lectures. Now I cannot see that lectures can do so much good as reading the books from which the lectures are taken. I know nothing that can be best taught by lectures, except where experiments are to be shown. You may teach chymistry by lectures. – You might teach making shoes by lectures!

When Duncan Macleod raises his eyes from this passage, he finds Mr. Parker watching him with a self-deprecatory grin, rather like the Cheshire Cat.

"Well?" he says. "You've got to admit that I recommend the book from which I take my own lectures, eh?"

"Are there any more like that?" Duncan enquires with unconcealed relish. "I mean – debunking lectures?"

"Oh yes," Mr. Parker informs him. "I can especially recommend

Adam Smith's *Wealth of Nations*, Book V, Chapter 1, Part III, Article II. 'Of the Expenses of the Institutions for the Education of Youth'."

"I thought Adam Smith's *Wealth of Nations* was economics," Duncan confesses. "I mean, I didn't think it was interesting."

"It is the most interesting book of moral philosophy in the world," Mr. Parker declares with fervour. "Smith looks at education, as he looks at everything else, from the point of view of the consumer."

"My point of view," Duncan murmurs.

"Precisely. Why not? The university authorities look at education from the producer's point of view. After all, they've got to find some excuse for paying stipends to learned men. Why not lectures?"

"Are you a lecturer yourself, sir?"

"My God, yes. How else do you suppose I make a living? You don't imagine that I could live on fees for supervising you chaps, do you? Morevoer, I shall expect you to attend my lectures with the utmost regularity."

"Certainly, sir," says Duncan. "I shall look forward to that, no end."

"I believe you mean it, poor fellow."

He does. He has already formed the opinion that there could be no more entertaining and enlightened don in the whole university than Mr. Parker. And, since this is what Mr. Parker wishes him to believe, they part on excellent terms. It is understood that young Mr. Macleod will wait on Mr. Parker with an essay on 'The Causes of the Fall of the Roman Empire' on the following Tuesday at five o'clock.

Returning to his rooms, Duncan Macleod's steps are no longer wandering and slow, but brisk and lively and purposeful. He feels that he now belongs to the educational system of the university. Scales have fallen from his eyes. Life is real, life is earnest. In the morning he will buy a copy of *The Wealth of Nations* and absorb a further dose of 'the consumer's point of view'. He waves his hand gaily as he passes the lighted windows of Dr. Smart and Mr. Silas Stock. He has, he tells himself, already got to the heart of the matter.

The Destructive Element

He hasn't. He never will. All he has done is to begin to articulate the skeleton of the Cambridge 'college system', with its perplexing and interlocking relationships of tutors, directors, and supervisors. He hasn't even conceived the idea of a Master, a dean, a bursar, a steward, a praelector, a chaplain, a librarian, or the underpinning structure of porter, butler, kitchen manager, college secretary, gyps, bedders, clerks, staircase men, gardeners, and waiters. A college is a world, and he has only touched its axis, its spinal column. He has mastered the part of the system that immediately concerns him as a newcomer in search of formal education. The rest will impinge upon his life, consciously or unconsciously, as he goes about his business over the next three years. He will, as likely as not, never conceive the idea of many of them at all. He will meet some of them as individuals: the Master at coffee or tea at the Lodge, the dean as a slightly aggrieved granter of permissions for this and that, the chaplain more likely at tea or coffee than in Chapel, the praelector when he matriculates, and again on that distant day when it falls to that gentleman to supplicate the Vice-Chancellor on his behalf for his degree. He will probably know his gyp and his bedder best of all, and after them the porter. He may never even remotely guess who is bursar or steward, or who is the watchful power that buys the food he consumes in hall, or cooks it, or mows the grass, or makes out his college bill. All these things he will take for granted as happening somewhere off-stage, like the government of the university itself. It is more than possible, indeed it is very likely, that he will never be able to put a name to more than two or three of the faces that he regularly sees on the distant plateau of High Table. The average undergraduate knows, and is content to know, very little about what, or who, makes his college tick, and still less about the hidden springs and sources of the life of his university.

There are exceptions. There are young men who are persuaded that it is their job to improve both the college and the university. Politicians, journalists in the bud with an assignment for some undergraduate paper on the poor standard of college meals, or the wretched inadequacies of college libraries, or the idle and inefficient methods of supervisors. Snoopers, spies, informers, professional belly-achers they are called by tutors, stewards and librarians; intent upon knowing everything and successful in understanding nothing. Returning the compliment, they call the world they know so well and understand so little, THE ESTABLISHMENT. Dons stand self-condemned as members of THE ESTABLISHMENT. It is a little difficult to know what else they could be members of. The future of their critics, however, is assured.

Duncan Macleod, like Daffyd Evans and Philip Hughes-Browne, and Messrs. Thwaites, Shalimar, Zogropolous, and Albert of Africa, discovers a large number of messages from persons and organizations of active and evangelical turn of mind awaiting him among the mail every morning during his first week at Cambridge. He hardly likes to throw them away without reading them, for in most cases the envelopes or wrappers are addressed to him personally in somebody's handwriting rather than in the machine-script of a circular. It is hard for a freshman to reject out of hand the overtures of anyone who appears to take an interest in him. So he consults Peter Plummer, next door. The worldly-wise third-year man suggests various base uses to which these missives should be promptly put.

Before taking his advice, however, Duncan Macleod spends a perplexing half-hour examining some of them. The first, in order of arrival as well as in importance of appearance, offers him sixteen cogent reasons why he should become a member of C.U.S.C., which apparently stands for the University Socialist Club. The next expresses a cool conviction that he is and always has been a Conservative and will wish to be kept informed of the vitally important activities of the Young Conservatives in the university. It will interest him to know that stocks of the Tory Club tie are on sale at all the leading university outfitters. There is also a brief and elegant slip of (apparently) handwritten stationery to remind him that the Liberal Party continues to flourish in the university, as is only to be expected in an intellectual atmosphere like that of Cambridge, and that 'thinking men' are automatically Liberals, so that there is no need to enter into boastful argument after the manner of certain other parties. . . . All the same, Mr. Macleod's adherence will be welcomed most warmly, etc. etc. . .

Mr. Macleod is also invited to share his personal experience of Jesus Christ with members of the Intercollegiate Christian Union (C.I.C.C.U.); to join in broad-based Christian worship with the Students' Christian Movement (S.C.M.); to attend a course of lectures on the claims of 'the' Church by the Dominican Fathers; and to remember that, although its inspiring pastor has departed for pastures new, St. Mary the Great is still the University Church. There is also a small and neatly printed folder-card informing him that the College Chapel is the centre of the religious life of the college, and that the chaplain is glad to see members of the college at any time, and is generally in his rooms at Chapel Staircase between the hours of 8.30 and 9.0 p.m. during full term. If Mr. Macleod is interested in Railway Operation and History he should join The Puffer Club; if he is interested in Unarmed Combat he should join the Judo Club; if he is a fencer . . . a beagler . . . a mountain-climber . . . an amateur actor . . . a musician . . . a sailor . . . a cinema-enthusiast . . . a Humanist. . . . In the end, Duncan Macleod decides that Peter Plummer's advice is sound, and takes it – rescuing at the last moment the college Chapel card, which he sticks on his mantelpiece.

When he meets Daffyd Evans, however, he wonders whether he has been precipitate.

"Man," says Daffyd, "you should come to C.U.S.C."

"All right," says Duncan. "I'll go with you sometime, just to see. . . ."

He goes to C.U.S.C. because he has come to like Daffyd, but he still doesn't 'see'. He goes to the Young Conservatives because he likes Philip Hughes-Browne, who, like the Junior Conservatives, didn't seem to invite him with any particular urgency. Among the J.C.'s he 'sees' rather more, because they seem to be saying the things that his father, and all good New Zealanders, always say. Scratch a Cambridge Conservative and you find a Whig. He goes to College Chapel, and decides that it is near enough to his Presbyterian Church 'at home' to give no offence to his native taste for plain common-sense Christianity. Besides, he likes the chaplain, whom his friends of the Anglican Communion call 'the plain-chap' because he is all things to all men. The chaplain is the more acceptable to Duncan Macleod because he once coxed the 'varsity boat, and Duncan has fallen in love with rowing. The chaplain has a pleasant way of making you think that Jesus Christ once rowed for the college, that he had known him slightly when he was up, and that even now he is the finest stroke that any crew could possibly have in the great Boat Race which is life. This notion, which Duncan Macleod would never dream of putting into words, causes him to argue quite firmly with Mr. Parker when he has read to him his first essay, on 'The Causes of the Fall of the Roman Empire'. For Mr. Parker suggests that the spread of Christianity may have had something to do with the celebrated 'decline' and that St. Augustine's equally celebrated attempt to refute the idea was what you might expect from a 'bloody-minded Bishop, the father of persecution', just as you might expect a cobbler to insist that there's nothing like leather, or a college tutor to crack up that unmitigated nuisance 'the college system'. This is the first time that Duncan Macleod has heard anyone deny the divine efficacy of the college system, and it shakes him almost as severely as the suggestion that the Christian religion had done more harm than good in the course of human history. It is intended to shake him. That is what Mr. Parker is paid for. Young Mr. Macleod returns from his supervisor's den with the salutary feeling that he has been turned upside down, losing all the contents of his pockets in the process. As Silas Stock would say: 'it's beginning'.

Meeting Daffyd Evans in hall that evening, Duncan Macleod presently asks:

'What sort of supervisor have *you* got?"

"Lousy," Daffyd declares with some force. "Man, he thinks Shelley was a poet."

"Well, wasn't he?"

"Not since Pyecraft took him in hand."

"Who's Pyecraft?"

"Man, where have you been?"

"On the river. Tubbing."

Duncan feels more thick this evening than he has ever felt in his life. Nosey Parker's iconoclasm, followed by an hour's tubbing at the Boat House, and now a pint of college ale, have together conspired to leave him feeling as stupid as any owl.

"Don't be so damn literal," he hears Daffyd protest. "I mean where have you been educated? Will you oblige me with the name and address of the putative educational establishment that can contrive, in this year of grace, to keep from its benighted pupils the name of the greatest living literary critic?"

"Greatest what?" Duncan yawns.

"L-i-t-e-r-a-r-y c-r-i-t-i-c," Daffyd bawls, spelling out the words against the surrounding din.

"What are you yelling about, Taffy?" Peter Plummer intervenes. As President of the Junior Tables, Peter enjoys the prerogative of intervention in any private *fracas* which threatens the decorum of Hall Dinner. From the dark fury on the Welshman's face he judges that his intervention is timely. "Some one been blaspheming your god?"

"Tell this clot of a Kiwi who Pyecraft is," Daffyd begs. "I can no longer trust myself to address him."

"Aloysius P. Pyecraft," Peter explains gravely, "is the god of their idolatry to all who are so mistaken as to read for the English Tripos."

"Not all," Daffyd corrects him. "Some there are, including my benighted supervisor, who hate and fear him."

"Good show," Peter rejoins. "But listen, Kiwi. This great god is the father and mother of a thing they call 'Eng. Crit.', specially designed for 'Eng. Critters' if you ask me. Anyway, Pyecraft is its High Priest. And, this year, he's come here as visiting Professor of English. He is called Pyecraft because, like the man in the H. G. Wells story, he floats about in an elevated position. You may see him floating about Cambridge at any moment. When and if you do, make the sign of the Cross and offer up thanks that you are in the same town with greatness."

Daffyd Evans has ceased listening. He has learnt to stop his ears against blasphemy. Besides, he has his own personal reasons for rage. He is seething with Welsh fury. Nurtured on the pure milk of 'Eng. Crit.', he has this day encountered a don who knows not Pyecraft, or pretends he knows not, for Daffyd still cannot quite believe his supervisor is as stupid as he makes himself out to be. In Daffyd's case, the assault upon orthodoxy produces a frenzied wrath which makes his dark Celtic face look like the face of St. Augustine at war with the Donatist heresy. Or so Duncan imagines. His own wrath in face of the

heresies of Mr. Parker now seems mild indeed, a mere passing discomfiture. He is inclined to put this down to the renowned sense of
proportion inculcated by rowing practice.

"You ought to row, Daffyd," he says now, with another yawn.
"Good for the bile."

"God save us," Daffyd retorts. "A world like this needs bile, and
plenty of it, I tell you."

And he waves his hand at the guzzling multitude, at the dons on the
dais serene, and at the university in general. Altogether, thinks Philip
Hughes-Browne, who has overheard the greater part of the interchange,
Daffyd the Welsh Trog is showing healthful signs of disillusionment
with the 'beautiful world' to which he has come. Blessed is he, Philip
thinks, whom ancestral experience hath taught to expect rather less,
for verily he shall not be disappointed. Yet, on the whole, he is inclined
to envy Daffyd his sharp experience of the clash between the ideal and
the real. There is something divine about his discontent, the clot.

How much, or how little, the undergraduate gets out of these
bouleversements of his early days depends upon the man. The important
thing is not that he should lose any beliefs that he brings with him, but
that he shall be compelled to defend them, and to defend them against
both his intellectual superiors and his equals. Cambridge, the university
of John Milton, is dedicated to the destruction of cloistered virtue. And
the good work is going on all the time. The demolition squad is composed not only of the middle-aged or elderly gentlemen who sit in
armchairs by their study fires and tear young men's essays to pieces.
The young men themselves lend a hand. Their contribution is the more
effective because they are left very much to themselves, authority
remaining, for the most part, discreet and aloof. Dr. Skinner's
favourite complaint that his colleagues fail in their duty to the young
men by remaining aloof is rather like the mistaken lament of the rate-
payer that the police seem to have nothing better to do than to stand
about at street corners. In effect, it is an unintended compliment to
donnish good sense. For 'aloof' is precisely what decent young men
prefer dons to remain, although of course they are too polite to tell
Dr. Skinner so. Thrown together within the four walls of a country-
house on the banks of a sluggish stream, lined with lawns and screened

by trees, housed and fed and ministered to by willing and largely unseen hands, with the greater part of day and night at their disposal to do with as they please, taught to call themselves 'men' rather than 'students', what more – what else – could they need in the way of suitable conditions for the progress of their civility? The greatest of all dons, though he practised the craft in the macrocosm of the world, of which a university is the microcosm, defined CIVILITY in his dictionary as: *the state of being civilized: freedom from barbarity.*

The endless talk that goes on in college courts and gardens, behind the lighted windows of undergraduates, and on the Sunday 'grinds' by Trumpington, the Meadows, and Coton footpath, is supplemented by the organized forensic forays of college clubs and societies. The great days of the Cambridge Apostles are gone, although the Heretics still flourish at Trinity, and the Jesuits still meet at Jesus. But the average undergraduates finds his own level in the multitudinous little gatherings that scarcely boast a great name in their title, often no more than mushroom growths sprung up beneath the hands of a few convivial spirits who seek excuse for pseudo-intellectual romps among the coffee-cups. These gatherings, indeed, often meet their chiefest enemy in a mistaken search after 'star performances'. Some over-efficient secretary takes it into his head to invite a bright young don to address the company. Within a term or so, dons, more or less bright, become the regular fare. Dons, of course, protest that they are too busy, but they seldom refuse. Most dons keep a file of some half-dozen 'papers' suitable for delivery to undergraduate societies, which go the round of the colleges. Then the more light-hearted, or light-minded, brethren tell themselves that the show is 'just one more lecture'. The audiences dwindle to a few utilitarian members on the lookout for 'tripos gen', and the end is in sight. In these days of examination-complex, college societies of the older and more healthful sort find it hard to keep going. People fall to the temptation to work, or confine themselves to properly university societies where an 'authority' delivers a lecture followed only by 'questions', or else they go to the cinema. It is a pity. The small, ill-organized, college society, with dons strictly barred except on the occasion of the inevitable annual dinner, was truly the mother of men. Here it was, and still is, in so far as these gatherings fitfully survive, that men 'talked for victory'. They talked a great deal of nonsense, and still do. Slightly 'elevated' gentlemen read papers on modest little topics like 'Modern Man and the Universe', 'Slavery', 'The Ethics of Persecution', or 'The Dreyfus Case' (two hours non-stop by a gentleman who will one day be Lord Chancellor of England). And here is the only place left in England where the future small-town solicitor can tell the future Lord Chancellor that he doesn't know enough Law to cover the head of a large-sized pin, and the future perpetual curate of Pimpleton can tell the future Archbishop of Canterbury that his theology is as wretched as his prose-style, and twice as tedious.

Cambridge Morning

The bedmakers come into College at dawn. At least that is the theory. Mostly they arrive at about seven o'clock, winter and summer alike. Only the porter on duty at the Lodge sees them come. They call at the porter's lodge for their keys which hang on several rows of hooks just inside the door. They all carry covered baskets, and ungrateful under-graduates say these receptacles are always much heavier when they leave again at about ten o'clock. It is the footfalls of bedmakers as they unlock gyp-rooms and cupboards that announce to the undergraduate, and the resident don, that the day is beginning. There is no reason what-ever to pay any attention to these sounds, for the 'bedder' has yet to make her pot of tea and smoke her cigarette before she starts her magnified imitation of the death-watch beetle on the door-panels and tunes up her cheerful voice to the chant of 'Eight o'clock, sir. . . . Half-past eight, sir. . . . Sir, it's a quarter to nine. . . . Goodness sake, sir, if you don't get up in half a minute, you'll get no breakfast. . . .' It used to be possible for the undergraduate to ignore these agonized cries until somewhere near ten o'clock, and still get his bed made and his breakfast-things washed up. It is so no longer. The modern bedder is resolute about quitting the premises at what she considers a proper trade-union hour. And there are no breakfast-things to wash up. You must race into hall before nine or go breakfastless which some still prefer to do.

Bedmakers are survivals of the age of the gentry. Many, indeed most, of them are still tolerant of the idle morning habits of the young. It is important not to provoke them beyond a certain limit, however, for they are hard to recruit, and the porter (whose problem it is) finds a legitimate source of grievance in a rapid turn-over in bedmakers. The main qualification for engagement as a bedmaker, apart from honesty, cleanliness and industry, used to be ugliness. It was laid down that such serving females must be 'horrific'. This, no doubt, descends from the time when the university consisted of a population of 'clerks' – clerks in Holy Orders, or on their way to them. The trouble appears to have been that these horrific matrons brought with them their daughters as 'bedder's-help', and the daughters helped the clerks. So there set in the days of the hags, which lasted until only yesterday, the days when bedders were a cross between the witches in *Macbeth* and Sairy Gamp. These formidable and hideous creatures were one of the traditional sources of Cambridge humour, of grisly legend, of endless anecdote. Henry Gunning has left us his portrait of the renowned Sal Elvedge, bedmaker to such celebrated wining and dining dons of the later eighteenth century as Thomas Adkin and Busick Harwood. 'This woman,' Gunning records, 'was much attached to her masters; and although she never scrupled supplying herself with coals, candles, etc. from their stores, yet she watched most perseveringly over their interests, in not allowing them to be imposed on in any other quarter.' Sal regarded her peculations as her perquisites, and Gunning makes the best case that could be made for the pilfering bedmaker of ancient times. Very poorly paid, they rather naturally established the custom of helping themselves to 'little necessaries'. Among other things, Sal Elvedge used to drink the spirits which Dr. Harwood left in a jug in his gyp-room after replenishing the preservative of his anatomical specimens. She swore that this practice saved her life on more than one occasion. Bold, boozy and endlessly voluble, she constitutes the Platonic Idea of the old-time Cambridge bedmaker. Varieties of Sal Elvedge still haunted college gyp-rooms well within living memory. Mrs. Bloggs told young Mr. Valentine, when he commented, not very long ago, upon the frequent breaking of his crockery, "It's Mrs. 'Awkins

the 'elp, sir. She's that deaf she can't 'ear when she's breaking things."
And there are still some surviving examples of that capacious covered
receptacle known as 'a bedder's basket'.

It was the dawn of the Welfare State and the onset of full employment that killed off the old bedders. Alternative and better-paid employment, together with the accompanying transformation of the
middle-aged and elderly women of the working-classes in the matter of
personal appearance and self-esteem, has made bedmakers scarce and
'superior'. Where they still survive, they can earn some three pounds a
week for two or three hours of room tidying and washing-up a day.
They regard this as 'pocket-money', or perhaps 'pin-money'. Nine
times out of ten the present-day bedmaker 'doesn't need the money',
as her grandmother needed it, nor would she 'lower herself' to make
away with her gentlemen's soap and sugar and tea. She is more like a
visiting housekeeper. She dresses smartly, and she is often good to look
upon. The notion that she must qualify for her job by ugliness departed
when the 'gentlemen' departed – the gentlemen who thought anything in a skirt fair game for gentlemanly diversion. The modern
undergraduate, as often as not, would find it hard to distinguish his
bedmaker socially from his sisters, his cousins and his aunts. The
bedmaker of to-day, like the undergraduate of to-day, is a type-
phenomenon of a silent social revolution. Likely enough she will
vanish completely from the Cambridge scene within a few years, along
with other survivals of the days before self-service and electric gadgets.

Likewise the 'gyp', the man-servant, her masculine counterpart. He
still serves in some colleges in his old capacity of body-servant to a
group of undergraduates living on his 'staircase', but he spends most
of his time nowadays stoking hot-water boilers, scrubbing out communal bathrooms and lavatories, sweeping stairs and passages, removing furniture, and waiting in hall. The 'staircase-man', with his
multitude of small tasks, is fast replacing the old-time valet. Some of
these men, haunting colleges staircases while generations of undergraduates come and go, have been among the best-loved landmarks
of undergraduate life: Charlie, and Jack, and Horace, and Sidney, not
to mention little Smithson, the ex-jockey; and Jeeves (it really was his
name) who could never retire, after sixty years of gypping, and had to

F

be allowed to come and sit in the gyp-room or the boiler-house during his last days because he was miserable unto death anywhere else. These men, along with their great exemplar, the porter, and their still more solemn exemplar, the butler, have often served the college from boyhood. They belong to it, they know about it, they love it (though they curse it often and long) more completely and continuously than anyone else in the place, not even excepting the oldest don. They constitute the communal memory. They are the fixed points in an ever-changing society, as undergraduates come and go like the flies of a summer, and as dons live their little day between fellowship election and departure for their suburban donnery. They live on small wages, they work at their own pace, and generally speaking they are among the very few people of a Cambridge college who have time to stand and stare. They have plenty to stare at, and they store it all up, and they excel even tutors in never forgetting a name or a face. It is impossible to decide whether it is a good thing, or a bad thing, that they rarely if ever write their memoirs. A don would be the first person to acknowledge that they are, after dons, the most important people in a college.

October days, for the undergraduate, begin with the not unobtrusive ministrations of bedders and gyps. They go on with hall breakfast (generally self-service in a queue at the service tables), and a fleeting glimpse of the court in the morning sunshine. It is at these moments, or as he goes on his way to lab. or lecture-room, that the undergraduate first feels that he belongs to Cambridge, or alternatively that Cambridge belongs to him. The sky is a misty blue over King's Parade and Market Hill as he flaunts his fledgling gown among the sauntering or hurrying crowds on their way to the formal business of the day. The streets are swarming with bicycles, bells chime high overhead, lecturers with long-tasselled caps and billowing gowns stalk remotely and with consciously closed faces towards Mill Lane, or the Divinity School or Senate House yard. Here, the youthful newcomer may well feel, something of everlasting importance to his life is going on. Or he may not, or not for long. He will certainly 'sit at the feet' of a few of the solemn stalkers in long gowns for a time, sampling their wares, if only to find out (as Mr. Parker recommends) 'where the stuff is coming from' before retiring to the libraries to read the books. But lectures are important for quite other reasons than those adumbrated by their warmest advocates and despite the animadversions of their sternest critics. To sit as one in a crowd for fifty-five or perhaps only fifty minutes while the performer up aloft does his best to make the nominal hour seem like three, to listen only half-attentively while someone who has been over the ground many times before goes over it again, to look up like a sheep that is not fed or is wearisomely stuffed: these things may, or may not, have academic value in terms of a widening and enrichment of the young mind. Generally, for first-year undergraduates, they have very little, since the lecturer is bound to be trying to do the impossible: to impart 'outlines' and still remain fresh and stimulating. All the same, even the *longueurs* of a first-year lecture in these early days have their lessons to teach, lessons quite other than those intended by the lecturer to be learned.

First, there is the man: that supposedly learned authority up there at the desk. He has been laid on to do this, and there is therefore an initial assumption that the activity is important; and anyway the State, or some other well-intentioned institution, is prepared to pay for you to hear him. You may even have heard his name at school, or read one of his books. This is the man behind the printed word. One of the two most ancient and dignified educational institutions in England has appointed him to address you. He may not be doing it very well, but the odds are that he is doing his best. You can, if you find his words trivial or boring, speculate about his home-life, his love-life, what he is like at board and in bed. You may choose to assess his present activity simply as a histrionic performance, or as a comic turn. You can time his jokes (one every ten minutes is the Cambridge average), and you can reckon what he paid for his suit, whether he puts on a clean collar every morning, or how often he shaves. The important thing is that you should get used to the idea that he is an ordinary human being earning his living, and that Cambridge is full of senior members exactly like him, and all slightly 'phoney'. Unless the undergraduate decides that his teachers are thoroughly inadequate, by reason of either foolery or knavery, at a very early stage of his career at the university, he will be wasting his time and opportunities. Only when he has got over this stage of experience will he begin to get the best out of the place. And the best, when he comes to it, is a great deal better than he can get anywhere else on earth. He learns this later, sometimes too late. It is best that he should expend his criticism, ill-informed and indeed ignorant as it is most likely to be, as early as possible, so that he may go on from there; and the best way to expend it is in the company of persons as ill-informed and ignorant as himself, in cafés and pubs after lectures in his earliest days at Cambridge. There he will hear the process of expelling bile, bilious disappointment, and generally ill-conditioned criticism going on at a tremendous rate to the accompaniment of Espresso-jets and swashing beer-engines.

"Still going to the Severn Bore? Good God, I gave him up after a week. . . ."

"Oh, Severn's not all that bad. Saves reading textbooks, anyway."

"I learnt all he told us in his first five lectures in a couple of hours at school."

"Kept wondering when he'd say something fresh, didn't you?"

"He's got his jokes written in the margins in red-ink."

"Did he lend you his lecture-notes?"

"Polly Severn told me. She's his daughter, you know. Reading Geography, to get away from Pop. She says he's got little notes on the margin, like 'If this one doesn't come off, try number fifteen.' Sickening, isn't it?"

"Did he introduce himself? Old Tar-baby does it every time. Sticks his chest out and opens his arms and smiles like a shark. 'I'm Tarbet of St. Mike's,' he says, just in case you didn't know."

"Exhibitionism of the first water."

"Why don't they take lessons in lecturing? I hear that no one ever tells them. They're just let loose on us."

"I shall give Shawms just one more chance. If it's no better after Thursday, I shall cut. . . ."

Cutting one's first lecture is an important experience. To stroll as far as the lecture-room and pass on while others are going in; to wander down to the Mill and sit on the bridge with half a pint of bitter; to imagine that one hears Shawms, or Tarbet, or Severn still drooling on distantly for the benefit of less brave and enlightened minds; to

welcome the poor slaves of routine as they come out at twelve o'clock
with a face expressive of complete indifference; to nurse the notion
that one can do this every day; to kid oneself that the only good don
is a dead one (or one who knows that he is dead), or one who has been
reported as saying that the young men educate each other: all this is
an important part of the process of growing up. It demands the company of other, like-minded, persons if it is to be enjoyable and to bear
fruit. It also demands that a lot of other people are hard at work while
one is doing it. When T. E. Lawrence was at the university, he has
told us, he used to work at night, when everyone was in bed. In the
day-time his mental processes were disturbed by the impalpable
presence of several thousands of minds all around him and all cerebrat-
ing at high pressure. Most undergraduates leave off work for less subtle
reasons. They do not complain of other minds functioning around
them. They applaud it. It lends an edge to their own enjoyment of
what, to the young, is almost a positive activity in its own right: the
activity of not being active. Some educationists have raised this to the
status of an educational theory. They talk of the value of university
life as providing an 'interim' between the slavery of school-days and
the slavery of earning one's living. A period of salutary incubation.
The only period in one's life when one has time to think. It is safe to
say that those who indulge in this active activity rarely act on any
theory. They simply happen to like it. It answers to some, generally
temporary, need of the growing organism. But they indulge in it far
less than once they did.

Cambridge in October, in autumn generally, should conspire to
encourage it. Whenever the sun shines in Cambridge people say that
the place looks at its best at this time of year. Twice in the year this is
true, impossible as it may seem: in mid-autumn and in early spring.
And, looking back in later years, it is the glory of October mornings
that chiefly glows in the memory. The summer heats have given way
to the cooling breath of the dying year. The sultry grey skies which
arch over the place in August have been ripped and rent apart by the
winds of autumn, and the vault is high and blue-bag blue and traversed
by the bulging white canvas of the sky-galleons which float endlessly
from the fens through the livelong days. This is the time, of an October

morning, to forget about time-tables and sit on a seat behind St. John's or Trinity or King's or in Clare garden. The trees in the Backs droop and swing in the processional shades of autumn's colouring, from the green that is almost black to the bronze and yellow and gold which will die underfoot with the first frosts. The pale grey bridges link the gardens to the meadows, and the empty river shines all the way from John's to Queens' like a clean, sweet strip of Venice. Now is the time to remember thankfully Richard Bentley, the Master of Trinity, who, under God, gave Cambridge the Backs. It is a good time, also, to stroll down to Garret Hostel Bridge and gaze reverently upon the spot where young Mr. Isherwood, having decided to give up working for the tripos, dropped Bishop Stubbs into the Cam. But that was in the good-for-nothing 'twenties, when young men cut lectures almost unto death, and thought the world well lost for an hour of idleness. No doubt the young Isherwood's act of immolation was observed by admiring crowds. In the present year of grace no one would be there to see. They would all be in labs and lecture-rooms and libraries. But then, there would be no Isherwoods, either. His opposite number, now, is sitting on the bridge outside the Mill, drinking half a pint of bitter and waiting for the crowds to come out of the Mill Lane lecture-rooms with death in their hearts and masses of information in their note-books, ready to grouse and grumble about the ineptitudes of the lecture-system, and equally ready to return for more. State pensioners, clients of the County Authority, keenly conscious of the competitive world that awaits them after their three years in this place, they have no time to develop a philosophy of idleness. Even the young man with the half pint of bitter will probably return to the Severn Bore or the Tar-baby on Thursday. Or won't he?

The River and the Fields

'*I remember . . . the glorious feeling of an eight-oar running with an even keel on a summer evening, and the sensation that death was near . . . .*'

HARRY GABB: Downing, 1895–8

On these fine autumn afternoons, the boats are out on the river, and the tow-path beyond the *Pike and Eel* is tuning up to the megaphonic tones of the rowing-coach.

"You're just not together. . . . What the hell's the point of stroke if he's got seven blind men behind him?"

"Easy all. . . . Now, if you think you're the rugger boat, you'd better think again. . . ."

"Give them ten, cox. . . . No need to rush it. . . . Long and clean. . . . Nice work, but there's still digging at five. . . ."

These are the eights, old crews re-forming after the splendours and the miseries of distant June, new crews coming into formation, scratch collections of raw recruits fresh from tubbing. Eight men and a cox don't, of themselves, make a crew. They have to be the right eight men, a product of trial and error, tempered and refined in the fires of many ardent afternoons between the railway-bridge and Grassy, eight specimens of young flesh and bone and muscle (not to mention brain) transcended into that most powerful and beautiful spectacle of human propulsion between sky and water, a racing crew at the top of its training. Rowing, for the man who gives himself to it, is not a sport. It is a religion, a philosophy, a way of life. It has its saints, its prophets, its messianic masters, headed forever by their legendary god, Steve Fairbairn.

"No harm in lectures," Steve used to say. "You can still keep your wrists turning, even when you are at lectures."

And it was Steve who gloomily foretold the death of Cambridge rowing when, walking along Jesus Lane behind two rowing men, he heard them talking about – poetry.

At Cambridge, rowing has to be done on that narrow and un-promising stream, the river Cam. A sluggish strip of water, beginning (for the rowing man) in sight of the gas-works and the bake-houses overlooking Midsummer Common, and winding away under the railway-bridge to Grassy Corner and Ditton and the willowy links towards Clayhithe. There are no hills to which Cambridge crews can lift up their eyes for help, only the gloaming flats and the willows and the little whale-back of Ditton. Practice crews have to crowd into the banks, and sometimes to ship their oars, in order to pass each other in the narrower reaches, more especially when the university crew in training for the tideway comes storming along with indefeasible prerogative to the right of way. A case of 'challenge and response', perhaps. Cambridge crews have to acquire a trim economy of space, a certain rigour in navigation, from their earliest days. Likewise, their races have to be run not abreast but in succession, with the crews chasing each other and registering 'bumps'. Twice a year, towards the end of the Lent and the May terms, the 'Lents' and the 'May Races' fill the river with these sublime spectacles of catch-as-catch-can by water, all between the roaring running crowds of the tow-path on the one shore and the tethered punts and barges on the other. The 'order of boats' for starting purposes is the order decided by the bumps of the previous evening, and there are four successive evenings. There are also seven divisions (in the Mays), in each of which a college may have a boat rowing, so that the proceedings may last anything up to three or four hours. To have your First Boat at the top of the First Division in the May Races is the Paradiso of every college Boat Club. Sometimes a college – in recent times generally Jesus or Lady Margaret – may stay 'head' for several years on end. When there is a change of 'head', Cambridge college deans cower in their rooms all night, dons living in college seriously think of getting married before next year's races, and the night-sky glows with old boats burning on the Backs or Jesus Green or the Common. It is generally to be observed, however, that more damage is done, and more rowdiness ensues, when a college has done badly on the river than when it has done well.

The prestige of a college still depends to quite a considerable extent upon the position of its boats on the river. Its 'firsts' in the tripos, and its Blues in other forms of sport, count for a good deal, but rowing triumphs still bear the palm. The first thing that many an old member of the college still asks, when he comes back to Cambridge, or meets another member somewhere in the wider spaces of the world, is: 'How is the Boat doing in these days?' And this not only among men who, in their day, laboured at the oar. Somewhere at the back of most men's minds there lurks the notion that they would have been better men if they had rowed while they were 'up', just as most men (according to Samuel Johnson) think a little the worse of themselves for never having been a soldier or a sailor. For rowing has not only the prestige of being a very ancient sport, even if its ancient devotees rowed in galleys because they had no alternative, but it has the prestige associated with all human activities, however apparently pointless, which demand the utmost rigour of physical endurance, more especially when the endurance is shared with a small and select band of brothers. The rugger man will often dispute the point, yet it remains true that with all his fierce exertion there are moments when he is not by any means at full stretch. The lonely sprinter, or hurdler, is mainly an individualist. All men engaged in strenuous sports may have to train hard, surrendering the pleasures of wine and spirits and tobacco for long periods, and going to bed at ten o'clock. But the rowing man will tell you that he not only endures all this, but he does it always with his friends, and he breaks his heart over his oar from the moment of the starting-gun to cox's cry of 'Easy all!' He probably exaggerates both the extent of his rigours and the unrelieved labours of the race. Cynics still tell of the Belgian crew that came to the Cam and caught the best Cambridge boat of its year at Ditton corner, after drinking its customary goblets of wine and throwing away its cigars at the starting-gun. 'Stumpy little chaps, yellow as spade guineas, and cheerful as larks,' the old story goes, 'while our chaps looked like Franciscan friars in the middle of Lent'.

Every now and then there are signs of revolt against 'the tyranny of the Boat Club'. After all, rowing is an expensive form of sport. Although it costs the individual oarsman only a singlet and a pair of shorts, it costs the college (the Amalgamated Clubs of the college, whose funds are a charge upon all undergraduate members, whether they play games or not) very large sums indeed. The beautifully-built shells in which the oarsmen perform their feats of endurance are the work of highly-skilled craftsmen. They cost several hundred pounds each. A college Boat Club may require half a dozen or more for regular use, apart from practice shells and reserves, and they are not long-lived articles. The boat house and the boatman have to be maintained. And there are funds for the annual visit to Henley, and other regattas, if the crew is worth it. The officers of other college sports clubs are not infrequently heard to grumble about their own 'starvation' for the better nourishment of the Boat Club, especially if the boats are not distinguishing themselves, or their crews are getting the Amalgamated Clubs into bad odour for rowdyism and damage to college property. The cure for grumbling of this kind is victory on the river. Every good Captain of Boats knows that he has the cure in his own hands and the hands of his men. And since the standard of leadership and zeal on the part of Boat Club officers is generally very high, rowing always makes its come-back amidst general acclamation. How a Captain of Boats goes about his business of building or maintaining the spirit that leads his club to victory is his own affair. The best Captains of Boats, one notices, are nearly always something else as well, and the very best have generally been intellectuals. There have been examples even of Evangelical captains, men who put down swearing and lewdness, men who could turn a training-breakfast into a prayer-meeting. The best-remembered of this breed actually improved the position of all his college's boats on the river by several places, and got the First boat its oars (i.e. stroked it to a bump on all four successive days of the May Races). Cambridge is, after all, the university of East Anglia as well as all-England, the land of Cromwell, and the New Model Army, and the Eastern Association.

Freshmen of an athletic type, like Duncan Macleod, and even small men from schools where nobody knows one end of a boat from the other, like little Thwaites from Lancashire, may easily fall in love with the river. One says 'the river' advisedly, for a great many men take up rowing not simply because they originally wanted to row, but because they sense something rural and idyllic about its setting. If they survive their early experience of 'tubbing' – the somewhat frustrating experience of sitting in a fixed tub ('bank tub') below the boat-house and pulling on an oar which makes no difference whatever to anything except the palms of your hands, the muscles of your legs, and the skin of your backside – having survived this, and a few further lessons in a moving tub, and then being promoted to an 'eight', they begin to feel the fascination of the river itself. The autumn air comes cold off the water, the everlasting river-smell gets into the nostrils, and on the homeward spell against the stream the receding reach between the willows spreads like a dusky rippling road towards the trees and the church and the little farms of Ditton. The day is dying in the high sky

over the flats. There are winking lights along the railway. The roofs
of Cambridge across Midsummer Common hold a dim promise of
tea and toast by the fire in the small hours before hall. You may feel
desperately tired, but even your weariness is sweetened by the blessed
sense of achievement. The coach on his bicycle, pedalling slowly beside
you on the tow-path, his megaphone slung mute on the handlebars
now, has said that you will probably make a Lent eight if you come out
five afternoons a week for the next six months. You are backing alongside the gravel slope in front of the boat-house, and Tom the boatman
is squatting at the bow with his hook, and everyone is keyed up for
the last lovely ritual of shipping oars and stepping ashore. Up goes the
shell, lofted over your heads and down again, just as you have seen
it done on Television by the 'Varsity crew on the tideway. A shower
and a change into slacks and a slow spin back to college on the bike,
and you know that you are a rowing man for life.

You need never have been in a boat in your life. If you are keen, and
willing to learn, they will teach you everything from tubbing to your
colours. Lesser men, back from the fields, know no such ecstasy, for
they have been playing the game they learnt at school. Out on the
college grounds beside Barton Road, Grange Road or Long Road, they
have been punting footballs or clashing hockey-sticks. "How're the
blisters?" they enquire, smiling when you lower yourself gingerly into
a chair. Or "Do they pay you to do it?" And again: "Oarsmen of the
world unite, you have nothing to lose but your chains." But you don't
care. You put up a good show of singing in your chains like the sea.

Organized games are a comparatively new thing at Cambridge, as
they are in general. Although both Trinity and St. John's had boat
clubs by 1825, and bumping races date back to 1827, football was for
long regarded as a mere boys' game, and investment in college sports-
grounds and their amenities only began in later Victorian times. Well
into the nineteenth century, the undergraduate took his outdoor
pleasures, as Henry Gunning took his, with a fowling-piece on the
marshes and meadows between Parker's Piece and Bottisham. They
walked, they rode to hounds, they fished at Clayhithe, they played
bowls or billiards at Chesterton. But their greatest sport was found in
rowdyism between Town and Gown. Indeed, it was partly to

discourage extravagance in horseflesh and tandem-driving, and to divert energies from horse-play of another kind, that colleges took to organizing games according to rules and to providing grounds where they could be played. An undergraduate of the Regency or the reign of George the Third, if he were able to re-visit Cambridge to-day, would be more astonished by the sports of the twentieth-century undergraduate than by anything else. The formalism, the organization, the almost ritualistic resort to team-play and rules would probably repel him. His world was divided into the two classes of 'reading men' and 'varmint men', of whom the first did the work and the second played games. The 'varmint' way to proceed to the B.A. degree was both popular and well-defined:

Cut Lectures, go to Chapel as little as possible, dine in hall seldom more than once a week, give *Gaudies* and *Spreads*, keep a horse or two, go to NEWMARKET, attend the six-mile bottom, drive a drag, wear *varmint* clothes and well-built coats, be up to smoke, a rum one at Barnwell, a regular go at New Zealand,[1] a staunch admirer of the bottle, and care a damn for no man.

The Varmint's day was a matter of dressing, drinking, drabbing and gamesmanship. It began with a lounge through the streets with his friends, visiting saddlers, milliners, barbers, bootmakers and tailors. If the day were fine, he would make up a water-party, dine at Clay-hithe, or Ditton, take a snack at Chesterton, and play billiards at *The Three Tuns*. In the evening, he thinks he will go for a ride, 'and without togging for the occasion, just puts on his tile and mounts his pad . . . urges his steed along the Trumpington Road, goes out by the Shelford Common, and returns home between eight and nine'. When he comes to his second year, the only difference is that 'he is now twice as gay as before, rides, courses, hunts, shoots, fishes, drives, drinks, fights, swears, rows, and gambles, more than ever'.

There are still survivors of the age of the Varmint Men at Cambridge, but they are few. The distinction between the Varmints and the Readers is almost gone. Everyone, almost, reads, and the reading men are as likely as not to be found on the river or the playing-field as in the

[1] Both Barnwell and New Zealand were, in distant days, the regions of the bawdy houses.

libraries. If a man wants to play games, there is nowadays no reason why he should not also be able to get some work done. The only really serious problems arise for the cricketers, whose long days at Fenners and on their own college grounds in the May term – the term of the Tripos examinations – call for a good deal of foresight in the winter months. The scientists with their long hours in the laboratories may feel the need to concentrate their exercise in the temporally economic games of squash and fives. When the cheerful little Mr. Thwaites, from Lancashire, finds himself under impressment as cox to the second boat, he sensibly consults his tutor.

"All I've done up to now, sir," he informs Dr. Skinner, "I've done by real hard work. Can I afford the time?"

"We shall expect you to cox the boat *and* get a First for the college," says that terrible taskmaster. "Better men than you have done it. I did it myself."

After that, Mr. Thwaites decides that it must be easy.

Matriculation

The college is settling down. Michaelmas Term is coming to the end of what Silas Stock calls its Second Movement. Night after night, from his place at High Table, the Senior Tutor's experienced ear detects the changing rhythm of the undergraduate orchestra. He claims that he could divine the time of term, almost to a day, from the timbre of that Hall full of young men at dinner. Mentally, he marks the score. Beginning with the tentative tuning-up of Beethoven's Ninth, proceeding to the steady jog-trot of the second movement of the Eighth, dashing into the Trio of the second movement of the Fourth (with its cock-crowings and its cheek), then fading into the nostalgic Adagio of the Fifth: thus goes the Freshman Term, quarter by quarter, from birth to death.

Even if, like Beethoven, he were stone deaf, he would be able to form a pretty accurate impression by using his eyes. As term goes on, and friendships are cemented in common experience and shared tastes, undergraduates tend to sit at table in small fraternities. The rowing men rather naturally congregate at one table, although they have no exclusive right to it, except possibly during training periods when a special table and a special diet are allocated to them. Again, it is natural enough that men reading a certain subject which keeps them together during the working day, at the laboratory bench or in the engineering shop or the anatomy school, should tend to maintain a certain amount of association at dinner. The same may apply to men reading Law or Economics or other technical, though not strictly scientific subjects, men who have been working in the hours before Hall in the same supervision classes or in the same section of the library. The most obvious individualists are the Arts men, historians, modern linguists and literary practitioners in general. They may be found sitting at different places on different nights. They are the spies, critics, observers of human oddity, the dissolvents of specialized conclaves in the interests of communication. They tend to plant themselves on the fringes of these conclaves talking their 'shop', and to ask questions which can only be met by recourse to fundamental principles. This is what they want. Having dragged the specialists into the open arena of principles, they produce an intellectual disorder. It is at this point that arms begin to wave, fingers to wag, faces to approach each other across the stewed gooseberries.

"It's impossible to hold an intelligent conversation with a man who hasn't read Plato's *Republic*. . . ."

"A man might *try*. . . . Anyway, how am I to talk sense to a man who doesn't know the Second Law of Thermodynamics?"

"All the same, we seem to be getting on quite nicely."

"This business of the Two Cultures doesn't worry you?"

"Not a bit. I'm for as many cultures as possible."

"I must say I think it's a good thing to know a lot about one thing rather than a little about everything. . . ."

"But, I say, what about integration and all that?"

"To hell with integration. Just another of those O.K. words."

"Let's say cross-fertilization, then."

"Cross-fertilization. There. Feeling better?"

"Obviously, reading History makes a man a cynic."

The players in this undergraduate orchestra, like the instrumentalists in any orchestra whatever, are scarcely aware of its total effect upon the inward ear of an experienced listener like Silas Stock. Unlike the harassed don, the ordinary undergraduate does not concern himself very much with the time of term, or even the time of day. Of course, he may possess the Cambridge Pocket Diary, that neat little volume produced annually by the University Press which contains all the main items of information useful to a member of the university in his diurnal life. On the other, he may not. It is, like most other publications of the Press, far too expensive for the undergraduate purse. Apart from the London train service and the order of boats on the river, it contains little to interest the average undergraduate. Dons, on the other hand, generally have it on order, from year to year, at their booksellers. Indeed, one of the most typical Cambridge gestures may be observed, wherever one or two senior members are gathered together, in the reach of fingers to the breast-pocket and the myopic scanning of flimsy leaves as they exchange invitations to dine in each other's colleges, or, more often, to consult together on some business concerned with the setting of examination papers. A freshman might possibly buy this little book in the first flush of his intention to set himself up as a *bona fide* undergraduate. If so, it is there, round about page forty, that he will come upon the mystic words MICHAELMAS TERM DIVIDES. Hitherto, he has been accustomed to talk about 'half-term'. At Cambridge, however, he now learns, term 'divides', like an academic worm. And just before term divides, in the very early days of November, he will discover another date which concerns him much more intimately. This is marked by the single word: MATRICULATION.

Occasionally, some over-innocent freshman, on spotting this date ahead, hastens round to his tutor to enquire breathlessly whether this means that he is in for an examination. He has a very emphatic notion that he took what parents call 'matric' while he was still at school. His fears are quickly banished by the information that all he will have to do on the day marked MATRICULATION is to parade with his fellow freshmen, under the guidance of the college 'praelector', to the Senate House in order to make his bow to the Vice-Chancellor. And when the day comes, and the rather tired-looking gentleman in the chair at the west end of the Senate House has nodded back at him, he will probably feel a dull sense of anticlimax. Is this all there is to it? A walk in crocodile in one's darkest suit and one's gown, with the 'Father of the College' (a term which one had imagined until now to mean the Master, and not this smiling old bird in hood and bands with the Latin title), a bow and a nod, and a walk back again? True, the praelector will probably make you a short speech in which to tell you that you are now a full member of the university by formal admission, and that you have (quite unknown to you until this moment) undertaken to observe the Statutes and Ordinances of the University (which you have never seen), as far as they may concern you (which you imagine must be very little), and to pay due respect and obedience to the Chancellor (whom you have never seen) together with the other officers of the university (whom, you rather rightly suppose, are summed up, for you, in the proctors, who were hanging about the Vice-Chancellor's chair when he nodded to you). So far as you can see, the only really profitable feature of the whole business is the Matriculation dinner or tea-party, or other refection, arranged for you and the rest of the 'intake' (the word seems irresistible), according to the time of day when it is your college's turn to matriculate – if you belong to a college that bothers with these things. It may be a more or less agreeable crush in Hall, where the Master and some Fellows turn up and ask you 'what you are reading?' Signing the Master's Admission Book generally accompanies Matriculation, though it may be nothing more than another item of clerkly business at the college office. There is also a photograph, a freshmen's group, posed against the background of Hall or chapel. In another six or seven years you will hang this memento in a thin black frame on the stairs of your family residence, or (if you have such a thing) in your study. And there it will hang to your dying day, to remind you that you were once a freshman, and to identify the faces of men whom once you knew and who have long since faded into the cloud of unknowing.

"How are you doing?" the president of the Junior Parlour wants to know, when he meets a bunch of the newly-matriculated at the bar before Hall. "Feeling a lot better for it, I hope?"

Aerial view of Cambridge, 1959

Entrance to Clare College Avenue, showing King's College on the right, c. 1815 by R. Ackermann

"Man, I feel like a card that's been fed into a computer."

"Come, come, due respect and obedience for the Chancellor, Vice-Chancellor, and all those set in authority over us. . . ."

"I pity that poor old blighter sitting up there nodding ten to the dozen all day. He'll catch a packet of fibrositis before he's finished."

"Don't worry. They make 'em tough, these Vice-Chancellors. Besides, there are deputy V.-C.'s to do a spell for him."

"My father saw him during the war, when he was unrolling his carpet in North Africa. I had expected to see a more military figure."

"Talking about Tedder? My dear Albert, you can hardly expect the Chancellor to come down and nod to a gaggle of freshmen."

"We have been fobbed off with a Vice, my dear chap. Never mind. They're saving up the Chancellor himself for the day when they give you an honorary degree."

"I wish I knew how this place works. Are we supposed to be a democracy, or aren't we?"

Mr Vice-Chancellor, and Others

How the place works is known to few. Whether or not the place is a democracy is an improper question.

Mr. Vice-Chancellor, the effective head of the university, is elected annually in June and enters into office on the first of October. Normally, he serves for two years, so that his election is only a real one in alternate years. He is elected by the Senate, or as many of the members of the Senate as care to turn up, for every Master of Arts, past and present, is a member of the Senate, and there are between sixty and seventy thousand of them alive. It is very necessary and proper that he should be elected from the Heads of Houses,[1] for he receives a very modest stipend, and he must have an income and a house large enough to enable him to keep up a suitable style and hospitality.[2] The smooth

---

[1] 'Heads of Houses' rather than 'Masters of Colleges', because not every college can properly be described as such (e.g. Peterhouse, which is only antiquatedly called 'St. Peter's college', and Trinity Hall, and Fitzwilliam House. Nor can every Head of a House be called its 'Master', for Queen's has its President, King's has its Provost, and Fitzwilliam House has its Censor.

[2] True, the Vice-Chancellor has his entertainment allowance, but he has no official residence.

and peaceable way in which this great office passes from Head to Head of the Cambridge Houses is a credit to all concerned. It was not always so. But, as with so many English elective institutions, the give and take of enlightened oligarchy has turned out to be the answer to faction fighting. The younger universities, with the exception of London, have solved the problem differently. With few, or no, component colleges from among whose Heads to choose a head of the university, they have sometimes adopted the institution of a permanant, or professional, Vice-Chancellor. By choosing a fresh Vice-Chancellor every year (in fact, every two years), Cambridge, like Oxford, is able to enjoy, or suffer, the rule of the amateur. The result is a succession of learned men, for the most part well-versed in the routine of academic life;[1] men a large part of whose lives have been spent in teaching and the pursuit of learning; men whose full energies will be turned again to such pursuits when their little term of administrative authority is over. Such men may do odd things in office, even to the extent of investing a man of science with the degree of Doctor of Divinity, or counting votes twice over at a Senate House election, or forgetting to turn up. But these are thought to be a small price to pay for the inestimable advantages of a succession of fresh minds at the head of university affairs. And, after all, the Vice-Chancellor has the University Marshal – the inevitable Jeeves – who combines the functions of King's Remembrancer and Court Chamberlain,[2] not to mention a large administrative staff or civil service whose whole duty is to make the system, and the Vice-Chancellor, work.

The Vice-Chancellor may be seen. Preceded by his attendant Esquire

[1] 'For the most part ...' is a necessary qualification, for it may happen that the candidate by rotation is the head of a house who has been only recently elected thereto, and who has spent many years away from Cambridge. Such a person can, indeed, decline nomination. If he accepts (as he generally does), he has a lot of homework to do, and depends considerably on the advice of his predecessors in office. If he is unfit for the office on other grounds than inexperience of university affairs, as was that hard-drinking, hard-riding 'squarson', the Rev. Mr. Barton Wallop, who was wished on Magdalene College as its Master by the patron of its Mastership in 1774, both Vice-Chancellor and university are in for an unhappy time. Fortunately, the end of patronage in appointing heads of houses has made the recurrence of a Barton Wallop situation inconceivable. (For the case of Barton Wallop, see D. A. Winstanley's *Unreformed Cambridge*, pp. 19-21.)

[2] Gunning tells us of the famous Bore who served as University Marshal in the eighteenth century. He wore a blue coat and a silver arm-band, and was known as 'the Blue Bore'.

Bedells, or mace-bearers, and with the University Proctors at his heels, he makes a sufficiently impressive, but not garish, spectacle as he goes to Congregation at the Senate House or to university sermons at Great St. Mary's. Heads are turned and caps go off as he passes, the grand embodiment of the authority of the university, latest of a line stretching back over more than four hundred years. Only one other surpasses him in rank and dignity, and he is but rarely seen. This is the Chancellor himself, that non-resident potentate for whom the Vice-Chancellor serves as deputy, that distant deity who only comes near the place on such rare occasions as when the university awards honorary degrees to distinguished visitors. There has been a Chancellor ever since 1246. Since 1514 it has been the practice to elect him for life, and since he took to spending most of his life away from Cambridge, while his 'vice' performed his duties there, his life has sometimes been unnaturally short. His was certainly a dangerous trade in the time of the Tudors and Stuarts. No less than seven Chancellors of the University died violent deaths (on account of activities outside the university) between the Reformation and the Revolution. The very first Chancellor to be elected for life, John Fisher, President of Queens', Lady Margaret Professor of Divinity, and Bishop of Rochester, died on the scaffold for his differences with King Henry VIII in 1535. His successor, Thomas Cromwell, Earl of Essex, went the same way five years later. After him, both the Dukes of Somerset and Northumberland, who held the Chancellorship of the university, lost their heads in quick succession; Mr. Secretary Cecil died in his bed. But Robert Devereux, Earl of Essex, was executed for treason. The Duke of Buckingham was assassinated for serving Charles I both too well and too badly. The Earl of Holland brought up the tragic tale to 1649. These fell occurrences, however, were not to deter such distinguished men of affairs as the Prince Consort, two successive Dukes of Devonshire, and Lords Balfour, Baldwin and Tedder from accepting the dignity in subsequent generations.

Much of the insignia and regalia borne by the Vice-Chancellor came in the shape of gifts from the university's more unlucky Chancellors. The maces which are carried upside down before the Vice-Chancellor by his Esquire Bedells (and right-way up before the Chancellor) were

given by the Duke of Buckingham, and the silver-gilt Cup, which the
reigning Vice-Chancellor likes to display at High Table in his college,
by the Earl of Essex. He also has two gold signet-rings, though he no
longer uses them, and a true medieval *cappa*, or cope (the only example
still in use) which he wears when conferring certain degrees, and on
other ceremonial occasions. All these things, and some more, comprise
the moderate pomps of a Vice-Chancellor when he performs his duties
in the University on behalf of the Chancellor.

His entourage on these occasions is likewise moderate though
dignified. His Esquire Bedells who precede him with the maces are
gentlemen-beadles, senior members of the university whose functions
are nowadays purely ceremonial, although in earlier times they took a
managerial part in the university examinations. Henry Gunning, whose
Reminiscences have preserved for us a treasury of gossip about the older
Cambridge, served in this capacity for many years. The proctors who
bring up the rear of the Vice-Chancellor's suite are likewise senior
members, but their functions are not only ceremonious but, like
KoKo's, 'particularly vital'. They embody the disciplinary powers of
the university, and they come second only to the Vice-Chancellor in
precedence. Nominated by the colleges according to a highly complicated rota, they are admitted to proctorial office at the same time as the
Vice-Chancellor. They attend him at the Senate House and at University sermons. They are the guardians of his dignity and authority. There
are four of them, a Senior Proctor, a Junior Proctor, and two pro-
Proctors for reinforcement on important occasions.[1] Wrapped in their
swathed gowns which always look as if they have been put on back-
to-front, and drawn up over the breast as if to provide a toga-like
swathe of black stuff to sweep across the face in times of conspiratorial
assault upon wrong-doers, they stalk upon the scene like figures of
doom, ancient birds of prey, harbingers of fines, rustication, and final
expulsion.[2] The proctor, accompanied by his pair of constables, or

[1] There is also a special pro-Proctor for motor-vehicles and aircraft.
[2] Rustication, or sending into the country for a time, means going out of residence
for the rest of the term, or more; a penalty which will involve staying up for a further
period, after one's third year, in order to complete the necessary period of residence for a
degree. Expulsion, or sending down, is the end, and is inflicted only in extreme circum-
stances and by the vote of the Governing Body of one's college after an opportunity to
offer a defence, either in person or through one's tutor.

bull-dogs (generally recruited from college servants, fleet of foot and strong of arm, in their top-hats and black coats and bearing on cere- monial occasions such proctorial impedimenta as halberds, partizans and linstocks) parading the streets after dusk in the interests of sobriety and good order, is one of the classic sights of Cambridge, a sight that the undergraduate always hopes to be able to show to visiting parents, providing that he is properly dressed for the encounter. Naked of a gown, he may be able to show them more than he bargained for. . . . The darting bull-dog, diverging from the track of his lord and master, making a swift descent upon the victim.

"Are you a member of the university, sir?"

"Er – yes – actually, I am."

"The proctor would like to speak to you, sir."

The proctor lifts his square. The victim wishes that he had some- thing to lift in return.

"Your name and college, sir?"

Down it goes, in his little book. Another square-lift, a murmur of salutation, and it is over. . . . Until the morrow, when a billet-doux arrives requesting that Mr. X of Saint Y's College, call upon the proctor at his rooms at Saint Z's at a certain hour. This call will probably resemble an episode in a queue at a railway booking-office. The gentleman seems to be reciting in his sleep: 'Six-and-eightpence,[1] please. . . . Next. . . .' Collectors of Cantabrigiana generally have their proctorial receipts mounted and framed for the edification of their children. Proctors have a great deal more to do than walking the streets after dusk in order to collect gownless undergraduates. Even their peregrinatory activities are more complicated than that. They visit cinemas and theatres and other places of public resort (generally on request of the management). They take a look into public-houses, keeping a specially watchful eye on such haunts as have been declared out-of-bounds to undergraduates. In the days when there were

[1] A university born in the Middle Ages still continues to inflict monetary penalties in terms of medieval currency. A mark is taken to count as thirteen shillings and fourpence. The commonest fine is half-a-mark, or six-and-eightpence. B.A.'s are generally fined double. But proctors may, if they see fit, inflict a fine regardless of these traditional niceties. A number of rowdies at the theatre were recently fined a pound apiece. Monies thus levied are paid into the University Chest, and are not, as is commonly supposed, pocketed by the proctors.

numerous bawdy-houses,[1] their peregrinations involved espionage, ambush, and the art of siege. The year 1960 is only the first centenary of the great de Freville *coup*, when the proctors waylaid an omnibus-load of undergraduates and dressmakers, together with a small band of music, as it passed by Parker's Piece on the way to the de Freville Arms at Great Shelford, where, the proctors had advanced information, breakfast had been ordered for the following morning.[2] To-day, it is rare indeed for proctors to find their somewhat humdrum lives diversified by more than the rough-and-tumble of a Guy Fawkes night or a barracking at a theatre. Proctors are rather preoccupied with problems of whether or not to grant proctorial permission for various forms of festivity or public meeting, or with problems of taste and decency in undergraduate journalism. They are, on the whole, courteous, tolerant, and well-meaning men. Anyone who knows a proctor in private life finds it a little difficult to take him quite seriously when he meets him, in bands and robes, walking the streets. The general public tends to regard him increasingly as a slightly comic character in fancy-dress, an antique survival, an anachronism in the welfare-state. The undergraduate on rowdy nights shouts 'Fascist!' and runs away. However, proctors are adequately paid, and they are unlikely to have to do more than two years' service in the course of a lifetime.

It is into the proctors' safe-keeping that the retiring Vice-Chancellor resigns his regalia, either to receive it back if he is at the end of his first year, or to transmit it to his successor if he has served two years. It is on this occasion, which always falls on the first day of October at 9.30 a.m., that the Vice-Chancellor makes his speech to the assembled Congregation of the Senate. The ceremonial language of the university is still Latin, but the Vice-Chancellor's address on quitting office, like the debates in the Senate House, is nowadays delivered in English. This is just as well, since a considerable gathering of Doctors and Masters are waiting with some impatience to hear what he has to say. What he generally says is something like this:

---

[1] *See* footnote to p. 92.

[2] One of the consequences of this episode was a case in the Court of Common Pleas between one Emma Kempe and Latimer Neville, Master of Magdalene and Vice-Chancellor. (*See* D. A. Winstanley, *Early Victorian Cambridge*, pp. 380-1.)

That the past year has been one of orderly routine and consolidation; or/one of outstanding events and notable changes.

That more than a hundred Reports have been made by various Syndicates to the University, not one of which has produced a division of the Regent House; or/several of which have produced closely contested divisions of the Regent House, notably a Report on the place of Latin in the requirements for university entry, etc., etc.

That a number of important university buildings are nearing completion; notably some new lecture-rooms, a new Chemical laboratory, a new School of Veterinary Medicine, Engineering, or Psephology, any one of which is at any time liable to be opened by a Royal Personage.

That schemes include a University Club and a new Tripos.

That a new college is (a) in prospect; (b) designed, and a site purchased; (c) named, chartered and blessed by the celebrated personage whose name it bears.

That all who value our ancient college system must fervently hope and trust that the new college will prove an asset to the perpetuation of that priceless system.

That the university is faced more urgently than ever by the problem of controlling the creeping inflation of numbers, in itself a very real threat to the perpetuation of the said system.

That the present financial state of the university finances demands austerity, economy, and the pursuit of stability, or – at the very least – a policy of wise spending.

That while the State pays large sums to the university, the colleges are still, God be praised, self-supporting; long may they continue to be so.

That it is a sad duty to record the deaths of some university figures; that some others have entered into retirement or departed to services elsewhere; and that it is a pleasant duty to welcome certain newcomers.

That it has been equally a pleasure and an honour to serve as Vice-Chancellor during the past year, and that it will be equally an honour and a pleasure so to serve in that office during the year to come; or to be succeeded by . . .

That no one but the Vice-Chancellor can adequately assess and record the debt which he owes to his numerous assistants and advisers, to all of whom he wishes to accord his heartfelt thanks . . .

The Vice-Chancellor's speech is in no sense to be compared with the Speech from the Throne at the opening of Parliament. The Vice-Chancellor is not a Prime Minister. He does not enunciate or celebrate a policy. University history is not in the habit of referring to 'the enlightened Vice-Chancellorship of X', or 'the inspiring leadership of Y'. The Vice-Chancellor is more like (though not very like) a Chairman of Directors reading his annual report to that corporate body known to the law as 'the Chancellor, Masters and Scholars of the University of Cambridge', in whose name all corporate acts are done and in whose hands all power and property rests. Nor are the legislative acts of the university to be compared with statutes. Statutes are given to the university by the Crown. Under these statutes, the university is enabled to frame and pass rules for the conduct of its own affairs, or 'Graces'. A Grace may deal with almost anything, high or low, from a proposal to abolish compulsory Latin for university entrance to a permission for an undergraduate to take an examination notwithstanding that his tutor has entered him for the wrong papers.[1] Graces are promoted officially by the Council of the Senate, an elective body which serves as a kind of Cabinet through which Graces proceed on their way to legislative enactment by the Senate. Most Graces pass the Senate unopposed. Vast numbers of reports to the university, produced by syndicates (equivalent to commissions of inquiry) are adopted by the Senate without comment or discussion. The formal assent of the Senate to a Grace takes the form of a 'placet' – which simply means that the Senate is pleased. If a section of the Senate is displeased, notice is given of a 'non-placet', which simply means that a number of people intend to 'divide the House' when the Grace comes up. As soon as a non-placet is intimated, circulars or fly-sheets go out, indicating the arguments upon which the dissentients base their case for it, arguments which are at once countered by fly-sheets from those who intend to vote placet.

On an issue of outstanding importance – such as the recent issue over compulsory Latin – this war of words will wax fast and furious. The limitless capacity of academic persons for contention, lobbying and the more gentlemanly forms of intrigue, is then displayed to the full. Stately figures are to be seen parading with heads close together between the Senate House and the Pitt Press, on college lawns, and in the precincts of laboratories and lecture-rooms. And when the day

---

[1] For an error of this kind, a tutor is required to plead *incuria*. His plea goes on record: another species of tutorial nightmare.

comes for discussion of the question on the floor of the Senate House, benches which are normally half-empty will be crowded with the gowned contestants. Not for nothing was public disputation for centuries the university's mode of examination.

Mr. A.   declares that the wretched standard of Latin in the Previous Examination has for too long been a byword and a scandal. He would prefer Latin to be maintained, but for decency's sake let it be Latin, and not a crossword puzzle with a dictionary.

Mr. B.   thinks it doesn't matter as long as it is Latin. There is no such thing as easy Latin. Any Latin examination whatever is better than none. Shall it be said that men and women come up to Cambridge totally unacquainted with the learned tongue of western culture over so many centuries?

Dr. C.   recounts his own boyhood sufferings in acquiring a few scraps of this sacred subject in order to get into a university where he promptly forgot every word of it – and has never felt a penny the worse.

Dr. D.   records his thankfulness that he was beaten into the acquisition of the rudiments. He admits that he has forgotten them long since, and has never in his academic life found any need for them. But he is sure that his youthful experience was good for him. It taught him application, precision of mind, and the grand lesson that all worthwhile learning is hard: lessons that have stood him in good stead ever since in a quite alien field of study.

Dr. E.   wants to know why it should always be supposed that these lessons are best learnt from fagging at a *dead* language? English itself, learnt properly, with parsing, grammar and syntax, could serve the same purpose equally effectively. He quotes Sir Winston Churchill's testimony, that acknowledged master of the English tongue . . .

Prof. F.   points out that even if the university were so ill-advised as to drop Latin as a requirement for entrance, the colleges could, and would, insist upon a reasonable proficiency in the language when admitting men to read certain subjects – such as History, Law, and (of course) Classics.

Prof. G.   reminds the last speaker that his argument implies a deepening of the unfortunate cleavage between Science and the Humanities. The discrimination of which he speaks seems to imply acquiescence in the Two Cultures . . .

Mr. H. says (in other words) to hell with the Two Cultures. The situation
        exists, let's face it, and anyway – who cares? Let the devotees of the
        so-called Arts subjects have their play-things. Science already rules
        the world, and the really worthwhile scholars in supposedly non-
        scientific fields are practising scientific method, anyway. Away with
        all this meaningless talk about Science v. the Humanities. We are
        all scientists, now.

Mr. I. thinks it high time to return to the subject under discussion. The
        matter can only be profitably discussed empirically. Does Latin
        serve a purpose, as a subject for entrance? In his opinion, it does. No
        other language possesses the same testing qualities for intellectual
        capacity. If he thought that Russian possessed them, to the same
        degree, he would be in favour of compulsory Russian. The only
        real point, in his opinion, is whether the standard required in past
        years was high enough. In his view it was not. Make Latin a real
        hurdle, or abolish it. He could see nothing else to discuss.

After a lady don has put up a case for compulsory Anglo-Saxon, the
discussion draws to a rapid conclusion. A discussion in the Senate is
never followed immediately by a ballot. When the day appointed for
the ballot arrives, it is all over very quickly. Out of a Regent House[1] of
one thousand four hundred and twenty-five members, only forty-two
per cent turn up to vote. Of these three hundred and twenty-five vote
'Placet' on the resolution that persons should in future be able to secure
admission to the University without qualifying in a classical language.
The 'Non Placet' vote comes to two hundred and seventy-eight.
The 'non placets' comfort each other with the reflection that the decision can still be reversed at a later stage, for a syndicate has been
appointed to report on the whole question of regulations for the
Previous, and anyway there is always the question of what to require
in place of Latin. Some hope for a revival of compulsory Greek. Others
spitefully hope for compulsory Chinese. The 'placets' congratulate each
other on having helped to usher the university into what they call 'the
modern world' – and high time, too. They are quite wrong.

Graces are voted upon, not by the whole body of the Senate – save
in some few specified cases – but only by those members of the Senate

[1] See next paragraph.

whose names are on the Roll of the Regent House. Every Master of Arts, resident or non-resident, is a member of the Senate, and if the voting on Graces were open to the Senate as a whole, and if the whole sixty or seventy thousand members turned up, thereby constituting what is called 'a Congregation of the undivided Senate', the meeting would have to be held, not in the Senate House, but at Fenners or on Parker's Piece. So, the Senate is divided, and those entitled to take an active part in the government and administration of the university come to a total of some fourteen hundred out of the senatorial total of about seventy thousand. They are known as members of 'the Regent House' – the House of Regents, which simply signifies Governors. They are the resident teaching and administrative staff of the university. The Roll of the Regent House, duly revised, is published every year.

It is all rather confusing, especially for the undergraduate who wants to know how, and by whom, he is governed. After all, anyone might be forgiven for supposing that a body bearing the august name of 'the Senate' was the repository of real power. But it is not so. The 'undivided Senate' elects the Chancellor, and votes on certain kinds of Grace, but that portion of the Senate known as 'the Regent House' does everything else. It is no longer possible, as once it was, for coach-loads of country parsons to invade the Senate House in order to put a stopper on legislation to allow women to be admitted to degrees or the abolition of compulsory Greek for university entrance. The university, in fact, is effectively governed by those who teach its junior members and run its day-to-day business. Much of the work is done by the 'administrative-type' don, who never taught an undergraduate in his life. Like all other institutions of a complex and complicated nature, the university tends to be run by its civil servants. Fortunately for the non-administrative-type dons (generally the loudest critics of bureaucracy), there is always a plentiful supply. 'A genuine love of learning,' wrote the late D. A. Winstanley, 'is not given to all men, and not even to all Fellows of Colleges, but at the present day, those who have not this interest can yet play an extremely useful and valuable part in the University as administrators.'

The Regent House is not really a house. Nonetheless, there still survives a portion of the Old Schools, behind the Senate House, which properly bears the name because the Regents used to meet there. This again may perplex the undergraduate, since there is another building situated in Regent Street (named after the Prince Regent, later George IV, of blessed memory) and nearly opposite Downing College, which bears the inscription REGENT HOUSE in stucco letters two feet high, above its second floor. At street level, it is a restaurant. Undergraduates instructed to report for examination in the ancient room in the Old Schools have been known to turn up, suitably gowned, at the doors of the Taj Mahal Restaurant at nine o'clock on a Monday morning in early summer.

November 5th and Poppy Day

With Matriculation and the division of term, early days are over. The days of a thousand anticipations and a thousand surprises are giving place to the days of some few things accomplished. The freshman ceases to worry about concealing his freshness. He has come to terms with the lecture system; learnt how to keep his supervisor quiet (although prepared for him to break out again any time); and put names to some of the faces at High Table (and even had tea, or lunch, or sherry with some of them). He knows the quickest way to the Mill Lane lecture-rooms, the Divinity School, the Law School, the labs in the labyrinth of the Downing site and off Corn Exchange Street. He also knows where to find *The Whim*, *The Little Rose*, *The Gardenia*, *The Florence*, and *Snax*. If he is very precocious, he may even know his way to *Daddy's*. His feet positively glide over the well-worn tracks to the Arts Theatre and the Arts Cinema, the Regal, the Central and the distant Rex. Even the Faculty Library and the University Library have now a shadowy presence. Both literally and metaphorically he thinks he knows his way around. It will be another year, perhaps two, before he discovers that he doesn't know Cambridge. Indeed, he may never discover this, even if he has been inside King's College Chapel, the Senate House, St. Mary's the Great, and the hall of Trinity.[1]

[1] See pp. 237-47.

The language problem is simpler than it once was, for much of the old terminology of Cambridge life is dead or dying. The passing of some of it is scarcely to be regretted. Having your brekker before going to a lekker, and throwing your notes into the wagger-pagger-bagger, deserved to die before it lived. Nor, it seems, does anyone nowadays trouble to tell the young that one does not 'live' in one's rooms, but 'keeps' there. The ancient habit of calling one's living-room one's 'keep-room' or 'keeping-room' passed away when separate living-rooms gave place to bed-sitters. Sticklers for an older elegance, like Silas Stock, are still known to remind their pupils that they live on 'staircases' not in 'blocks', and that staircases lead down to 'courts' not to quads, let alone campuses. A questionnaire would probably reveal that scarcely one man in a hundred knows nowadays that 'sporting your oak' means locking your outer door; which is not really surprising, since few people apart from dons any longer have an outer door, or oak, to sport. As for that ancient Cambridge figure of fun, the policeman, he is no longer a 'Robert' or a 'Bobby' but a 'Copper' or quite simply a Policeman. This amendment probably represents one feature of the impact of northern England upon the south. It is a curious anomaly when one considers that undergraduates have a passion for calling each other by their Christian names, and that every undergraduate Bob is now a Robert, every Dick now a Richard, and every Jim now a full-blown James. The habit of referring to everyone by his Christian name and his surname together is probably a tribute to democracy, just as the same habit has come into the sporting prints with the breakdown of the old distinctions between amateurs and professionals.

Abbreviations of the names of colleges go on unaltered. Emmanuel and Pembroke are still Emma and Pemma. Fitzwilliam is still Fitzbilly. St. Catharine's is lingeringly Cats. Some few still refer to Peterhouse as Pothouse. No one ever rows for St. John's but for Lady Maggie, and no doubt the waters which flow along both sides of Trumpington Street from Hobson's Conduit and the Nine Wells by Shelford, are still known as the Pot and the Pem. Until fairly recently, freshmen learnt in their earliest days of the tipsy don who fell into one of these kennels and declined assistance from his friends with the adjuration:

"Never mind me. I can swim. Save the women and children first." It came the way of young Samuel Taylor Coleridge in 1792. Only Coleridge, being Coleridge, the legend was retailed in a letter home as involving himself.

I add a postscript on purpose to communicate a joke to you. A party of us had been drinking wine together, and three or four freshmen were most deplorably intoxicated. (I have too great a respect for delicacy to say drunk.) As we were returning homewards, two of them fell into the gutter (or kennel) We ran to assist one of them, who very generously stuttered out, as he lay sprawling in the mud: "N-n-n-no – n-n-no! – save my f-fr-fr-friend there; n-never mind me, I can swim!

Undergraduate 'jokes' are eternal, and this one, which is also to be found in Gunning's *Reminiscences,* has probably been told as long as the water-ridden town of Cambridge has had freshmen. Tales of the tipsy habits of dons, however, are far less frequent, and probably far less keenly relished, than they used to be. Thirty years ago, every under-graduate heard in his first year of the college tutor who was discovered sitting in the middle of the lawn under an umbrella after a Bump Supper night announcing that he was a mushroom, or of the lecturer who was discovered by his class sitting in a hip-bath with another bath on his head announcing that he was an oyster. The decline of the tipsy don story may possibly have something to do with the changing character of dons. It is much more likely to have something to do with the changing character, and tastes, of undergraduates. No longer does the mention of brewing in a lecture on economic history make the rafters ring and the floor resound under stamping hoofs as once it did.

The dean, making a discreet perambulation of the court in the company of the chaplain, on the night of November the Fifth, expresses the opinion that the college has settled down well, and that it looks like being an industrious and peaceful term. He always gets the chaplain to accompany him on his nocturnal stroll around the college on the Fifth. It is an undergraduate maxim that 'they' hunt in couples. But in truth 'they' are not hunting to-night, for they know full well that any-thing that may happen on Guy Fawkes night invariably happens on

Market Hill or in the streets thereabout, and that the night of the Fifth in college is one of the quietest nights of the year. This is the night of the proctors, not of college dons.

"There are even some people working," the dean remarks, observing lighted windows here and there around the court. "Quite encouraging, I must say."

"Sheer carelessness," says the chaplain. "They're always leaving lights on when they go out."

The frosty grass crackles softly under their pacing feet. The world beyond the dark line of the roofs around them is faintly rosy with fire, as if the town were stealthily burning. There is a tiny tang of burnt powder in the air. Cracks and bangs and thunderous explosions crepitate and rumble distantly. The sporadic fusillade has been steadily swelling into a bombardment since dusk. At frequent intervals the sky is ripped by the soaring course of a rocket, spangled by the cascades of red and green and golden rain.

"It always seems astonishing to me," the dean reflects, "that they do so little damage."

"You won't remember that night just after the war when some idiots set off dynamite and smashed the windows of the Senate House; 1948, I think it was."

"I gather from proctorial observations that most of the real hooliganism, where it occurs, is the work of townees, Teddy-boys, even lads coming in from the villages, all trying to persuade themselves that they are undergraduates."

"Not all of it, I fear," the chaplain sighs. "And oddly enough, when any of our men get into trouble, it's nearly always quiet little chaps who have got caught up in some mob. They go out simply to see what other people are doing, and half an hour later they find themselves doing it, and then a constable picks on the nearest and runs him in, generally because he hadn't the sense to run away."

"Good-night," says the dean, loudly and firmly, as two gowned figures cross the patch of lamplight on the path from the Porter's Lodge. "Two of yours, padre, I think," he adds *sotto voce*, having recognised the faces of Mr. Shalimar and Mr. Thwaites.

The chaplain, as acting tutor for the absent Alistair Wynne's pupils, feels obliged to accost the returning wanderers in suitably paternal fashion.

"None the worse for wear either of you, I hope?"

Mr. Shalimar speaks for both. He is supporting little Thwaites, who seems to be walking in his sleep.

"Oh no, sir," says Mr. Shalimar, his beaming eyes almost entirely eclipsed by his high padded cheek-bones. "The town is very quiet to-night, sir. We decided to return early."

"At proctorial suggestion? What's the matter with Thwaites?"

"He struck his eye on the elbow of a police-constable, sir. He is such a little man."

Mr. Thwaites is heard to murmur something about a 'bloody copper', as he hooks himself more securely within Mr. Shalimar's protective arm, and the two friends make their way slowly in the direction of K Staircase.

"East is East, and West is West," says the dean, as he falls in beside the chaplain to pace the grass once more. "The rest of the observation is plainly untrue."

"All the same, I hope that little Thwaites won't make this kind of an ass of himself too often," the chaplain sighs. "He's the most promising cox we've had up in years."

In the morning, when the tutors ring each other up to exchange notes, they find that they can congratulate themselves that no one has had to be bailed out at the Police Station this year. At the same hour, Peter Plummer's friends are congratulating him on the addition of a policeman's helmet to the trophies that adorn his rooms. After all, this is his third year, his last chance. 'Third time lucky,' is his own summary of the night's proceedings.

'Rags', at Cambridge, are not what they were, as old members tell each other when they come up for Association dinners.[1] The fact is that they have been sublimated. In earlier times there was a 'rag' several times a year. Enormous energy and ingenuity were expended on suit-

---

[1] Even the term 'rag' is going out of fashion since the younger universities have taken it over. A correspondent in *Varsity*, in a letter discussing the proposal to institute a single day in the academic year when funds should be raised for charities in general, to replace the single-purpose 'Poppy Day', recommends that 'every effort should be made to avoid the provincial overtones of calling the new day a 'rag day'.

The Backs – Barges and Punts and a view of King's College Chapel and Clare Hall (after *The Itinerant*, J. Walker, 1793)

King's College Chapel – Interior floodlit

able celebration of events like the visit of Kitchener after the South
African War, the rejection of degrees for women or the Revised Prayer
Book, or the opening of the tomb of Tutankamen. The whole Bench
of Bishops paraded through the streets, pushing prams. The most
extraordinary assortment of objects were brought up from the under-
ground lavatories on Market Hill by kilted and varnished Egyptians.
Long processions of cabs and carriages followed the hearse and coffin
to the station when an undergraduate was sent down. And there were
the hoaxes, as when the Sultan of Zanzibar was met at the station and
conducted to the Senate House to be received by suitable university
'authorities'; and when, too, workmen, digging up the road, were told
that a body of undergraduates disguised as policemen would shortly
arrive to put a stop to their operations, and the police were told that
a body of undergraduates disguised as workmen were digging up the
road. All these abounding energies, all this misplaced ingenuity, is now
concentrated on the great constructive effort of Poppy Day.

The undergraduate body sets up its standing Poppy Day committee,
and each college sets up its committee for its own special effort. There
is intense rivalry between the colleges to raise the largest sum. From
the crack of dawn to the fall of dusk on the Eleventh of November,
or whatever day is appointed for the commemoration of the Armistice,
hordes of wolves and hawks armed with rattling collecting-boxes turn
the city of Cambridge into an enormous engine of extraction. Tumbrils
full of powdered aristocrats rumble down to the guillotine set up outside Trinity Great Gate; cages full of white-slaves from Girton and
Newnham are driven on lorries with the cracking of whips; satellites
go up from brewery-waggons; there is a bull-fight on Parker's Piece;
kilted Highlanders pipe their way in solemn formation through all the
main highways; every car is stopped at barriers by highwaymen with
collecting-boxes; every pavement has its 'mile of pennies'; and as dusk
falls a gentleman clad only in a mackintosh soaked in paraffin leaps in
flames into the river from Magdalene Bridge. All work stops; somehow the city struggles along with its business; and when the tumult
and the shouting dies, there is another £12,000 in the Earl Haig Poppy
Fund. There are some who think that the proceeds should be devoted
to a wider variety of good causes.

H

The Working College

From an Open Letter to an Undergraduate:

Do you ever do any work at Cambridge? You are 'up' for six months in the year, in three spells of two months, and whenever we hear about you you are rowing, or ragging, or debating about birth-control, or (as far as your dons are concerned) performing on the telly. We can only charitably assume that you put the blacking on your boots at Cambridge, and spend your time at home polishing it. Considering the vast sums that we, the tax-payers, spend on you, we are bound to wonder whether it is worth it.

It will be time to go home in two or three weeks time, and it is as well to be prepared with an answer. It is best not to quote Greek, even if one is up to it. Not a bit of good telling them that the Greek word for leisure is the origin of our word for school, and that true learning begins where work leaves off. This would be suspected as special pleading. Don't quote the Senior Tutor on how the young men 'educate each other'. They will want to know why in that case dons are paid two thousand a year, and then it will be necessary to point out that a college is defined in its Statutes as 'a place of education, religion, learning and research', and that the education of the young is only one out of its four functions. Probably attack is the best form of defence. Ask them, as the Oxford don asked the Trade Unionist:

"What do you do when the hooter goes for knocking-off time?"
If they have been well-trained, they will reply:
"We go home."
It is then time to deliver the body-blow. Simply say:
"We don't."[1]
If this doesn't finish them, the only thing to do is to wrap up in a warm overcoat, or a couple of blankets, and lock oneself in one's bedroom for six hours a day for five days a week, and end up by getting a First in the tripos. One would be well-advised to do this, anyway.

Many an undergraduate asks his tutor, or more often his supervisor, how many hours a day he ought to work, and the answer is always the same: it all depends on the kind of person you are. Some people can get more out of a couple of hours reading than others can get out of half

[1] The *locus classicus* for this gambit is Dacre Balsdon's *Oxford Life* (1957), p. 207.

a day, or a whole day. Some people never really discover how to read at all. They can follow the words on the page, and they can make out what they mean, but they take their reading as others take knitting – so many rows to be accomplished before the piece is rolled up and put aside with a warming sense of duty done. Or they take books as bottles whose contents have to be poured into their minds. In either case, reading is something that has to be 'done', not something to be experienced and made part of oneself. And it is very difficult to teach people to read profitably. Some dons don't even try. They expect the young man to know. They set him an essay, or a piece of work, and suggest a few books that he should 'read' in order to write it. The unpractised scholar assumes that he has to summarise the contents of these books and turn the product into a *précis*, which will constitute his 'essay'. Nine times out of ten, of course, confronted with this boring and barren task, he will turn to a text-book summary or some lecture-notes, where he will probably find the subject treated with such necessarily generalized brevity that all the real issues are distorted and all the possible solutions boiled down to one. He has not learnt, perhaps he will never learn, how to use books; that profitable reading is not a matter of ploughing through, but a matter of digging out; that a book is best used when you know what you want to know; that profitable reading, for scholastic purposes, is primarily a matter of knowing what questions to ask of your authority. It is this posing of profitable questions, rather than the supplying of 'correct' answers, that a supervisor is there to assist. And this is something that comes out of a lot of patient talk, speculation, suggestion; for a supervisor is properly not a teacher in the sense of a purveyor, but an assistant in the process of self-education. It is scarcely possible to measure this work in terms of time.

Thus 'work', at the university, is in the first place qualitative rather than quantitative, and more than enough of it can be achieved in the intensive activities of six months in Cambridge to serve for the digestive and elaborative processes of the rest of the year. But, of course, it is very difficult to put this across to friends and relations who still think of 'work' as acquisition of knowledge, and who equate the knowledge acquired quite simply with time spent. The overcoat and the back bedroom are far more convincing.

It is towards the end of the Michaelmas Term that one first gets the sense of belonging to a 'working college'. The newcomers have had time to settle down, to get to know what it is all about, and they are alive to the fact that there are only two or three weeks left in which to put on the blacking that may profitably be polished in the vacation. Those who began by despising lectures may even attend a few at this time of term. Those who have gazed remotely at the tall and blunted tower of the University Library with its thin streamer of smoke (for they say that the librarian burns surplus copies of horror comics in there),[1] and wondered whether they would ever dare to venture within those massive tiled and glass-eyed labyrinths, may now cross the river at Clare bridge and wander slowly through Memorial Court. They may even enlist the good offices of a second or third year man in order to creep inside without looking, and feeling, too unutterably lost. Duncan Macleod, intent as ever upon enjoying what his father calls 'the privilege' of being a Cambridge undergraduate, goes in under the wing of Peter Plummer. He is astonished to discover that he, an undergraduate of less than a single term's standing, can wander at will among the open 'stacks' and carry off any books that take his fancy to read in the airy comfort of the great Reading Room. He is not at all surprised that he will not be allowed to take books away until he has taken a part of his tripos, and then only through his tutor. The very idea of being able to browse along these miles of shelves strikes him as wonderful, as indeed it is.

"Down there," says Peter, pointing to the left when they come to the first floor, "down there is Anderson."

"Who's he?" Duncan whispers.

"Chap who keeps the dirty books," Peter informs him, and disappears in that direction, leaving Duncan to fend for himself with the aid of the threepenny *Reader's Guide* which he has bought at the entrance desk. 'Anderson', he soon discovers, is the name of the room where the reserved books may be read, ranging from Frank Harris's *Life and Loves* to manuscript 'Penitentials' of the Middle Ages. Peter, he

---

[1] By the Licensing Act of 1662, the University Library at Cambridge, the Bodleian Library at Oxford, and the King's Library at Windsor, were entitled to receive a copy of every book printed in the King's realm. This was reaffirmed by the Copyright Acts of 1709 and 1814.

decides, was merely showing off. He doesn't know that the clerk's son from Norwich, who has already one First in the classical tripos to his name, is looking beyond his coveted First in part II towards the promised land of 'research'. Duncan spends a happy afternoon on the prowl, finishing up with tea in the basement tea-room, where he meets Peter again and puts on an act of taking all these newly-discovered privileges in his stride.

"It's a pity they built the place so far from College." he complains.

"You don't suppose they'd have been allowed to build such a monstrosity anywhere else, do you?" Peter demands. "It's easily the most hideous building in Cambridge."

As a 'colonial' (a term that he doesn't in the least object to), Duncan knows that he will be in Cambridge for a good part of the vacation. That will be the time, he tells himself. He will more or less live in the University Library over the Christmas vac., and really do some reading.

"How many books did you say there are?" he asks Peter as they cycle back to college in the early darkness.

"Oh, about a million and a half. Thinking of reading them all?"

He is. The fantasy expresses his jubilation at the opening of endless horizons. Speeding along under the blackening trees of Garret Hostel lane, he scarcely sees the grey face of Wren's library with its arcade looking down the lawns from Trinity. He supposes it is the chill air of the wintery Cambridge evening that has started the tears from his eyelids.

"We are, after all, a working college, my dear Alan," Silas Stock remarks to the second tutor as they slowly cross the court after Hall. "Observe the lighted windows. Allow the studious silence to sink into your soul."

"Nonsense, my dear Silas," says Dr. Skinner, "They're playing cards, or they've gone to the cinema and left their lights on to fox us. The bursar is always complaining about that."

All the same, there is a hushed air of industry about the place on these late November nights. The lamps at the angles of the court burn steadily until midnight, and when they are switched off the court still gleams with the white light of the window-panes. The footfalls of some late-comer drift over the gravel and fade on the stone of a staircase.

Once and again there is an agonized howl from the upper darkness where someone's party is still in progress. Bells chime away the small hours, the stumbling sound of clashing cymbals comes down the wind from the station-yards, owls go hunting with little shrieks in the Fellows' garden, and all night long the fountain sings in the midmost darkness of the court. And still there are lights aloft, diminishing one by one as the night passes onward to another day.

Daffyd Evans closes his Nonesuch Donne and strolls across to the window.

"The lights are going out all over Cambridge," he says, pressing his nose on the pane.

"About time, too," says Philip Hughes-Browne, dropping Tanner's Tudor Documents beside his chair and knocking out his pipe.

"They'll be lighted again, to-morrow and to-morrow and to-morrow," Daffyd groans, and drinks off the last of his beer. "Like that Yorkshire chap when the guide told him how many gallons of water go over Niagara every day, I can see nowt in partic'lar to stop it."

"Why do you want to stop it?"

Philip recalls the lighted enthusiasm of the Welsh face at his side when they had come here, six – seven – weeks ago.

"Cambridge is hell," Daffyd declares gloomily. He has been reading a lot of Isherwood lately. "Insidious hell . . . Cambridge is a monster, a blood-sucking blasé monster. It attacks you when you are off your guard, and before you know where you are all poetry and individuality have been drained out of you, and you become a motor-bike or history maniac. Beware of the daemon of history, Philip bach. It is merciless. It eats the flesh and heart and leaves the bleaching bones. History, history, hysteria!"

"Oh, shut up, you Welsh rabbit."

"I tell you, man, I shall only get this insidious Cambridge out of my system when I get back to Llantovery and primary production. Ah Philip bach, how my soul yearns for the smell of a slag-heap."

End of Term

The end-of-term feeling is in the air. The trees are bare in the Backs. The ditches beside Garret Hostel lane, and beside the frosty lawns, are choked with the blackening debris of autumn foliage. The river is laced with the black crepe of the leafless willows under the low grey skies of December. Lights go on in the court at tea-time, and it is dark in the Cury by half-past four. From beyond the candle-lighted panes of chapel windows there come the high pure tones of college choirs practising for the end-of-term carol service. In a few days there will be mountains of luggage outside the Porter's Lodge, flat caps and gutter-crowned hats will come out of store, taxis will roar round Hyde Park Corner and the War Memorial. Michaelmas Term will die without drama or festivity. Tripos examinations are still six months distant. Bumping races belong to Lent and Easter. 'Cuppers'[1] begin after the New Year. Michaelmas Term ends with neither a bang nor a whimper. Not even a college concert. Only a carol service.

The dons have done sharpening their knives for the Scholarship boys several weeks ago. Now it only remains for the victims to arrive on the scene of their immolation. The very trains that bear away the seven thousand undergraduates disgorge the two thousand schoolboys. Towards dusk they are to be seen, hatless, raincoated, grip in hand, scanning college gateways, doubtless wondering why a Cambridge college omits to set its name above its portals. They will only ask their way surreptitiously, and of persons who are plainly townsfolk. There is something touching, and a trifle forlorn, about the aspect of these unobtrusive wanderers in the land of heart's desire. Within a few hours, of course, they will be swinging along in little companies, putative undergraduates, would-be conquerors. Their aspect, then, in the eyes of those who watch them from the fastnesses of the citadel, will be more touching still. For many of them, this brief taste of Cambridge is all that they are ever destined to enjoy. For the rest, all unknown to themselves, it is a foretaste of the life to come. And who is who, or

---

[1] 'Cuppers' are matches played in the knock-out competition between colleges for the rugger cup, the soccer cup, etc., as distinct from friendly fixtures. Cuppers are played in the second term, by which time the college teams have been welded into practised sides, and have also had the opportunity to take the measure of each other. (*See* pp. 204-5.)

which is which, is on the lap of gods known as examiners, at present keeping pace, hour by hour, with the paper outpourings that go on in Trinity Great Hall, or the engineering laboratories, or Mill Lane. So intensive is the labour of these arbiters of destiny that they may have parted the obvious sheep from the obvious goats even before the last session of the written examination is over. For this final session is 'the general paper' which all candidates must take, whatever their specialised subject. The more ghoulish examiners have been known to watch their victims coming away from this concluding session with a sense of watching the dead walking.

The work of examining these schoolboy competitors for the scholarships and exhibitions offered by the colleges of the university is some of the most intensive and exacting that goes on in the academic year. This is as it should be, for a young man who wins a college scholarship goes on to the 'foundation'. He becomes a member of that corporate body, 'the Master, Fellows and Scholars' of the college, in whose name the corporate acts of the college are done. Moreover, to win an 'open award' entitles the successful candidate to 'supplementation' by the State: his scholarship may be worth only £100 or £60 per annum, and his exhibition only £40, but its value will be made up to such a total as will cover all his fees and his living costs (provided family financial conditions justify it). In a very real sense, therefore, the examiners for open awards are telling the State on whom it should spend public money. Again, the responsibility involved is very great vis-à-vis the college. Examiners are selecting the man who, it is fairly confidently to be expected, will do it honour in university examinations at a later stage. They may also feel, with some justification, that they are selecting the men who will some day be the future Fellows of the college. A large proportion of the Fellows of colleges at any one time may be said to have made their academic debut in open scholarship examinations. On the other hand, of course, a considerable number of successful candidates in open scholarship examinations turn out to be quite ordinary second-class men in their university careers. Some prove to have shot their bolt at this early stage of their academic life and never shine again, either at the university or anywhere else in particular.

No academic examining is infallible, but in order to ensure that it is as reliable as possible in point of accuracy and judgment, the colleges have formed themselves into groups, each composed of some half a dozen colleges, and each of which appoints examiners who take part in the examination of all candidates who chose to enter for a college in the group. Thus the work of a candidate for an award at any one college in the group will be seen by examiners from four or five other colleges besides. This ensures, it is hoped and believed, the maintenance of a common standard. A successful candidate will thus have run the gauntlet of some half a dozen diverse and experienced minds. His work, and that of all candidates who survive the first eliminating round of the competition, will have been discussed and weighed and compared with considerable care and exactitude.[1] When the group examiners have drawn up their classified lists of scholars (major and minor) and exhibitioners, it is up to the component colleges to adopt them. A college will normally 'honour its first preferences', as the saying goes: that is, it will elect those who have given it their 'first preference' on the entry-form, to scholarships or exhibitions at the college according to the examiners' recommendations. If a college finds itself with more successful candidates than it can take for any particular class of award, in any particular subject, it will signify its intention to 'drop' this man or that, and he will 'fall through' to the college of his second choice, and so on down the list. There are always some successful candidates who fall through thus to colleges of their second, third, or other preference. The negotiations between the colleges of the group on these matters are conducted at a meeting of college representatives (normally tutors) on the day after the examining is concluded. This meeting is known as 'the auction'. The name might seem to have a slight ring of the slave-market about it. In fact, however, it is a perfectly fair and reasonable way of seeing that all successful candidates are taken on at some college, and as closely as possible to the declared preferences of the candidates.

When all this is over, and it takes some ten to fourteen days to complete the work, examiners can feel that the labours of the Michael-

---

[1] This, at least, is the ideal. In subjects like history it is also the reality. In some subjects, however, it is rumoured that the job is done with a pair of scales and a slide-rule.

mas Term are over. Of course, tutors are still faced with the work of informing successful and unsuccessful candidates alike of their fate. Perhaps within three or four days of Christmas Eve, everyone concerned feels able to relax. The thousands of young men who went home at the end of term probably imagine that dons stop work the moment their train has puffed out of Cambridge station. This is only one of their manifold illusions. Nor is it really surprising that the Fellows of the college see fit to indulge in a Christmas dinner on a rather more elaborate scale than their customary dinner in Hall.

A satire from the Cambridge Review *on 'The Women's War' (see page* 232)

Interlude – Cambridge Christmas

Where do dons go in the winter time? They go to Twickenham, in the first place. Even while the schoolboys are writing their examinations dons by the dozen set out in the grey December morning to join the vast caravanserai converging on Twickenham for the Rugger Match. As Universities, Oxford and Cambridge meet only in the fields of sporting contest, and the Rugger Match is the first major fixture of the academic year. It has not a little of the character of a ritual, for the Twickenham stands contain not only whole generations of the Rugger world, but old men and beardless boys, women and children, dons and College porters, gyps and groundsmen, town and gown. These roaring ranks of worshippers keep up a tumult which lasts all through the short winter afternoon while the battle of the fifteens sways to and fro. Second only to fox-hunting, Rugger affords the very image of war with its racing lines, its falling bodies, its heaving head-down scrums and its leaping line-outs. 'This is a rough game, papa,' cries little Polly Donling, aged six and a half. 'I think I shall enjoy it.' A game for cads played by gentlemen, some one once called it.

But, after Twickenham, where do dons go? In the distant days of resident and unmarried dons, they commonly kept Christmas in college with the Master, like the household of a manor-house. The Twelve Days of Christmas, when a foundation like Trinity College kept open house, were once famous. Nowadays they mostly spend the greater part of Christmas Day, and the adjoining days, in the bosom of their families. Many of them go away immediately after the Fellows' Christmas dinner and their place knows them no more until very nearly the first day of the Lent Term. Even Mr. Stock, in these days, goes to his sister at Walthamstow on Christmas Eve and returns on Boxing Day. He grumbles about this, gloomily predicting the arrival of the day when the steward will drive resident Fellows on to the streets and into public eating-houses on the last day of full term. The steward has to consider his kitchen staff, and greatly hopes that resident Fellows will contrive to get themselves invited to the households of friends and relations for at any rate a few days. Increasingly he is in the habit of sending round a notice to announce that High Table will close down on such-and-such a day and re-open about ten days later. But Fellows will stand on their privileges, among the most cherished of which is their privilege of dining at college expense on every day of the year. The dictates of Trade Unions and Catering Wages Boards, they will *in extremis* declare, are none of their business. They are, however, very much the business of the steward, and this tug-of-war between college stewards and resident Fellows is, in many colleges, still unresolved.

Of course, in this, as in so many other contests that afflict college relationships in a changing world, there is right on both sides, and reasonable compromise has to be reached. The point of principle involved is the ancient character of a college as an institution which shares in what Burke called 'the mode of existence decreed to a permanent body composed of transitory parts'. Properly speaking, a college never 'closes'. There is no single day in the three hundred and sixty-five when the gates are locked, the curtains down and the carpets up. A college is a house, not a hotel; a home not a hostel. True, where there is a road or a path through a college, the gates will be closed and locked for one day in the year in order to preserve it from the establishment of a right-of-way by the general public. Passage through such a college, its courts and gardens, is permitted to the public by courtesy of the Master and Fellows, under certain light restrictions such as the prohibition of bicycles, prams and dogs; and on the whole, the Cambridge colleges are generous in these things. But if there is a single day in the year when gates are closed and locked, it is generally Christmas Day or Boxing Day. Then, and especially towards the festive hour of noon, life there comes nearest to the total ebb. Even the porter, or his deputy, seems to have left the telephone; and, peeping through the gate-bars or the keyhole, the unlikely visitor would probably see, and feel, something as uncanny as any sight in all the world: a college holding its breath in the brief trance of suspended animation.

Cambridge at Christmas has a life and a beauty all its own. The weather is generally mild and sunny, and the pale sunshine lends to brick and stone a fragile charm uncharacteristic of the place at any other time of the year. For a moment, this most masculine of universities wears the pale tinted smile of an ageing beauty. The strong

Tudor-rose brick of Trinity Street bears the pretty pink of the dog-rose; the tawny lion-gold and brown of Christ's and Corpus and Pembroke fades almost to lime and lemon; the grave pewter greys of Clare and King's, the Senate House and Emmanuel, are lighted to the smile of silver. At any moment one expects to see the neo-gothic spikes and crockets of the wedding cake at the back of St. John's close the vista across the Backs with dreaming spires. Wren's work at Pembroke and Trinity comes into its own with the grateful pellucid light of wintry sunshine. Even William Wilkins' cumbrous cubes at Downing are lightened as the sifted splendour brings forth the softer tints of pink and grey and rose from Ketton stone. Flagged pavements and winter grass lie like quiet shores at the feet of these serenely shining cliffs. Hour upon hour they give up scarcely the sound of a passing foot as they dream in the sun of the departed throngs of terms innumerable that are over, of throngs that will return with Lent and Easter and the Long. It is this dreaming peace of Christmas present that is broken by the voice of the boy-chorister singing of Royal David's City in King's College Chapel on Christmas Eve.

To many millions of people, all the world over, Christmas is symbolized by the familiar lines of the chapel of King Henry VI. Wherever English-speaking people dwell on the face of the earth, the message of Christmas comes to them on Christmas Eve in the voices of the King's choristers in the service of Nine Lessons and Carols. Few of them have ever seen, or will ever see, in their bodily presence, the simple splendour of its setting, the glory of glass, the grace of branching stone, the miraculous spread of the fan-vaulting which canopies the whole like the frozen fronds of a towering forest which meet and interlock with infinite grace beneath the mid-winter sky. The short day is dying over river and fen. The greens and golds and purples in the high windows melt into a universal black, and only the radiant blue collects the remaining light. The candles brighten to flickering founts of ochre. The forest leafage high overhead is almost gone into night. Crouching aloft on the great screen at the crossing, the organ puts forth its soft and trembling thunder from below the uplifted golden trumpets of the seraphim. The great throng of the congregation rises to its feet as the boys and the young men in their surplices come threading through its midst, leading the last anthem in a chorus of universal praise. Behind them come the slow-stepping Provost, the Vice-Provost, the Fellows and the Scholars and the visiting lesson readers from the city and the city's churches. The voices die into silence, the organ breaks into the parting voluntary, and the great crowd streams out into the December dusk. All across the town, little groups of worshippers peel off into the maze of streets, and the ranks of waiting cars in King's Parade strip off their radiator-rugs and blankets and go purring into silence. Soon the great Chapel will be dark and silent, too, waiting through the quiet night for the bells that will ring out from St. Mary's tower and all the city belfries on Christmas morning.

LENT TERM

Second Year Men

Lent Term begins early in January, and before the New Year is a fortnight old Cambridge is full again. It happens unobtrusively, almost surreptitiously. Swallows and daffodils had their dramatic and delightful days in September and October. In January, with its meagre hours of daylight and its Siberian blasts, it is a matter of the returning tide.

> Far back, through creeks, and inlets making,
> Comes silent, flooding in, the main.

Townsfolk tell each other: 'the men are back.' Everyone is too busy keeping warm to bother.

"As I was saying, gentlemen . . ." the Severn Bore reminds his audience as he opens the folder which contains his Lent Term lecture notes.

"When was that?" Mr. Hughes-Browne whispers to Mr. Macleod.

"Last year," whispers Mr. Macleod in his literal fashion.

For there are lecturers who take a deep breath over a comma in December only to expel it again in January. Men resolved, it seems, to make manifest the continuity of History.

"I am Tarbet of St. Tom's," the Tar-baby announces, opening wide his arms above the rostrum. "It is just possible that some of us are still strangers to each other. . . ."

"Surely not," whispers Mr. Macleod.

"Sure as fate," whispers Mr. Hughes-Browne.

Mr. Parker smiles diabolically as he pins a notice on his door announcing that he will be unable to see his pupils until Thursday week. He has been invited to take part in a session of the television Brains Trust.

"Do 'em a power of good to set themselves their own essays for once," Mr. Parker tells himself as he sports his oak.[1]

[1] 'Sporting the oak'. See p. 109 above.

"The sheep look up and are not fed," Silas Stock observes, to no one in particular. He has just caught sight of a little queue that has been steadily forming since nine o'clock outside the entrance to Alistair Wynne's rooms on H Staircase. "Nor perhaps is this to be regretted when one reflects upon dear Alistair's notions of nourishment."

Dr. Skinner, crossing the grass at high speed on his way to the college office, also observes the unfed sheep. He tells himself for the three hundred and sixty-fifth time that the election of Alistair Wynne was a mistake, that the man has not justified his place, and that he doesn't pull his weight. Dr. Skinner's pupils have been steadily working at back tripos papers from their first supervision in October, and will go on doing so until the last supervision of their last term.

Ten minutes later, Alistair Wynne's long and elegant figure, clad in charcoal-grey suiting, appears on a bicycle. He pedals slowly round the court with the sombre grace of the Swan of Tuonela. The bursar glares out of the top window of the bursary staircase and nearly swallows the ends of his military moustache in baffled rage. He has been conducting a campaign for the last twelve months to discourage the Fellows of the college from exercising their privilege of riding bicycles in the court. Alistair waves up at him, drops one foot to the gravel under the steps of H Staircase, and lets his bicycle fall into the clutches of the nearest of his waiting pupils.

"Happy New Year, gentlemen," he greets them in the resonant tones which once, and unavailingly, resounded in the Court of Queen's Bench. "Come on up, the whole crowd of you. I can just as well say my piece to ten as to one of you."

The queue vanishes into H Staircase and up the stairs like rabbits scurrying into a burrow. Ten minutes later they all come tumbling out again. Thus the tutorial method of Alistair Wynne. Instead of the slow-motion conveyor-belt process, by which a succession of individuals is fed steadily into the tutorial sanctum, where each is given a handshake, asked whether he has enjoyed the vacation, whether he has got any work done, whether he has any problem for tutorial solution, and then gently eased out of the room (with or without having consumed a glass of sherry, according to the size of the waiting queue): instead of this process, with its emphasis on 'the personal note which distinguishes the tutorial system of the older universities' – Alistair employs what he quite unashamedly calls 'mass-production methods''. He decided quite early in his career that 'the personal note' in a college of four hundred undergraduates and three tutors, was a piece of anachronistic humbug; a subtle form of self-flattery for tutors, a slow-motion sausage-machine for undergraduates, and a waste of time for everyone. Chiefly it was a waste of time for dons who, in Alistair Wynne's opinion, should on no account be encouraged to lay the flattering unction to their souls that tutoring is a full-time job. It should rather, he conceived, be a side-line to scholarship, which it always was until the recent appearance of the 'professional tutor'. Alistair therefore has taken his own line, to the scandal of his colleagues and the rejoicing of his pupils. If the college possessed a peal of bells, Alistair Wynne's pupils, rushing up H Staircase at the beginning of the Lent Term as into a belfry, would ring the changes for a whole hour to celebrate the return of their tutor from the New World to restore the balance of the Old.

The most fervent bell-ringers would be the second year men. If to be left alone is the undergraduate dream, it is more especially the dream of the second year men in the Lent Term. For the Lent Term is their term in a quite peculiar way. If life at Cambridge be not a rich and rare thing now, they feel, then surely it never will be. With all the experience of freshman's year behind them, and with a whole term's experience of second year splendours, they are in a position to enjoy an increasing sense of maturity together with a lingering sense of *insouciance*. They have had four out of their nine lives. After this present term there will be four more. Any third year man will tell you that he lives on a *glissade*. There is a haunted look in his eye. Only the second year man, with spring and summer before him, can afford to forget about past and future. . . .

> Unborn TOMORROW, and dead YESTERDAY,
> Why fret about them if TODAY be sweet!

Of course, the second year man does fret, he does remember, he does look forward with trepidation from time to time. So did old Omar,

otherwise he wouldn't have spent so many sweet stanzas in recommend-
ing total forgetfulness. But it still remains true that the second year
man, *nel mezzo camin del sua vita*, has the edge over everyone else in
the matter of living in the present. There is no longer such a thing as
the care-free undergraduate, but the second year man in the Lent Term
is about the nearest thing to it.

Second year men are the solid keel of the undergraduate body. They
are the responsible officers of clubs and societies: not presidents, perhaps,
but – what is far more important – Hon. Secs. They have made their
way into solid membership of those coteries where undergraduates
practice the kind of activities they hope to engage in when they leave
the university. They form the hard core of Union Society debaters if
they are making for politics or the law. They cultivate crew-cuts and
brisk manners as cub reporters or special correspondents for *Varsity* if
they aim at journalism, or they cultivate beards and a 'beat' look if
they more vaguely want to 'write'. Thousands who no less vaguely
want to be actors, producers, librettists, song-hit writers, comic men,
scene-painters or stage-technicians, join up with the A.D.C., the
Marlowe Society, the Mummers, the Footlights, and scores of more
ephemeral groups for the promotion of song and dance and mime.
'Dramatics' of some kind or another absorb endless time and energy
on the part of both male and female undergraduates, to the abiding
distress of their tutors and teachers. Nor are they content, as once they
were, with amateur status and standards. The 'professional' undergraduate has replaced the old-time dilettante. They aim to sell their
Cambridge productions to London managers. London agents, critics
and talent scouts come down to watch their shows, and it is by no
means uncommon to hear the undergraduate addict of the arts refer
to 'my agent . . . in town. . . .' As for music, the old University Musical
Society (C.U.M.S.) is only the doyen of musical life in the university.
College musical societies, choirs, madrigal clubs, orchestras large and
small, afford an almost limitless field for choral and instrumental talent.
Not only the quantity but the quality of the musical life of the university is far higher than it has ever been. The fashion is for polyphonics
and counter-tenors, sewing-machine rhythms and castrati-wailings,
and every variety of syncopation from old-fashioned Jazz (now regarded

as serious music, worthy of historical research, and respect), to the moribund rock-and-roll, antique jive, and the latest thing in washboards and guitars. Politics, more especially party politics, which flourished so exceedingly in the 'thirties, play a comparatively minor role among undergraduate activities nowadays. Instead, everyone acts or sings or plays the flute, the trombone or the clarinet. Those who don't (and even some who do) prefer a prayer-meeting to a political party. 'Religion' is in again. Everywhere, on doors, over mantelpieces and beds, some one recently complained in *Varsity*, you see crosses, seeming 'to presage an untimely resurgence of Christianity'. Life, it seems, has become too serious for politics.

Undergraduate life is one proliferating mass of 'little platoons' dedicated to social, artistic and religious activity. Sponsoring 'causes', putting on 'shows', ministering in a multitude of ways to the insatiable appetite of the young for good works, gaiety, faction, exhibitionism, gossip and friendship. The only difference between the young and their elders in their indulgence of these passions is that the young indulge them in public. And everywhere, the second year man – and woman – is in the lead. Now, they seem to say, is the time (if ever) to grow the beard, to dress like a tramp, to combine a 'beat' aspect with frenetic energy. Part I of the tripos is still (for most people in their second year) some four or five months away. The really vital Day of Judgment, or Part II, twelve months beyond that. Work can be fitted in, is fitted in. Games, in the playing-field and on the river, go alongside the rest. There never was such a time, or such a place, for the cultivation of *l'uomo universale*. There is room, indeed, for a *Varsity* edition of Arnold Bennett's handbook on 'How to Live on Twenty-four Hours a Day'. It is remarkable how successfully instinct supplies instruction in this perennial problem of managing one's time without disaster. It is not at all remarkable that second year men are ready to ring the bells for the return of such a tutor as Mr. Wynne.

The freedom of the second year man to get on with this important business of living his life in his own way is much enhanced by the fact that he generally lives out of college. In digs in Chesterton Lane, or Maids Causeway, or beyond Parker's Piece, or even out in the wilds towards Cherry Hinton or Barton, beyond the immediate range of vision of college authorities, he can go his own way with considerable independence. He will (unless he can produce some reason convincing to a reluctant tutor) be obliged to come into college for most of his meals, or at any rate he will have to contribute towards 'kitchen over-heads' involved in producing meals that he does not eat, much to his indignation. His landlady will have to vouch for his keeping decent hours, although there is a movement on foot to entrust undergraduates with latch-keys and the task of making their own gate-bills. All rooms let to undergraduates have to be vetted by the University Lodging Houses Syndicate, and landladies who depend on letting for a living are naturally careful. But the landlady who cherishes her 'young gentlemen' as the mainstay of her livelihood is rarer than she used to be. In a town where flats at five, six and seven guineas a week are snapped up readily by people who have nothing to do with the university, she can afford to be independent, and colleges are often at their wits' end to find rooms for their undergraduates. The answer, as college tutors see it, is to put up more college buildings so that a larger proportion of men live in college for a greater proportion of their time. Whenever this is done, however, it simply means that colleges take more men, so that the problem remains as before. Colleges always swear solemn oaths that they will not allow this to happen: that they will employ the new accommodation in college to reduce the number of men in digs. But there is a kind of Parkinson's Law by which the numbers of undergraduates expand to fill the space available. When this has happened, tutors blame the bursar, that greedy man who is always grasping at the opportunity to get hold of more fees. The bursar blames the tutors.

Tutors make their case, to their own satisfaction, by breathing the holy words 'college spirit', or 'community life'. The notion that many men prefer to live out of college is rarely admitted to their councils. A century and more ago it was argued that living in digs was morally harmful. A certain Mr. Lawrence Dundas, an undergraduate of Trinity College, returning from a dinner-party in lodgings in Bridge Street, fell into a ditch in a state of intoxication. Trying vainly to climb out, he tore off most of his clothes, and was found next morning frozen to death. An Evangelical clergyman then composed a pamphlet en-

titled 'The melancholy and awful death of Lawrence Dundas, Esq.'
in which he argued that immorality among undergraduates would
never be checked as long as they were allowed to live in town lodgings.
The argument appears to have convinced large numbers of senior
members, and the Master of Trinity, Dr. Christopher Wordsworth,
at once set about persuading his college to build a new court. This was
in 1818. The first stone was laid on the King's birthday, 12 August,
1823, and George IV, who had often been drunk but had not yet died
of it, gave £1,000. The band played *God save the King*, and *Rule
Britannia*, and Trinity College soon had the King's Court at a cost of
over £50,000. It is sometimes said that nobody, either inside or
outside the college, knows precisely how many junior members
Trinity has at any one time.[1] But it is safe to say that the proportion
living within the college is no greater than it was before Dr. Wordsworth's building campaign in the cause of morality. It is also safe to
say that few would argue the case for more college buildings on that
basis to-day. Tutors, at least, would be more likely to complain of
undue domestication than of immoral excess. It is complained that
undergraduates in digs tend to live more and more with the family,
that they sit around watching the family telly, that they even help
out with odd spells of baby-sitting. It is rarely acknowledged that the
present-day undergraduate in digs lives very much as he lives in his
own home, and that the home in which he lives is in most respects
indistinguishable from his habitat at Cambridge. Apparently it is to be
deplored that he enjoys it.

The second year man sees through all this rather readily. He has very
little time for 'college spirit' factitiously engendered by tutors. There
are, too, even in these days of mass living (perhaps even because of it)
a considerable number of solitaries by taste and preference. They are
supposed, far too often, to be 'brooding' in enforced loneliness out in
the wilds of the Newmarket Road or Romsey Town, 'missing all the
best things that life at the university has to offer'. How infrequently
does a well-meaning tutor realize, when he offers a pupil a second
year in college as a reward for having done well in his first-year
examination, or because he is secretary to some college club, that the

[1] The current edition of *The Student's Handbook* (1959–60) gives a total of 805.

young man would much prefer to 'go out', simply because he feels that he has had enough of his neighbours for a while, or because he wants peace and quiet to do some reading, or even some writing? More 'Cambridge novels' are begun out in digs by second year men than anywhere else in the world. Some of them even get published. They all begin with a second year man staring out of a window on to Parker's Piece or Midsummer Common and cursing 'the college system' in his heart for trying to kill the unique quality of his own soul. A year in college has awakened within them a suspicion that they are coming under the impress of 'the Cambridge stamp', and they don't like it. That insidious enchantment of the Cambridge world which William Wordsworth and Edward Fitzgerald resented and resisted in the past, and that young Daffyd Evans is beginning to declaim against in the present, is breathing down their necks. Clutching to their bosoms the inviolable shade of some earlier and more vital passion, for poetry, or republican virtues, or simply for slag-heaps and primary production in South Wales, they seek some extra-mural solitude wherein to nurse the unconquerable hope . . . 'The man actually *wants* to live out,' his tutor notes. 'God knows why. . . .' Indeed, God knows. In tutorial eyes, the motives for such a preference must always remain sinister.

The average second year man, however, is not like this. He goes out of college into digs with initial reluctance and then, stretching his wings, he comes to like it. The undergraduate *moyen sensuel* likes most things he comes upon at Cambridge by habit and slow experience, and what he doesn't particularly like he finds means of tolerating or evading. Thus Jonathan Fowkes, coming back to his digs on Maids Causeway at the beginning of the Lent Term, feels that he has been rather clever to get himself into Mrs. Gathercole's first-floor set, with the trim strip of garden under the front windows and the tree-fringed expanse of Midsummer Common across the road. As he stands there, looking out into the orange-tinted darkness of the January evening,[1] Jonathan thinks not of the undergraduate novel of resentment and revolt, but of the note he has found waiting for him from the President

---

[1] Orange-tinted by sodium-lamps, not the sunset. Cambridge sunsets, once so splendid, have been banished by this modern form of street-lighting.

of the Union Society. The crucial words lend to the glare of the sodium lighting on the Causeway the glory of a halo . . . 'if you will lead for the opposition to Jeremy Sprake's motion of no confidence in the present Government. . . .' Jonathan has not hitherto had his name 'on the paper'. He has generally managed to catch the President's eye towards the tail-end of the evening. Now, at last, he has his big chance. He is terrified, and at the same time jubilant.

He thinks first of his father. His father is an old-fashioned family solicitor at Hastings, and Jonathan is reading for the Law tripos because his father secretly expects him to become Lord High Chancellor of England. Jonathan's ambitions are more moderate. He wouldn't mind being Recorder of London, or legal adviser to the Corporation of Hastings, and he has been given to understand that 'making one's mark at the Union' is an indispensable step in the right direction. But he is essentially a modest and rather conventional young man. He went to a Woodard School, and he goes to Little St. Mary's on Sundays and Saints' Days, very much as he goes to the Union Society debates on Tuesdays. He wears charcoal-grey suits, silk waistcoats, single-coloured ties and socks, and he brushes his pale gold hair back in a thick but well-ordered mane. He has a softly musical voice, perfect manners, and a tendency to pimples. He models himself on his tutor, Alistair Wynne, has a habit of opening most of his sentences with 'I must confess . . .' and (when he doesn't forget) keeps his eyebrows raised in a rather nonchalant expression of incredulity. Everyone in the college likes him a good deal.

"Sheer waste of time," declares Christopher Cattermole, his neighbour, when Jonathan casually imparts to him the glad tidings. "Bunch of gas-bags playing at parliament, those Union types. Little pifflers spouting big piffle."

Christopher's superiority arises, Jonathan reflects, from his having played the part of Bardolph in the A.D.C. production of Henry IV at Christmas.

"Still, congratulations, old lad. I suppose you have to do these things if you're going to be a lawyer. I shall come and hear you."

"Thanks," says Jonathan, without enthusiasm.

At the Union

Jonathan Fowkes will prepare his speech with infinite care. He has read somewhere that the first Lord Birkenhead once confessed to having prepared only two speeches in his life: his maiden speech at the Union Society, and his maiden speech in the House of Commons. Needless to say (though his Lordship said it) they were both brilliant. Coming from a man who attained the Woolsack at the age of forty-seven, these reminiscences make a deep impression on Jonathan's already anxious mind.

To bracket the two occasions is natural enough. The Union Society is the House of Commons writ small. On its floor, aspiring men of politics and the law rehearse their part, learn the manners and conventions of public debate (not of public speaking, merely), and discover their own limitations and potentialities on their hind legs. The Union resembles the House of Commons not only in its rules, written and unwritten. It bears some resemblance to it also in its temper. If anything it is an even more exacting critic. The House of Commons is celebrated for its kindness to maiden speeches, although it may turn cruel when it is tried too high, as the young Disraeli discovered. The Union also tries to be fair, but it is not weighed down by a sense of legislative responsibility. Nothing much hangs upon the outcome of its deliberations. The young men who address it have not come there through the fiery ordeal of election, nor need the House assume that their futures depend upon their success or failure in that place and at that time, although the young men themselves may choose to think so. Many a young man has been shot down in flames at a Union debate and gone on to glory elsewhere. Many have shot their bolt in glory at a Union debate and never been heard of again beyond a schoolroom or an administrative cubbyhole. The House is ever ready to laugh, and it expects its speakers to make it laugh, with them and not at them. Its risibility is extremely infectious. Solemnity, when and if it comes, must be led up to with immense and lightsome care. Mere rhetoric is fatal. The House debates, it does not listen to orations. The President, with his bell, will see fair play, but the speaker must play fair with the House on its own terms, and its terms are far more elusive, far more temperamentally determined than those of the House of Commons. The difference can most readily be seen when some distinguished parliamentary hack comes down as a guest speaker and treats the House to his vintage brand of guff. He is, of course, received politely, as a guest, but the silence that reigns is sometimes appalling.

Guest speakers, men of every variety of eminence, come down to speak second and fourth to the undergraduate leaders. Many, of course, are old Union officers, ex-presidents whose stars began to shine in this place. Many have never been near the place in their lives, nor would ever have imagined to find themselves invited. These last are always received with especial tenderness and often turn out an enormous success. No one who was privileged to hear the late Edgar Wallace second the motion 'Chicago delenda' while confessing that he had no idea what the words meant, or to see the late Jimmy Thomas swinging his fist at the House like Mr. Polly denouncing the universe from his stile, or Harry Pollitt charming the House with the cogent persuasiveness of a Jesuit at the Court of the Emperor of China, will ever be likely to label, or libel, the Union Society as a bunch of elderly schoolboys playing at parliament, or little pifflers spouting big piffle. Piffle there is, in plenty, but a House that can listen with sympathy and delight to so many and varied protagonists of piffle other than its own, delivered upon so many and varied types of motion, is something more and something better than a pale parody of the House of Commons. Outwardly, physically, the form is the same: the ranks of benches facing each other across the table with its 'despatch-boxes'; the President enthroned aloft in impartial authority like the Speaker in his chair; the tellers at the two doors, marked Ayes and Noes on either side of the entrance; the gallery with its seats for visitors and its press desks, forming no part of the House and expressly banned from comment or even applause; the motion-papers; the rules of address – always 'Mr. President, sir . . .' and never 'Gentlemen . . .' – always 'the honourable member from Queens' . . .' or wherever he comes from, and never surnames. All this is familiar enough. But, since the House is happily exempt from the burden of governing England, the inward spirit is as different as it could be.

For one thing, although the officers of the Society tend to be elected along party-political lines, so that the prevailing 'colour' of Union Society politics reflects fairly faithfully the prevailing colour in society at large (the Left largely dominating the nineteen-thirties, and Conservatives staging a big come-back since the War), neither the motions nor the characteristic interest of Union debates are predominantly political. Political motions are, of course, more frequently debated in times of great political excitement. Home Rule for Ireland, Votes for Women, Collective Security, Hating Hitler, Understanding Russia, Colonialism, all have had their turn. More commonly, however, the visitor to the Union finds himself listening to cogent reasons for preferring Girton to Newnham (the most cogent, of course, being that it is farther away), or for preferring Manners to Morals, or for regretting the monopoly of brains by the two ancient universities at the expense of Red-brick. Francis Bacon's aphorism, that the only great source of political phophecy is to be found in the speculative principles of young men between the ages of twenty and thirty, may or may not be true. But it would be unwise, to say the least, to assume that the Junior Intelligence of England, or even of Cambridge, is to be accurately adjudged from the debates of the Union Society. Less than half of the undergraduate members of the university belong to the Society, and it is rare for a House of eight hundred to record its votes. Very large numbers of young men only turn up to hear 'star performers', mostly visiting luminaries, and after the fourth speaker has sat down there is generally a thronging exodus through the middle door, between Ayes and Noes, simply because this is the quickest and easiest way out. Quite apart from the multitudes who never join the Society at all, there are the crowds who never make use of their membership save to read the papers, or borrow books from the library, or play squash or billiards, or frequent the excellent bar and restaurant. The voting on Motions before the House represents only a sample of a sample. To pay very much attention to such decisions would be unwise, and might even be disastrous. It has sometimes been said that undue attention to a successful Motion to the effect that a House of undergraduates declined to fight for King and Country (though the House was in another place than Cambridge) disastrously misled Herr von Ribbentrop, and thereby Herr Hitler, about the youth of England.[1]

The characteristic tone of the Cambridge Union Society is one of intellectual liberalism, which is the characteristic tone of Cambridge, from Paley and Simeon and Hort down to Sidgwick and Maitland and Pigou. It was founded[2] in the days when the surviving liberal hopes of the Age of Reason were threatened, even in England, even in Cambridge, by the illiberalism of the Holy Alliance. One of the earliest experiences of the little group of 'reading men' who held their debates in the room in Falcon Yard, behind the *Red Lion*, in Petty Cury, was the invasion of their premises by Dr. Wood, the Vice-Chancellor, and his proctors, to demand the dissolution of their society. They were, at that moment, debating the question: 'Is the increased attention which has been paid to our army likely to have a good effect on society?' A 'leading question', indeed, in the days of the Holy Alliance. The Vice-Chancellor and the powers that be, like Lords Castlereagh and Sidmouth, scented sedition everywhere, even behind the *Red Lion*, for after all the name 'Union Society' was a common description of those Radical working-men's societies associated with the name of Major Cartwright, Sir Francis Burdett, and the suspected English Jacobins. The Cambridge Union Society, however, did not waver in face of intimidation. Its president, William Whewell of Trinity, set a classic example for all future presidents. No doubt recalling, like a Good Whig, the demeanour of the Speaker of the House of Commons when King Charles I arrived to arrest the Five Members, he told the Vice-Chancellor, courteously but firmly: 'Strangers will please to withdraw and the House will take the message into consideration'. The Vice-Chancellor withdrew, but for the next four years the Society lapsed into a mere reading club. This was the nearest the English universities came to suffering the rigours of the Carlsbad Decrees inflicted upon the German universities by Prince Metternich. When, in 1821, the Union Society was revived as a debating society, it was only on

---

[1] As the less frivolous of the two ancient universities, Cambridge considered a proposal to debate the motion that 'This House declines to fight for King and Harper' – a well-known firm of garage-proprietors whose premises adjoin the Society's buildings.

[2] The Society's day of foundation was 13 February, 1815. Its earliest Minute Book is for 1823.

condition of its leaving alone all political questions since the year 1800. Nevertheless it got along quite nicely by framing its political motions in historical terms. Thus, would the Greeks have been justified in asserting their independence in 1799? Or should the House of Commons have been reformed at the end of the eighteenth century? The last relics of restriction were removed in 1830.

Conceived in sin and born in obliquity, the Society grew to youth and manhood with the triumph of the middle-class liberalism of nineteenth-century England. Apart from a brief flirtation with the Toryism of Young England in the eighteen-thirties, and a phase of what has been called 'all my eye and Kingsley Martin' in the nineteen-thirties, it may be said to have held to the plain liberal line (with the small 'l') for a hundred and fifty years. Even its Conservatives have been old-fashioned Whigs under the skin, while its Socialists have been men of conscience rather than of ideology. Among the Society's officers during the nineteenth century, it is difficult to find a name that was to appear in the ranks of a Tory, or Conservative, Ministry, with the notable exceptions of Richard Cross and Austen Chamberlain. During the same period, the names of future Liberal ministers include Fawcett, Gorst, G. O. Trevelyan, Dilke, Lansdowne, and C. F. G. Masterman, not to mention the brilliant array of liberal lawyers and publicists: Henry Sidgwick, W. K. Clifford, F. W. Maitland, Courtney Kenny, J. K. Stephen, Edward Jenks. In the present century, the lists gleam with the same brand of liberal intelligence: Keynes, Wilson Harris, Arnold McNair, Norman Birkett, Dennis Robertson, the Ramseys and the Butlers. Undoubtedly the most brilliant period of the Society's history is to be found in its first fifteen years, from 1815 down to 1830. In that short space of time, we find the names of no less than twenty-five of its officers who were to attain to the provisional immortality of an entry in the Dictionary of National Biography. William Whewell, T. B. Macaulay, Mackworth Praed, Charles Austin, Charles Buller, John Sterling, John Kemble, Edward Bulwer, Alexander Cockburn, all these, and many more, shine out in that remarkable dawn. There followed a comparatively dull period, down to the 'forties, and then a second great epoch of liberal light and leading was to signalize the heyday of Victorian England from 1850 to 1880. This splendid flowering was heralded in 1851, the year of the Great Exhibition, by the passing, with a single dissentient vote, of the happy motion:

> That the political and social history of England since the peace of 1815 has been one of real and great social improvement, and there is reason to trust – unless by the wilful fault of the present generation – the future will be still happier than the past.

The strength of liberalism as the informing spirit of the Cambridge Union has outlived the eclipse of Liberalism as a party name. This has proved of enormous importance with the growth of extremism in the politics of the present century, more especially in the 'thirties when the Presidency often appeared to be the perquisite of the Socialist Club, and again in the 'forties when Conservatism took its toll upon the Society with almost monotonous regularity. The kind of men the Union presidency contributes to Conservative Administrations can be adjudged from the examples of Mr. R. A. Butler (President, Easter Term, 1924) and Mr. Selwyn Lloyd (President, Michaelmas Term, 1927). Sir Hugh Foot, though not a Minister of the Crown, might well be adjudged along with them: he was President (and a Liberal) in the Easter Term, 1929. The Society's presidency has still to supply a Prime Minister. Apart from Mr. Butler, the nearest to attaining the office has been Sir Charles Dilke. That unlucky ex-president (he held the office twice, Michaelmas, 1864 and Lent, 1866) is chiefly remembered by the Society for his energetic part in getting it housed in its present buildings, those irremediably hideous red-brick premises perpetrated by Alfred Waterhouse behind the Round Church, 'thirteenth century Gothic', according to the *Saturday Review*. Had Dilke succeeded in keeping out of trouble, and had the premiership passed to him from Mr. Gladstone, the Society would have had the distinction of supplying the Crown with its first Radical Prime Minister.

Were there ever such Union nights as those of the middle 'twenties, when the present Archbishop of York (then known as the Honourable Member from Magdalene) and the present Mr. Justice Devlin (then known as the Honourable Member from Christ's) seemed to revive the classic contests of Gladstone and Disraeli? Arthur Ramsey seemed even then to bear the marks of the man of God, with his heavy head, his slight stoop, and his rather nasal twang. Patrick Devlin, red-headed, his bony wrists seeming ever to escape from sleeves that were too short for his gracefully flourishing arms, was all fire and air. Uncle George, a Christian-Communist from Thaxted, scowled down with weary tolerance from the gallery. Afterwards, he said that it was terrible that decent young men should be encouraged to carry on this sham fight within the ruling class. Uncle George was probably right, in the middle 'twenties. Whether he would still think himself to be right in the middle 'fifties is far less certain. For behind a Union debate to-day one still feels, and one is more inclined to value, the persistence of the classic tradition of the Victorian age, the lingering ghost of a unique epoch of liberal prepossession in a world of reviving tyrannies. For here persuasion can still count its victories, here parliamentary manners and language still contain passionate conviction within the bounds of decency and good sense. It may be that the forms of parliamentary debate are dead or dying in the world at large; it is certain that they never lived in the greater part of the world at any time; it is no less certain that changing forms of social life must devise their own ineluctable procedures for carrying on the business of men. Yet, for as long as men remain interested in the outward forms and the inward spirit of political procedures in the great age of the English liberal intelligence, to attend a debate at the Union will instruct them more happily than a thousand pages of Erskine May. There they will discover in miniature, preserved but not embalmed, a heritage.

So Jonathan Fowkes prepares his speech with infinite care, rehearses his gestures before the looking-glass, dresses himself in immaculate dinner-jacket and gown, and goes off to dine with the President. His seconder is a large and somnolent Under-Secretary of State who tells him, over the dinner-table, what a brilliant affair the Union was in the days of Patrick Devlin and Arthur Ramsey. It is hardly to be expected, Jonathan gathers, that the debate this evening will attain those classic standards. Nor does it, of course. It is extremely tedious. And Jonathan is told why in the next number of *Varsity*. It has something to do with the way in which Mr. Fowkes models himself upon the style of

The Union

The new Chemical Laboratories in Lensfield Road (1960)

Union debaters of the nineteen-twenties. All the same, Mr. Fowkes should try again. Mr. Fowkes is sure he will. And again. And again.

Amal. Clubs and College Meetings

Inter-collegiate politics blossom at the Union. College politics, so far as concerns the young, have their forum at the 'Amal. Clubs'. This term is a shorthand expression for the college 'Amalgamated Clubs', a union for common convenience of all the clubs and societies which go to make up that congerie of multifarious activities which is a college. Every undergraduate member of the college is *ipso facto* a member of the Amal. Club, for which membership he is charged a subscription on his college bill. Theoretically, the individual can contract out of it, if he cares to make a fuss, like a Trade Unionist contracting out of the political levy of his Union. In fact, he doesn't, since membership of the Amal. Club carries eligibility to almost any college organization to which he may wish to belong.

Amal. Club politics are the politics of the little platoon, or the parish pump, and therefore vastly more serious than any other. At Amal. Club meetings a man is in his own agora. Here he knows everybody, and everybody knows him, supposing that he cares to attend. Here real things are decided, the things that come home to men's businesses and bosoms: whether to vote the Boat Club a subvention to send a crew to Henley; whether to build another squash-court; whether to petition the Governing Body for permission to have a May Week Ball again this year; whether to have, or to stop having, the *Daily Worker* or *British Union* in the Junior Common Room; whether to send yet another deputation to the steward to discuss the quality of the prunes or the spinach served at Hall dinner.

Amal. Club meetings are an excellent example of 'guided democracy'. For one thing, they are not allowed to settle anything important. Anything remotely connected with the wider purposes of the college as 'a place of education, religion, learning and research' is the exclusive business of the Master and Fellows as the statutory Governing

K

Body of the college. In the second place, almost everything that the
Amal. Club may want to do involves spending money from its funds,
and the treasurer of the Amal. Club is a don, generally a tutor. This
officer, formally nominated by the Amal. Club but virtually appointed
by the Governing Body, exercises 'treasury control', which is the key
to all good government whatsoever. He also serves as liaison officer
between the two bodies. Like Sir Robert Walpole, sometimes known
misleadingly as the first Prime Minister, who served as candlestick on
the see-saw of King and Commons, the Treasurer represents the
Governing Body at the Amal. Club and the Amal. Club at the
Governing Body. The arrangement works excellently, providing that
the senior member who serves as treasurer is capable of enacting the
role of Mr. Facing-both-ways with sufficient skill and tact. When the
Master and Fellows sit in solemn conclave at a college meeting, they
normally have one item, or group of items, on the agenda before them
under the heading 'Amalgamated Clubs business', and this will be
explained to them by the Fellow who serves as treasurer. He will
explain to the old men what the young men want; he will put their
views as faithfully as he can; in doing so he will make it pretty plain
what he thinks of them; and the old men will make up their minds in
these matters very much on his advice. Thereafter, it will be his business to go and tell the young men of the Amal. Club what the old
men think of their proposals and representations. . . . No, they can't
have a May Week Ball again this year. . . . Yes, they may hold a raffle
for the Henley Fund, under the following conditions. . . .

In the third place, the Amal. Club, like every other institution in
a well-governed community, tends to develop its own oligarchy. There
are certain people who always attend its meetings, and a great many
more who wouldn't be seen dead there. The result is something like
a Communist-dominated Trade Union. The serious politicians turn up
and manage to corner the offices and frame the business. The rest let
them get on with it and then complain that the Amal. Club is simply
a stooge for the Boat Club, or the Rugger Club, or whatever, which
are forever monopolising the Amal. Club's funds for their own low
purposes at the expense of other, and possibly more cultural, activities.
The treasurer, reporting to his fellows on the Governing Body, is

usually said to have his ear to the ground, his finger on the pulse of
the young men, in fact to know pretty accurately what the young
men are thinking and feeling. In fact, he knows what the active
minority of gamesmen are thinking and feeling. The rest are either
not thinking or feeling at all, or setting up transient cliques of their
own for heckling and barracking in corners. But, since no one on the
Governing Body would dream of taking over the treasurership if he
could possibly avoid it, the treasurer's reports on the health of the body
politic are always accepted with complete confidence.

Governing Bodies resemble Amal. Clubs in that they, too, are con-
cealed oligarchies or 'guided democracies'. Business is really conducted
on all Governing Bodies by some few active persons who bring along
the rest. The rest kick and struggle, but they are brought along. Some
Governing Bodies, however, admit the oligarchic principle openly by
surrendering the greater part of their business to an inner council.
When the Fellowship of a college comes to exceed twenty, a Governing Body tends to clumsiness, however skilfully the more active
members may organize the expediting of business beforehand, and
however skilfully the Master may exercise his function as chairman.
It soon becomes obvious that two meetings are going on at once, at
the top and the bottom end of the table respectively. Elderly gentlemen
give up in despair of hearing what others are saying, while less elderly
gentlemen come not to care. So, after much havering, the glorious
day arrives when the college revises its Statutes in order to equip itself
with powers to set up a council. The day expands into many months,
for any revision of college statutes must be lodged with the university
authorities for examination and possible objection, and thereafter with
the Crown in Council and both Houses of Parliament for approval.
How the college chooses to devise its council will depend very much
upon itself, but generally speaking it will arrange that certain officers
– the Master, bursar, tutors (or one of them) – shall be *ex officio* members,
and the rest of its members shall be elected from time to time by the
whole body of Fellows from among themselves. Of course, the whole
Governing Body will continue to meet at intervals. It will in any case
retain ultimate authority and control, more especially in all matters

concerning elections to college offices and stipends. But the bulk of day-to-day business will pass into the care of a statutory oligarchy. And since dons may be fairly easily divided into two categories – the politicians and the rest – everyone is fairly well satisfied. It is sometimes said that all dons are inveterate politicians, and it is true that the mildest and most scholarly men will sometimes show an astonishing gift for intrigue where college politics are concerned. But there are always some who are content with the semblance of power, or who cherish above all else the opportunity to get away from active business for at least occasional spells in order to devote their time and energies to their scholastic concerns. To these, the prospect of a college council holds the promise of a happy release.

The college at large is generally made aware of an impending meeting of the Governing Body, or its council, by the sight of certain senior members pacing the grass in pairs in solemn converse. The middle of the sacred grass of a college court is the most private place in the world.

"There they go," Mr. Stock mutters, as he glares down from his window. "There they are, intriguing, while I work."

Mr. Stock gave up intriguing on the grass many years ago. He leaves it to Skinner, and the bursar, and the one to whom he always refers as 'that ass, Tompion'. Cyril Tompion is not really an ass. He is the second – some would say the first – mathematical philosopher in Europe. But he combines mathematical philosophy with a passion for college politics. The college has never yet entrusted him with even the most minor of its offices. At the age of seventy-five (for he was elected before the statutes which require Fellows to retire at sixty-seven, and is therefore safely in possession of his Fellowship for life), he still marks his agenda with detailed notes, from which he will speak exhaustively and with the cheerful authority of Senior Fellow, more especially where small items of expenditure are involved, or where verbal precision can be made to darken counsel. A Governing Body meeting, to Cyril Tompion, is a cross between a parlour game and a paper-chase. Most Governing Bodies have a Tompion.

There is an unusually long agenda for the first meeting of the Lent Term. Business has been piling up over the vacation. This delights the

Master who knows that long agendas make for short meetings. Long meetings take place with short agendas, when everyone is trying to spin things out in order to justify calling for tea at four o'clock. Of course, everyone knows that tea will arrive at four o'clock whatever is happening, but it is nice to feel that one has earned it. Worst of all are agendas which consist of a large number of small items, when everyone is concerned to turn small questions into big ones.

"I have received one apology for absence," the Master announces when he has signed the Minutes of the previous meeting and disposed of certain minor matters 'arising' therefrom. "Mr. Parker writes to say that he has an engagement at the B.B.C. this afternoon."

"Brains Trust," Dr. Skinner scoffs. "Who'd have believed it?"

Faces around the table assume expressions of mute disapproval tempered by resignation, as who should say: 'there, but for the grace of God, go I'. Everyone present, with the single exception of Alan Skinner, has broadcast at some time or another, but no one has ever been able to rival Keith Parker in making it an alibi for attending the Governing Body.

The Master proceeds cheerfully to report on sundry letters of thanks, condolence and request. A letter from an old member of the college requesting a donation towards the Restoration Fund of his fenland parish church, provides the first snag in the quickening stream of the Master's business. The snagsman, of course, is the Senior Fellow.

"I fail to see, Master," says Cyril Tompion, who in fact has never yet failed to see anything, "I fail to see why the college, which consists of persons of all religious denominations, or of none, should allocate any portion of its income to the support of the Church of England."

"I agree with the Senior Fellow," says Silas Stock, a statement which surprises even himself. "We shall be paying Peter's Pence next."

"Chaplain?" The Master raises his eyebrows in the direction of the best authority in these matters.

"Perhaps I should remind the Governing Body," says the Chaplain, "that while under the Universities Tests Act of 1871 the university and the colleges are prohibited from imposing religious tests for admission, we are still required by our statutes to maintain religious worship and instruction in our Chapel according to the tenets of the Established

Church. This, perhaps, would indicate that a certain – shall I say? – concern for the welfare of the Church of England is to be expected of us?"

"Personally, I have no more concern for the Church of England than I have for the Church of Rome, or the Coptic Church, or the Church of the Latter-day Saints," Cyril Tompion announces, warming to his subject.

Disregarding the smiles and murmurs which greet his repudiation of sympathy with the Mormons (for everyone knows that Tompion has had half a dozen wives, and not strictly in succession), he sticks up his fuzz of perfectly white hair and sets out on an exposition of latitudinarianism which involves reference to John Locke, Pierre Bayle, and John Stuart Mill. It is only when he pauses for breath at the end of five minutes that the Master gently inserts the end of a spoke by asking:

"May we assume, Senior Fellow, that you would adopt the same attitude to a request for a donation from the Society of Humanists?"

Tompion is ready for this.

"No, Master. I should not. Humanism is not a denominational religion. Indeed, it is not a religion at all."

He is about to explain what it is when Dr. Skinner comes up with the ambulance which he always holds in readiness for these occasions.

"May I propose, Master, that we set up a standing committee to deal with subscriptions and donations?"

Mention of a committee, as always, produces murmurs of assent.

"Whom would you propose as members?" the Master asks.

"The Bursar, a tutor, and – if he will consent to serve – the Senior Fellow."

This, after some haggling over membership, is carried unanimously, and Cyril Tompion finds himself a member of just one more college committee.

It is now nearly three o'clock, and proceedings have not yet advanced further than the Master's preliminary items. This means that the remainder of the Master's business, involving as it does the long-standing question of 'taking powers to set up a college council', invites somewhat summary treatment.

That great lover of committees, Alan Skinner, puts the case for a council. It is obvious to the meanest intelligence, he declares, that the Fellowship is going to increase – must increase – over the next few years. Any increase must mean that college business cannot be despatched with either expedition or efficiency. A small college, with a small Fellowship, is a thing of the past. A large college, with a large Fellowship, and a council, is a necessity of the future.

"We simply cannot afford to remain a small college, as regards Fellowships," he insists. "We have to expand – or die."

"Hitler used to say very much the same thing about the Third Reich," Silas Stock reminds him, "and look what happened to him."

"I consider that remark to be in very bad taste, and quite irrelevant."

"I must confess," yawns Alistair Wynne, "that I find it hard to understand how a remark can be both irrelevant and in bad taste. Or is it simply my stupidity?"

"I would not care to venture an opinion on that, Master," says Cyril Tompion, who always takes linguistic distinctions as addressed to himself for adjudication. "I would, however, point out that much bad taste – in architecture, for example – is connected with the proliferation of irrelevant detail. Kohlhammer, of Munich, indeed, has defined dirt as matter in the wrong place."

"I think, Senior Fellow, with your permission we will pass over Kohlhammer, and return to the question of the expansion of our Fellowship. In Dr. Skinner's view, that expansion is inevitable. Personally, I regret it. Although we are among the oldest of the colleges in the university, we have always been a small Fellowship, and have managed to keep our total population within decent bounds, and I am convinced that much that is valuable is lost when numbers necessitate delegation of powers. Personally, I should regret very much the passing of our regular meetings, as a society, round this table. . . ."

The best, or the worst, of the Master, men say, is that you never can tell when he is serious. But the somewhat wry and charming smile with which he offers this last remark serves to restore a certain amity to the proceedings. Anticipatory nostalgia has a way of soothing present rancour. Silas Stock, however, has still a shot in his locker for Alan Skinner, and he is determined to deliver it.

"We are constantly told that there must be more Fellows," he says now. "But I have yet to hear a single convincing argument for the proposition."

"Well, for one thing," Dr. Skinner snaps, "there is quite a considerable number of modern subjects which are not represented at this board. We have no one to represent Geography, or Economics, or Mineralogy, or Crystallography, or Soil Science. . . ."

"But," protests Silas Stock sweetly, "is it really to be argued that one elects men to Fellowships for their subjects? Are we, in fact, going to turn the college into a High School?"

Dr. Skinner is now fit to burst. "No," he hisses, letting each word fall like a drop of cold water on the top of a red-hot stove, "it is not proposed, so far as I am aware, to turn the college into a High School. It is simply proposed to make it clear to Headmasters, and other important persons, that we can teach the men they send to us."

"What we can do, or cannot do," Silas Stock reminds him, "is best shown by what we – round this table – actually do in the cause of scholarship and humane learning, and not in the least by percentages of first, second or third classes in the tripos. Thus it has always been, and thus, in my poor opinion, it should always be."

"In other words," Alistair Wynne puts in, with customary aplomb, "headmasters be hanged."

"I don't think any of us would go quite as far as that," says the Master. "Nor do I think that we are likely to get very much further on this important question by prolonging our discussion to-day. I have thought for some time that there is a very good case for holding a special meeting of the Governing Body to go into the whole question of a council at our leisure."

This suggestion is greeted with acclaim. A date is fixed, after a lot of scrabbling in pocket-diaries, and the lull permits feelings to subside.

"Senior Tutor?" The Master bows in the direction of Mr. Stock. "You are, I see, to report to us on the results of the Group Scholarship Examinations in December."

The Senior Tutor presents facts and figures, largely the product of Dr. Skinner's statistical work at the tutorial office. He makes his perennial comment that while the college was given first preference by a very large number of candidates, the quality of the work submitted was disappointing.

"I could wish," he sighs, "that the proportion of good candidates to the total number of candidates who express a first preference for the college were rather higher than it is. After all, to be able to boast a superiority in first preferences over all other colleges in the group is a somewhat hollow boast unless we can also show a high number of awards. It smacks of self-advertisement, and a college of our eminence should, I think, have no need of it."

"If the Senior Tutor can suggest some way of discouraging candidates who prefer to come here rather than to go elsewhere," Dr. Skinner remarks, "I for one should be delighted to hear of it. After all, this is an open competition."

"Other colleges manage it, somehow," Mr. Stock replies calmly. "It is up to us to discover how they do it."

"Another case for a committee?" murmurs Alistair Wynne.

"Surely the tutorial committee is the obvious place . . ." someone suggests.

This brings the tutors together in a solid phalanx. Any criticism of tutors, or a tutor, always had this effect. Mr. Stock says that the tutorial committee will give the matter the most careful attention.

Lastly (before tea) the bursar and new buildings. This is a matter of spending £150,000, and it is disposed of fairly quickly to the accompaniment of tinkling tea-cups in the buttery. The question of housing more undergraduates for a larger proportion of their time in the 'domus', has been on the *tapis* for a number of years. All that is required to-day is to authorize the bursar to authorize the college architects to authorize the contractors to make a start. The bursar has hung up on this decisive step – literally dragged his feet – for as long as he can. He has made quite sure, for some three years, that the Governing Body understands the extent of its financial commitments. Personally, he thinks there is a lot to be said for undergraduates living out of college. He lived out of college for two out of his three years, and has never felt the worse for it. However, as he insists, like a good military man (he commanded the South Cambridgeshire Regiment for twenty years before retiring to the more belligerent life of bursar of his old college),

he is under orders from the High Command. His not to reason why. . . .
If the college wants new buildings, it must have them. It does want
them, and before the butler has finished laying out the tea and hot
scones, it has made sure of getting them.

"One is led to suppose," the high cracked voice of Cyril Tompion
is heard to declare over tea, "that the word 'domus' has a special and
rather sacramental significance. . . ."

The only really important decision to be taken, when the meeting
resumes at four-thirty is whether to hold a Guest Dinner during the
present term, or whether to rest content with the annual Audit Feast
in March. It is decided to have them both. Dr. Skinner's request, as
treasurer of the Amal. Club, that the young men should be allowed
to hold a May Week Ball again this year, is dismissed with the contempt
it deserves.

Shrunken Heads

Everyone feels better for a good 'G.B.'[1] Those who have done the
talking have a sense of release, of power expended without loss. Those
who have simply sat and doodled on the blotting-paper feel great
thoughts fructify within them, for there is nothing like a G.B. for the
purposes of incubation. Those who have won their points go away
reciting their best verbal strokes with satisfaction. Those who have lost,
or (what is far more common) conceded victory under the forms of
compromise, enjoy a belated sense of triumph in thinking of all the
things they ought to have said and didn't. Those who never said a thing,
and heard very little, rejoice simply that there will not be another
meeting for a fortnight or three weeks.

Only the Master, the Head of the House, who has sat for some two
or three hours like patience on a monument, goes away with a heart
bursting with baffled fury and despair. You would never think it, to
look at him. Only his wife, waiting at the Lodge with a second dish

---

[1] College slang for 'Governing Body' or a meeting thereof. When used as a transitive
verb, to G.B. anything = to bring a matter before the Governing Body (Tutors' slang).

of tea, knows what he suffers. She collects pot dogs, lunatic-looking poms and pekes, with pop-eyes and pendulous ears, which sit bolt upright in a row on the mantelpiece in the front hall. Each bears, secretly, the name of some member of the Governing Body. The Master, coming in swiftly from the darkening court, passes them with averted eyes. He hangs up his gown and square, and bolts into the drawing-room. He kisses his wife like Lemuel Gulliver returned from the land of the Lilliputians, warms his hands at the fire, and collapses into an armchair.

"You must be tired, dear," says the Master's wife. "Put your feet up. Would you like a couple of aspirins with your tea?"

As usual, the Master declines the aspirin. He knows very well that half an hour in this quiet handsome room will do him more good than all the drugs in the world.

"Pekes and poms all present and correct, I suppose?"

"Don't be irreverent, darling."

"I never can understand what they find to bark about for three whole hours."

"Nor can I."

The Master, who was elected from the Fellowship of another college rather late in life, is deeply attached to the college of his adoption, and, like a good Master, he keeps its secrets even from his wife. But he does sometimes wonder, on these occasions, what he is doing *dans cette galère*. When people ask him how he likes being Head of a House, and more especially of this particular House, he has sometimes been known to reply:

"Well, it's a very nice house, anyway."

By which he means that he likes living in the Master's Lodge. And, after all, who would not – with the possible exception of the Master's wife who has to cope in this year of Grace with the domestic problems presented by a mansion designed for an age when servants were numerous, dirt-cheap, and feudally-minded? The Master's wife gets along with a married couple, displaced persons from East Germany, and a succession of Scandinavian damsels who come to Cambridge 'to learn the language'. Trial and error have cured her of Latins and Irish, and taught her to engage girls of pure Nordic descent. "Really," she sometimes tells the younger Fellows' wives, "Hitler was right in some things." Her problems are somewhat simplified, also, by generosity on the part of the college in the matter of fixtures and furniture (especially in carpets and curtains), fuel allowances, and part-time help from the college gardeners. Such generosity on the part of the Cambridge colleges towards their Masters is not quite disinterested in these days, since it has become increasingly difficult to get desirable men to assume the burdens of Mastership. Neither college nor university stipends have risen in anything like proportion to the increased cost of living. The problem is not a new one. The Mastership of a college has always been an office of dignity and influence, but it has never been an office of very much financial advantage. The stipends of most Heads of Houses were fixed by college statutes at a time when £6 was considered a not inadequate annual payment.[1] Even in the later eighteenth century, the Masters of Corpus Christi and Jesus Colleges were entitled to little more than £100 per annum. The Heads eked out their living by seeking preferment to benefices, sometimes in plurality, or election to professorships that were virtually sinecures. Not a little of the shameless place-seeking of Heads in former days was the consequence of genuine financial hardship. 'I have always understood the value, reckoning the advantages, to be about £120,' wrote a candidate in declining the Mastership of Jesus, in 1789, 'but when the removal of a family, the furnishing of a house, and the living in some sort in a publick way are the conditions, I know too well how little that sum will do towards it.' Only the increased value of college property in terms of rents and produce, and the sharing of a large part of the surplus among Master and Fellows in 'dividends', enabled stipends to be increased to counter the fall in the value of money. However, it is in the nature of things that there should always have been periods when the time-lag hit the fixed-income groups particularly hard. Our own time is one of these, and it is proper that colleges should cherish their Heads in whatever ways they can devise.

The Master, drinking China tea with his feet up, while his lady chats

[1] Of course, these antique statutes have long been revised, but it is nevertheless true that even in the sixteenth century the emoluments of the Masters of Corpus, Trinity Hall, Christ's and Jesus (£6 13s. 4d. per annum) were (as Winstanley would say) 'not over-generous'.

gently about pekes and poms, both canine and otherwise, rests in the presence of his ancestors. The centuries look down from the brown varnished portraits on his walls, and if he is a man of historical sense and imagination,[1] he cannot fail to be stirred every now and then by the grandeurs as well as the miseries of his lot. They are a mixed crowd, those old Heads of Houses whose physiognomies, capped and ruffed and periwigged, look down upon the latest of their line. Taken *en masse*, they might be the academic equivalents of the baronets of Ruddigore, a representative sample of the Bench of Bishops, a decent delegation from the Royal Society. Saints and martyrs like John Fisher[2] and Nicholas Ridley; Archbishops like Grindal and Whitgift and Parker; Tory tyrants like Roger Long at Pembroke and Whig tyrants like Richard Bentley at Trinity; gentle neo-Platonists like Benjamin Whichcote and Ralph Cudworth. Providentially, and prudently, the Cambridge colleges do not wait for their Masters to die before they hang their portraits, nor do they necessarily wait until their Masters retire. Thereby it is quite possible for a Master literally to see himself in his historical perspective. Whether or not this is a chastening experience, only a Master can tell.

In any case, if he is wise (and what Head of a House is otherwise?) he will know that he can never hope to be as great a power in the university as even the least of these. For Heads have shrunk in these latter days. They still supply the university with its Vice-Chancellor, but there was a time not far distant, when they effectively ruled the university. The Elizabethan statutes, which remained in force until little less than a century ago, officially constituted them 'a distinct and separate estate of the university'. In their hands lay the interpretation of statute, the nomination of all the principal officers (not only the Vice-Chancellor, but the librarian, the registry and the Public Orator), and the composition of the 'caput', that small and autocratic body which really ran the university before the institution of the elected Council of the Senate (1856). The Heads used to meet, quite un-

---

[1] Four colleges have historians as Masters at the present moment (1959), and several others have men whose work is closely related to that field.

[2] John Fisher was President of Queens' from 1505 to 1508, but if his present-day successor wishes to see his portrait he must visit the Combination Room of Christ's, the college – along with St. John's – he did so much to establish for Lady Margaret Beaufort.

officially, in the vestry of the University Church after Divine Service in order to advise the Vice-Chancellor, and since most Heads had at one time or another been Vice-Chancellor themselves, their advice was indispensable. They held themselves aloof from lesser men, like a caste highly conscious of their power and dignity, and it was said that one never encountered anyone below the rank of a professor at their tables. Little wonder that Heads continued to wear wigs long after other heads had ceased to do so, well into the nineteenth century.

All, or most, of this is no more. The Head of a House still has his day when, and if, he becomes Vice-Chancellor.[1] But he is no longer *ipso facto* an officer of the university by virtue of his being Head of his House. His sphere of influence is for the most part confined within the walls of his college, and even there he is *primus inter pares* in all but his social functions. He is essentially a constitutional monarch, although his personal character and his initiative still enable him to do much to make or mar the fortunes of his college. But with the decline of his once enormous authority in the university at large, his superiority within the walls of his own college has quite naturally tended to diminish. The age of the Angry Old Men – of Heads who delighted to carry on a perpetual warfare with their Fellows – has long passed away. Even the enlightened despotism of an Isaac Milner is scarcely possible any longer, while the rampageous tyranny of a Richard Bentley is unthinkable. Milder manners have done as much as revised statutes to bring about the shrinkage of the Heads. There are colleges where the Head of the House only dines at High Table at the invitation of the Fellows, while the Senior Combination Room is presided over by a president chosen by the Fellows from among themselves. Indeed, it is not unusual when a Master dies, or retires nowadays, to hear voices raised (in Combination Room, not at the board of government) for the abolition of the office altogether.

"Now's our chance," says the Bright Young Fellow, "to get rid of an office which has been becoming an anachronism for years."

"Have you considered how the college is to be represented in the wider life of the university?" asks the Dull Old Fellow.

[1] See pp. 97-100.

The B.Y.F.: We have half a dozen professors and senior lecturers who sit regularly on boards and syndicates, and it isn't very often that we are not represented electively on the Council of the Senate.

The D.O.F.: Is it nothing to you that the college should supply the university with its Vice-Chancellor from time to time?

The B.Y.F.: Not very much. I have long thought that the university should have a permanent and professional Vice-Chancellor. After all, Red-brick gets on all right that way.

The D.O.F.: For how long have you thought that? I think you must have been reading Charles Hotham.

The B.Y.F.: Charles who?

The D.O.F.: Charles Hotham was a Fellow of Peterhouse who sent a petition to the House of Commons in 1651, arguing that the Fellows could quite well rule the college without a Master. He was a republican. But I am afraid the fact is that Charles Hotham, and the Fellows at that time, were chiefly moved by their dislike of Lazarus Seaman, a high-handed Master who asked for trouble by staying away from the college very often, thus putting ideas into their heads...

The B.Y.F.: Oh, I wouldn't argue from a doctrinaire basis.

The D.O.F.: In my opinion, it's the only basis from which you could argue. Now that Heads of Houses can do so little, for good or ill, you can hardly argue from any other. And, after all, we choose them ourselves. . . . Wouldn't you agree that we get the Masters we deserve?

Heads of Houses are mostly elected by the Fellows (or by those Fellows denominated 'electors' by the college statutes) and often (though by no means always) from their own body. The rather painful kind of fun and games that may conceivably go on when the Fellows of a college elect a Master from their own body have been portrayed by Sir Charles Snow in his novel *The Masters*. The portrait might well persuade the candid reader that there is something to be said for compelling colleges to adopt a candidate from beyond their own society, or even for a surrender of their electoral powers to some external authority. Colleges do sometimes in fact go outside for a Master, and even beyond the university itself. The late Field-Marshal Sir William Birdwood, Lord Birdwood of Anzac (Master of Peterhouse, 1931-38) and the late Admiral Sir Herbert Richmond (Master of Downing,

1936-46)[1] are recent examples. The principal objection to this is always said to be the undesirability of having a Master inexperienced in university business in case of his being elected Vice-Chancellor. The real objection is the celebrated 'college spirit'. A college likes, wherever it can, 'to take care of its own', in electing to both Fellowships and the Mastership. In either case, the cost of patriotism is sometimes high, but who shall presume to tell a college what is good for it? In the case of Trinity College, which has on the whole done rather well in the world, the Crown (or the Prime Minister) tells it. The Master of Trinity is given to the college from on high, although one need not doubt that the high powers take the trouble to find out from Trinity the kind of gift that Trinity would prefer to receive. Something of the same kind happens at Magdalene, whose Master is presented to the college by the owner of Audley End. This may lead, and sometimes has led, to odd situations, as when Lady Portsmouth posthumously wished the egregious Barton Wallop on the college in 1774, or when the heir to Audley End was an undergraduate at the college, and the undergraduate population rejoiced at the prospect of the Master being appointed by one of themselves. At two colleges, Peterhouse and Jesus, the Master was appointed by the Bishop of Ely until as late as 1882, even though his choice was limited in practice to nominees sent up by the Fellows.

The lengths to which the Fellows of a college will go in order to have a Master of their own choice are well illustrated by the extravagant goings-on at Peterhouse in 1787. In submitting two names to their Visitor, the Bishop of Ely, they were resolved that he should have no choice but to appoint the candidate they preferred. The Bishop, it was known, wanted to appoint Daniel Longmire, an ex-Fellow and Vicar of Linton. The Fellows preferred George Borlase, Fellow and Tutor. It was evident that if they sent up the names of both Longmire and Borlase, the Bishop would appoint Longmire. The thing to do, therefore, they conceived, was to 'nominate a stale' instead of Longmire: someone who was not a serious candidate and whom the Bishop could not reasonably choose. This practice of 'nominating a stale' was quite common in university elections as a means of forcing the hand of

---

[1] Although Richmond held the Vere Harmsworth Chair of Imperial and Naval History, and was a professorial Fellow of Jesus, when Downing elected him as Master, he was not in the original sense a university man, and had spent most of his life in the Navy.

Bumping

"Women's War" poster of 1897, see p. 232

electors by effectually depriving them of a feasible alternative candidate. The lot fell upon Francis Barnes, Vice-Provost of King's, who had no wish to be Master but who was prepared to lend himself to the office of 'stale', or what would now even less elegantly be described as 'stooge'. The Bishop saw through the trick quite easily. He declared that the Fellows had broken their statutes by nominating Barnes, a candidate from outside the college, while others within the college were willing and available. By this, of course, he meant chiefly Daniel Longmire. The Fellows having behaved unstatutably, he declared that the right and duty of appointing a Master of Peterhouse devolved upon himself without further reference to their wishes, and he did there and then declare the Rev. Mr. Longmire, B.D., to be Master. The fat was now thoroughly in the fire, and it continued to sizzle fiercely for some months. In the end, the Fellows secured a mandamus from the Court of King's Bench compelling the Bishop to choose between their original nominees, Borlase and Barnes. Deprived by a trick of his power to appoint his favourite, Longmire, the Bishop retaliated by appointing Barnes. The unfortunate 'stale' or 'stooge', despite his angry protests, found himself Master of Peterhouse. The Bishop had veritably sold the college a dummy, and a dummy of their own packing. And not for a time, merely, but for nearly fifty years. Dr. Barnes lived as Master of Peterhouse to the age of ninety-five. 'The experience of fifty years,' wrote one Fellow of Peterhouse, when the aged Master died in 1838, 'has too lamentably demonstrated to the college how little he was qualified for the discharge of any duty which required the exercise of high notions of morality and a careful regard to what is just, decent, and venerable.' After all, they might have known.

The imposition of a Master upon a college from without (although 'imposition' is generally too strong a word) may lead to unfortunate experiences, but for the most part it seems that those colleges which have received their Heads in this manner have had little to complain of, and a good deal to be thankful for. 'Its evil consequences,' Winstanley has said with typical understatement, 'can easily be exaggerated.'

Past Masters

Our vision of the men of larger, bolder outline, who once ruled the Cambridge Houses, and the university itself, is largely the product of the gossip of Gunning, the pencil of Rowlandson, and the pen of Hilaire Belloc. The result is an odd combination of absurdity and magnificence. And, since Nature has a way of imitating Art, the historian can readily produce examples of both. Rowlandson's portrayal of the absurdity – rounded, gnome-like figures staggering about in the Senate House or falling off ladders in the University Library – pot-bellied men, pug-faced men, men with curly wigs and billowing gowns – who should better exemplify this than Lowther Yates, Master of St. Catharine's (1779-1799)? Waddling along King's Parade to attend Divine Service at Great St. Mary's, he looked exactly like a turtle on its hind-legs.

> Gadzoons, gadzoons,
> Lowther Yates in pantaloons –

So sang young Mr. Charles Valentine le Grice, looking down from his rooms where he was entertaining his friends to breakfast. The Master was extremely angry, and Mr. le Grice apologized, but the song was to become a classic at the Catch and Glee Club of Huntingdon forever after. The magnificent (but still jolly) Head of that generation might best be seen in Dr. Richard Farmer, Master of Emmanuel from 1775 to 1797. Portly, affable, yet of true magisterial dignity, Dr. Farmer loved all the things that a good Head of a House should love: Shakespeare, punch, tobacco, play-going, and the poor. He was one of the few men, outside his tiny circle of bottle-companions, who could make the Younger Pitt talk, and even laugh, at his ease; and, as might be expected, he was on civil terms with Dr. Johnson, with whom he shared his Shakespearian scholarship. In Farmer's day, the hospitality of the Parlour at Emmanuel was famous, and not to be foregone by any celebrity on visiting the university. The Doctor was also a notable reveller at Stourbridge Fair, where he delighted in the Shakespearian performances at the theatre, taking his full share in all the jollifications that went therewith. As college curate at Swavesey, he would trot out

to the fenland parish of a Sunday morning on his favourite pony,
Taffy; always punctual, always meticulous in his conduct of Divine
Worship, always ready to indulge the company at the village inn
thereafter with punch and tobacco after his chop-lunch. Then, back to
college at six for Sunday evening in the Parlour. It was Dr. Farmer
who, as librarian, saw to it that the fine portrait of John Nicolson, the
old Cambridge book-vendor known to all as 'Maps', was placed on the
staircase of the library.[1]

Loving the good things of life as they did, it is yet the size of their
heads rather than the size of their bellies that lends to these old Masters
their abiding fame. Those heads were, they must have been, enormously swollen. Dictatorial, opinionated, riding rough-shod over their
Fellows, regarding opposition as a form of treason, the old Masters
came near to constituting a race of academic *condottieri*, and they made
Cambridge loud with their battles. They fought their campaigns in
their Lodges, at college meetings, on the floor of the Senate House, in
the press, and in the Courts Chancery and King's Bench. Sometimes
they fought for personal supremacy, or for the mere love of disputation.
More often they did battle for larger causes, the honour and fame and
greater good of the Houses over which they ruled, and whose well-
being they readily equated with their own. The merely factious, or
peculiar, might be found in such Heads as Roger Long, Master of
Pembroke from 1733 to 1770, or Thomas Browne of Christ's, Master
from 1808 to 1819. Roger Long was born in the time of Marlborough's
wars and lived to see the beginnings of the American Revolution,
which must have annoyed him very much. He was an autocratic Tory
of the pre-Hanoverian world who was supposed, in 1760, to be waiting
with hope deferred for the arrival of a Patriot King. He kept up inter-
necine warfare with the Fellows throughout his Mastership, not, it
seems, on behalf of any cherished ideals of a better college, but simply
in the cause of universal subordination to mastership. Toryism, to men
like Roger Long – as to Samuel Johnson – was not merely a political
creed, but a cosmic principle. It involved a Hobbesian horror of 'that
dissolute condition of masterless men'. Long was a learned and

---

[1] The portrait now hangs on the left hand wall of the entrance to the new University
Library, splendidly bridging the old world and the new.

ingenious Professor of Astronomy, and he loved all things mechanical. He set up the first planetarium in the college garden, a sphere within which thirty people could sit to watch the revolving heavens. The heavens revolved at the command of the Master of Pembroke, operating through a boy-demiurge who turned a handle outside. Astronomical ingenuity on the part of Heads of Houses has always afforded opportunities for the wits. When William Whewell, the Master of Trinity, published his *Plurality of Worlds*, in 1853, to dispose of the notion that there are other inhabited worlds than our own, it was suggested that his object was to prove that

> . . . through all infinity,
> There was nothing so great as the Master of Trinity.

After Roger Long, Thomas Browne of Christ's appears merely quarrelsome, and rather mean. He had the unpleasant habit of removing his enemies from the Fellowship by calling meetings of the Governing Body while they were absent from Cambridge, whereby they forfeited their titles.

Isaac Milner, President of Queens' from 1788 to 1820, was a Tory of a different stamp. Pursuing that *carrière ouverte aux talents* which is sometimes imagined to have been made possible only by the French Revolution, the weaver's boy from Leeds had come up to Queens' in 1770 as a sizar, or third-class college citizen, to attain eminence not only as Professor of Natural Philosophy, and of Mathematics, but as President of his college. 'The University perhaps never produced a man of more eminent abilities', Gunning was to write of him. In principles, Isaac Milner may best be described as a Tory Evangelical, which really means that he was a type of Oliver Cromwell in academic dress. Milner was determined to have his own way under the authority only of his own conscience, and he got it. Having his own way meant making Queens' College, and the University of Cambridge, worthy of Isaac Milner. The first thing that the new President must do, therefore, was to get rid of Jacobins and infidels from the Fellowship. This he achieved in a remarkably short time. Before very long, Gunning tells us, he had acquired 'such entire ascendancy over the Fellows that no one thought of offering the slightest opposition to his will'. Instead of fighting the President in a series of pitched battles, as the Fellows of Trinity had fought Dr. Bentley, the Fellows of Queens' resigned, retired to parish livings, or got married. One of them, indeed, got himself transported. Anything, it seems, was preferable to serving as a Fellow of Queens' under Isaac Milner.

The President himself has told us how, and why, he achieved his victory. 'I was positively determined to have nothing to do with Jacobins or infidels,' he wrote in 1801 to William Wilberforce, the arch-Evangelical. It was within his power as President to appoint the college tutors, providing he appointed them from among Fellows of the college. But 'the clever Fellows' who were, so to say, of tutorial timber, were also, in the eyes of their President, 'disqualified on account of their principles'. So he took the extremely bold step of looking elsewhere for suitable recruits. 'Our own being very unfit, we went out of College, sorely against the wish of several; however, by determining to make no jobs of such things, but to take the very best men I could find, I carried the matter through in no less than three instances.' No doubt these excellent Fellows, recruited from outside the college, became the President's devoted followers, and, with the retreat of the aforesaid clever but wrongly-principled Queens' men, there is little cause for wonder that he achieved complete personal ascendancy in his own House. It was the triumph of a bold, not to say despotic, temper in the cause of an ideal. He had 'converted Queens' from a home of Whig and latitudinarian principles into a stronghold of Toryism and evangelicalism'. As such it was to remain long into the nineteenth century, a breakwater of the Protestant university against all but the more trivial ripples of the Oxford Movement. Beyond the walls of his own college, however, Milner was a less god-like figure. As an examiner in the Schools, Gunning remarks with some asperity, he was impartial 'except when a man of his own college or of Magdalene was concerned'. As Vice-Chancellor, he complained over the excessive burdens of the office, and did his best to get a physician's certificate to testify that a second term would injure his health. He would drive to the Senate House in a closed carriage, though Gunning reports that his private dinner-parties were far from those of a valetudinarian, 'uproarious' in fact.

The King of all Cambridge's past masters, however, is without doubt Richard Bentley, the Master of Trinity from 1699 to 1734. Bentley, like Milner, was a Yorkshireman and of comparatively humble origins. Likewise, he same up as a sizar. But Bentley came up to St. John's, and, as he liked to say, by the aid of his God he jumped over a wall – into the Master's Lodge of the adjoining[1] college. His name and fame were already made in the world beyond Cambridge. Denied a Fellowship in his own college,[2] he had spent some years as a school-master and then as Keeper of the King's Library at St. James'. It was during these years that he came to take a leading part in the great intellectual controversy of the day: the battle of the Ancients and Moderns. His *Dissertation on the Epistles of Phalaris*, and on *Aesop's Fables*, marked only the beginning of a career which, year by year, was to establish him as the greatest among the critical scholars of classical learning in that age, and perhaps of any age. Lord Macaulay, arguing for a statue of Bentley in the ante-chapel at Trinity,[3] described him as 'the greatest man in his own department that has appeared in Europe since the revival of letters'. By the time he became Master of Trinity, Bentley was also famous for his Boyle Lectures in Defence of the Christian Religion against Infidels (1692), in which he undertook to show how the *Principia* of Sir Isaac Newton was truly (as the great man himself claimed) the work of a man 'having an eye upon such principles as might work with considering men for the belief of a Deity'. Indeed, his biographer claims that Bentley was the first 'to lay open those discoveries in popular form and to explain their irresistible force in the proof of a Deity,' and that Sir Isaac himself highly approved of his endeavours. It is therefore not difficult to understand why the

---

[1] Trinity and St. John's are the celebrated Cambridge back-to-backs. For many genera-tions they jealously maintained their stance of mutual hostility, mentally as well as physically. Johnian 'pigs' were a byword to the Trinitarians. Not the least of the offences of Christopher Wordsworth as Master of Trinity was his habit of quoting 'the swinish statutes of St. John's'. Trinity on one occasion refused to employ a butler because he had served next-door.

[2] At that time, St. John's, like some other colleges, had a county quota restriction on elections to Fellowships, and the Yorkshire quota was already full.

[3] Perhaps it is unnecessary to add that the statue was not erected. Macaulay was arguing in 1856, little more than a century after Bentley's death. Another century has passed, and still Trinity has left Bentley uncelebrated in its place of greatest honour. No doubt he is very hard to forgive. It is perhaps significant that the college's portrait of him was given by himself. It appears to be the original of the one in the National Portrait Gallery. Roubilliac's bust may be seen in the college library.

two Archbishops and the four Bishops, to whom William III had entrusted such royal appointments after the death of Queen Mary, should have chosen Richard Bentley unanimously as Master of the royal College of the Holy and Undivided Trinity in Cambridge. They knew him as his country's most brilliant critical scholar of ancient literature, and its more celebrated champion of the Christian religion under the aegis of England's latest and greatest contribution to physical science. It is only fair to say that Bentley's other, and less reputable, titles to fame, or notoriety, were not in evidence until after his installation. Even if they had suspected an unduly masterful temper from the tone of his celebrated controversial writings, they would doubtless have accounted it a fault on the right side. Trinity just then needed a master as well as a Master. They could not have been expected to anticipate how soon it was to forfeit any claim to be either Holy or Undivided.

The first-fruit of the Reformation in England, Henry VIII's foundation, had risen rapidly from infancy to maturity as a home of learning, but during the troubled period of the Stuarts it had fallen upon evil days. Civil strife and intolerance in the nation at large had had their repercussions within its walls. Despite great individuals like Barrow and Newton, the Fellowship had declined in intellectual distinction, discipline had been relaxed to the detriment of decorum and letters, Cromwell's parliamentary commissioners had inflicted upon it unworthy men for political and sectarian interests, and even more unworthy men had been intruded by Charles II and James II. The old Scholastic discipline had lost favour, and nothing vigorous had yet come to replace it, so that the college existed in an 'indeterminate state of torpor'. Whatever was to happen under the new Master, torpor was certainly to be banished. During the next forty years and more, the College was to be an academic bear-garden. The sounds of battle from beyond the Great Gate were to resound not only throughout the university, but in the law courts and even in the higher ranges of party politics. Whether Bentley's variegated prescriptions for dispelling torpor were worse than the disease may still be disputed. Perhaps it is best to recite the judgment of a Trinity man, Vice-Master of a later day. 'Bentley certainly did much temporary harm to Trinity,' wrote the judicious Winstanley, 'and was frequently guilty of the most discreditable sharp-practice, but his activities were not entirely selfish or pernicious, and his influence on the College was in some respects extremely beneficial.'

Bentley

The new Master's earliest concern (and it was a concern that was to occupy him, off and on, for many years) was to provide himself with a domestic setting of suitable amenity. The first thing he did was to tear down the aged and decaying tapestries from the walls of the Master's Lodge and install the latest fashion in wainscot, sash-windows and marble chimney-pieces. He also installed the handsome and very wide staircase which is still one of the glories of the Lodge. He set himself up with a handsome study, similarly apparelled, and it was suspected that he had designs on the Fellows' bowling-green which, being situated under his study windows, threatened to disturb his scholarly meditations. His double-vaulted wine-cellar, his garden-terrace and walks, his elegant summer-house, and his commodious granary on the river-bank (to receive the produce brought down from his rectory at Somersham[1]), were subsequent projects upon which he spent much time and money. Nor could the Fellows have failed to applaud the enhanced dignity and amenity of their Master's environment had he not expected the college to pay for them. The atmosphere was scarcely improved when it was suspected that his enlightened move to set up a chemistry laboratory was a device to provide the Master with a new green-house. It was discovered fairly soon, moreover, that he regarded the college servants, the butler, the cook and the porter, as appendages to his own household. And he expected the college to buy his produce, for he was (as Rector of Somersham) both a farmer and a maltster. Rumours were soon rife that the bad beer complained of at college Feasts was brewed from the Master's malt, which had been spoilt by weevils. This was probably a libel, but it is nonetheless true

[1] He enjoyed the living of Somersham as an appendage to the Regius Professorship of Divinity, which he acquired by a piece of remarkably sharp practice in 1717. It was chiefly a matter of voting for himself (despite disqualification) and taking advantage of the absence of a sufficient number of the electors.

that he used his magisterial powers to get a better and more certain market for his produce. When things came to a head over the bursar's refusal to pay for the Master's granary, he simply appointed a new bursar, a favourite of his from Upwell in the fens, one Richard Walker, henceforth known as 'Frog-Walker', who paid for the granary and contrived so to mix up the Master's accounts with those of the college that no one was ever able to disentangle them.

It was typical of Bentley that while he was thus enhancing his own (and future Masters') amenities, and taking every possible measure, honest and otherwise, to enhance his own income, he was at the same time laying the foundations of some of the best things that Trinity was to offer for the greater glory of Cambridge. He contrived the repair, remodelling, and decoration of the Chapel, that sombre monument to the rational pieties of Walpoleian England. He led off the subscription-list for this with a donation of £200, and proposed that every Fellow should sacrifice one year's dividend (either £50 or £20) to the cost. The total cost came to some £6,000, and the Master's financial proposals well-nigh ruined some of the junior Fellows and landed many others in debt for years to come. Resolved that the college should celebrate to the world its great pride in Newtonian learning – Queen Anne had knighted the man of genius at the Master's Lodge on her visit in 1705 – he built an observatory over the Great Gateway of the college in the following year, and installed the most promising of Sir Isaac's disciples as Astronomical Fellow to live there. On the strength of this, and perhaps of his getting Vigani of Verona (who had been made Professor of Chemistry in 1702) transplanted to Trinity and fitted up with a laboratory there, he has been called the founder of the Natural Sciences at Cambridge. Be this as it may, he can certainly be called the second founder of the University Press.[1] He also contributed much to the beauty of the University's setting, for it is primarily to Bentley that we owe that especial glory of Cambridge, 'the Backs'. He found a fen and he left a garden, adorned with lime avenues, groves and walks. This priceless legacy to the future was made in the years 1717-18. It cost the college £500, and for once no one complained. It is

[1] The reparation of 'that noble presse which my worthy and most learned friend.... is with greate charge and industrie erecting now at Cambridge', as John Evelyn wrote, was undertaken before he became Master of Trinity, and while he was the King's Librarian.

characteristic of the man that he also leased the South Meadow from the Fellows (they used it for grazing their horses) at a quarter of its economic rent, drained and hedged it, and used the proceeds of sub-letting to finance his annual fishing-party at Over, the college rectorial estate. This piece of business met with a somewhat different response, and he was checked (only just in time) in carrying out the further design of erecting a summer residence at Over for the exclusive enjoy-ment of the Master and his family.

The junior members of the college had some reason to applaud the Master's innovations, although he made an unpopular start by sending down an undergraduate promptly, and single-handed, and therefore contrary to statute, for being found in a bawdy-house. This lawless celebration of his entry into supreme power, like that of James VI of Scotland when he hanged a cutpurse without trial on his progress to London as James I of England, at once aroused forebodings about the new Master's attitude towards constitutional restraints. But most of his high-handed actions were at the expense of the Fellows, and the young rarely shed tears over the discomfiture of their elders. Indeed, some of the Master's earlier innovations were directed to the undergraduates, benefit, and perhaps to winning their alliance. For instance, he secured their admission to the college library and allocated increased funds for the purchase of books; meat suppers were provided in Hall on Fridays, whereas there had been no supper in Hall on that day; leave was given to undergraduates to rise from table before grace-after-meat instead of their being required to sit and watch the prolonged eating and drinking at High Table; noblemen and fellow-commoners were docked of their privileges of exemption from chapel and certain Latin exercises; and freedom to come and go at late hours was incidentally made a good deal easier by the Master's monopoly of the time of college servants. Meanwhile, the Fellows suffered agonies by the Master's inroads upon their privileges and by his downright bullying tactics. He made no attempt to conceal his contempt for them as a hoggish, poor-spirited and immoral crew. He cut the stipends of bursar and steward, reduced the service of commons in Fellows' rooms, and secured the expulsion of any Fellow guilty of *crimina majora*: one for cutting up the college plate, and another for committing adultery in Berkshire. He even tried to deprive them of their Combination Room, which afflicted him as a centre of mischief, dissension and intrigue. Expulsion, discommuning, financial ruination, abusive language, insult piled upon injury – these things aroused a sullen hatred which the Master chose to attribute to the factious spirit of the age. Bentley was a Whig, and most of the Fellows were Tories. 'If in this age of parties and divisions some few dislike me on that account,' he said, ''tis impossible to help it.' As for their perpetual talk about their privileges, he preferred to believe that this was simply an excuse for their resentment at the high price of claret. Their anger was to be attributed 'not to lessening their privileges but to increasing the price of claret by one shilling a bottle: this naturally hit them hardest,' he said, 'because this was the chief item of their expenditure, book-bills being forgotten among them.' When Edmund Miller, a lay fellow, came to the college for Christmas in 1709, he found the Fellows, after ten years under the new Master, terrified, scarcely daring to speak to each other, and looking like prisoners expecting execution or decimation. Mr. Serjeant Miller was to take a leading part in arousing them to resistance. Indeed, he became such a thorn in the flesh of the Master, that the infuriated tyrant had to install constables in the Lodge in order to exclude him from a meeting of the Seniority.

Bentley's attitude to the restraining powers of statute was a mixture of chicanery and unconcealed contempt. When he met resistance he would hint at a 'strict construction' of old rules which might again be brought into force to his own advantage, or he would refer to what he called his 'rusty sword'. More generally he preferred 'loose construction'. In order to secure the essential object of a statute, he would argue, it was often necessary to deviate from the letter of the law: 'it must be broken in order to be kept'. Either way, he invariably had the best of it. He had six law-suits before the Court of King's Bench in the space of three years, and won them all. He was still pursuing a contest with his bitterest enemy, Dr. Colbatch, Rector of Orwell, over the sum of 3s. 6d. in the Consistorial Court of the Bishop of Ely in 1738. It really seemed, wrote his biographer, that 'these grey-headed litigants were so habituated to a state of controversy that the excitement of a law-suit had become as necessary to them as that of hazard is to the inveterate gamester.' Bentley insisted on defraying all the expenses of his litigation from the college funds. The total amounted to nearly £4,000. The 'Frog-Walker' and other bursarial allies worked hard to improve the income of the college from its estates, and both Bentley and Dr. Colbatch refrained from dividends and dues for several years in order to ease the burden. But it was long before Trinity extricated itself from the debt incurred by the Master's career at law. The college came near to libelling the Courts of Justice when it complained that while the merest peasant could secure redress for his grievances, 'a body of learned and worthy men, oppressed and injured daily', could not get a court in England to receive their complaints. It was only when the Master's conduct upon the larger scene of the university (principally as Regius Professor of Divinity) brought upon him the wrath of his fellow Heads of Houses that he suffered nominal defeat. For he treated the university with little more respect than he treated his college. His brethren among the Heads had reason to complain of his tongue. Not only did he call Dr. Sherlock, the Master of St. Catharine's, 'Cardinal Alberoni', and Dr. Gooch, the Master of Caius, 'the empty gotch of Caius', but he asked Dr. Ashton, the Master of Jesus, who requested a slight delay because something was 'not quite clear to him', whether 'we are to wait here until your mud has subsided?' Dr. Gooch, the Master of Caius, had something more than words to complain of. It was suspected that the Master of Trinity had tried to put an end to the Master of Caius at the hands of a hired assassin. It certainly looked as if a bullet, fired from the direction of Trinity College, had passed through an open window of Dr. Gooch's Lodge and buried itself in the wainscot. When the wall was stripped at a later date, a spent bullet was discovered there.

Of course, there came a time when it was possible to believe almost anything of Richard Bentley, a time that has not yet passed away. Most of the less believable things are nonetheless borne out by perfectly good evidence. For instance, that he made his liability to catch cold his excuse for not attending Chapel for twenty years; that he left the college livings uninspected for thirty-seven years; that he imposed a Trinity man on the parish of Over without (on his own admission) ever having seen his face, and on the man's engaging to marry

Mrs. Bentley's maid; and that he secured a college Fellowship for his son, Richard Bentley (a young man of unimpeachable character), at the tender age of fifteen. Nonetheless, there were always those in high places, generally outside the university, who stood by him with unswerving loyalty and esteem, professing to regard him as a great man pestered by a swarm of academic midges. For one thing, all through his many campaigns, he continued to produce works of fine scholarship. His reputation in the European world of letters seemed to increase in direct ratio to the diminution of his moral reputation in Cambridge. Indeed, there is good reason to believe that he planned his triumphs in the world of learning as strategic moves – diversions, perhaps – in his battles with the Fellows of Trinity. At any rate, whenever his fortunes reached a fresh crisis, he came out with some contribution to critical learning whose brilliance might have been expected to deter, if it did not disarm, his domestic enemies. Lord Carteret, who loved learning more than he loved statesmanship, described the anti-Bentley uproar as arising from 'the distempered frenzies of cloistered bigots', and when he read the Articles exhibited against the great scholar in order to deprive him of the Mastership in 1734, his Lordship gave it as his opinion that 'no man of tolerable sense or learning could with a grave face expel a Master upon this charge; nor even admonish him without the censure of dullness and incapacity, and the amazement of mankind'.[1] But then, Carteret was often drunk, and he read his classical authors not within the walls of Trinity, but at his own fireside with his feet on the fender.

It should be remembered, too, that this was the great age of Whig supremacy, and that Bentley stoutly upheld the cause of Whiggery in a university a generation behind the times, an academic world still impregnated with the Toryism of the age of Queen Anne. Even during the brief Tory revival in the last years of the last Stuart sovereign, Bentley had managed to sustain himself at Court by 'address and good fortune'. He dedicated his edition of Horace to that keen collector, Robert Harley, Earl of Oxford, the Queen's Lord High Treasurer, and survived in good odour until the rising sun of Hanoverian Whiggery

[1] The candid reader can make up his mind for himself on the point by consulting the Articles where they are printed at the back of Monk's *Life of Bentley*.

emerged from behind the clouds in 1715. And when, in 1720, a Royal Commission was appointed to settle the disputes in the university, it proceeded to do precisely nothing, for the Whig ministers advised his Hanoverian Majesty against interference in academical feuds. Indeed, the House of Hanover was good to Cambridge. At the instance of Viscount Townshend, George I purchased the 30,000 volumes of the Bishop of Ely's library and presented them to the university. He subscribed £2,000 to the building of a new Senate House. He founded a liberally endowed Chair of Modern History. Cambridge was wooed and won as the university of the Protestant Succession, the breeding-ground of sound Whig politics. And Richard Bentley, even in the midst of his sins, was its prophet. It must have been a touching spectacle to see the ageing Master of Trinity standing beside the King's chair at High Table when the second George dined in Hall on his visit to the university in 1728. No one has ever asked why he did not receive a knighthood.

Richard Bentley was, in the end, deprived of his degrees and sentenced to be deprived of his Mastership, but he died in the Master's Lodge. The Vice-Master, whose duty it was to carry out the sentence, could never bring himself to the task. It would doubtless have been necessary to carry out Bentley, feet first. This was only done eight years later. He was buried in the chapel sanctuary under a plain stone inscribed: RICARDUS BENTLEY, S.T.P.R.[1] OBIIT XIV JUL. 1742. AETATIS 80. No reference was made to his Mastership. He had spent the closing years of his life in the Master's Lodge in amicable domesticity. He sat by the fire in his dressing-gown, reading his beloved authors, thee-ing and thou-ing his household, Yorkshire fashion, as he had always done, and spoiling his devoted grandchildren. He took to smoking at seventy, and he developed a discriminating taste for port-wine. He thought he would like to live to be eighty, an age long enough, he held, for a man to read everything that was worth reading. He did.

'We may strip him of his titles,' Conyers Middleton had written, years before, 'but we never can of his insolence; he has ceased to be a Doctor, and may cease to be a Professor, but he can never cease to be Bentley. There he will triumph over the University to the last; all its

[1] Sanctae Theologiae Professor Regius (Regius Professor of Divinity).

learning being unable to polish, its manners to soften, or its discipline to tame the superior obstinacy of his genius.'

When the Head of a House in our time looks back upon the long shadows of his predecessors, he is unlikely to regret the passing of the age of the giants. He may lament, as Niccolo Machiavelli lamented when he looked back to Republican Rome, that the Princes of the modern world can never be so great as the heroes of antiquity. It is improbable that he will accept Machiavelli's counsel to imitate their actions in order at least to 'savour' their greatness. He is more likely to regard them as awful warnings.

In this, he is in danger of doing injustice to the great dead. Within their age and generation (roughly from Queen Anne to Queen Victoria), they wielded the great authority entrusted to them by ancient statutes, and they frequently enlarged their authority to suit the magnitude of their ambitions. Yet they accomplished much that lesser personalities might have allowed to die from inanition or timidity. They deserve at least as much respect as the so-called Enlightened Despots who ruled so much of Europe in their time. This may not be saying very much for them. And perhaps, as Royal Commissions and revised statutes proceed on their remorseless and efficient way, we shall come to appreciate these men only for their entertainment-value, or as freaks of human nature, grotesque examples of what men may become at the hands of an environment that is no longer possible to our experiences, and scarcely possible to imagine. Yet, any account of Cambridge life as it is lived now, must involve some account of Cambridge life as it was once lived, for Cambridge is a place made big with legend and tradition, and the shades of the men who once lived there are something more than shadows. They stand about us like the buildings they once inhabited, and they affect our lives with the cumulative force of historic association. Burke's observation, and recommendation, that we act always as if in the presence of canonized ancestors, may look like very great nonsense when we think of the peculiarly uncanonical shades of Bentley or Roger Long. Nevertheless, no one is fit to understand Cambridge present who rejects from his perspective even the more disreputable ghosts of Cambridge past. He knows not Cambridge as she is who knows not Bentley as he was.

Winter Evening

Où sont les neiges d'antan?

They have a habit of arriving just when Cambridge folk are beginning to congratulate themselves on a mild winter. In the teeth of all experience Cambridge folk do this, more especially elderly dons and college servants. Bedmakers coming into college over icy pavements in the dark of February dawn; gyps and kitchen porters crossing arctic courts in their ministrations from staircase to staircase; dons crossing the lawns to dine in Hall when the lights burn low in the lamps, fringing the snowy wastes with ice-blue edges. Diagonally, between the resident don's staircase and the steps of the Hall entrance, a winding pathway is worn across the whiteness. Its winding tells a tale. The tale is told in the college magazine, with a back-view of a heavily shrouded figure plodding along, and a caption: AND QUIET FLOWS THE DON.

The snow comes late, like an afterthought of winter deposited on the very doorstep of spring. For a few days the heavy sky has lain like a grey blight, low over the town. Presently it softens into a feathery, smoky, colourless haze. Then the first flakes fall, melting into sleet as they reach the warmer world. Finally, the wind settles in the north-east, the Siberian wind, slicing across the fens and flats as if legions of professional knife-throwers have settled down along the Norfolk coast-line with King's College Chapel as their target. 'Operation Knife' generally begins late on a February afternoon. By nightfall the whistling breath of the knives has frozen everything in its path. Now the falling flakes survive their contact with the earth. They settle in a thin rustling carpet which thickens as the night goes on. By morning the world looks sheepish, and men come out with spades and brooms and carts to sheer away the fleece from paths and highways. But on lawns and roofs and towers it lies inviolate, save where the birds have left their tiny broad arrows or a privileged person has taken his short-cut over the sacred grass. It is, as they say, 'waiting for some more'. And some more comes, much more, spell after spell of drifting fleece, until the cold sky is empty and the earth is silent under burial. It will stay like that for a week, two weeks, perhaps a month, a frozen world under a freezing, windless sky.

Cambridge in winter is one of the coldest places on the face of the earth. Measured in degrees of frost, its coldness may not look impressive. Experienced on the nose, the ears, the cheek-bones and the finger-tips, it has the savagery of red-hot steel. It is the quality of the cold that strikes you. It is a cold that gets into the bones, ravages the sinuses and all other cavities of the human skull, closes round the body like a suit of chain-mail. Mittens, balaclava helmets, leather jerkins, double layers of woolly pants, fur-lined boots, these things may temper but cannot defeat it. For the cold has got into a shallow windless trough at the foot of the Gogs, and nothing but the rise of a strong wind from the south-west will move it. Coal-fires make a milder arc for some six feet about the hearth. Oil-stoves in distant parts of the room, or in the passages, may induce a feeling that one is indoors and not outside. Central heating, where it exists, will create a comforting fug and a headache. The one thing that Cambridge colleges will never do is to install double-windows, diffused heating, air-conditioning, effective lagging, inside plumbing, and all the devices that make life tolerable in lands where severe winter conditions are accepted as 'official'. The academic world, whose climatologists live in super-heated laboratories, prefers to go on regarding a severe winter as exceptional, just as its historians and political thinkers prefer to go on describing the English as 'an essentially temperate people, disinclined to go to extremes, etc. etc. . . .' It is odd that these myths are perpetuated in Cambridge – Cambridge crouching on its open, naked, unprotected plain, Cambridge with its Siberian winds, Cambridge with her back to the wall of the Gogs and without a rampart between her frozen nose and the Ural mountains. Perhaps there is a spurious warmth to be derived from a sense of Spartan virtue, or from a lingering loyalty to some outmoded ideal of scholastic asceticism.

Only the aesthetic sense finds comfort from Cambridge under snow. The white wilderness of lawns and courts sets back the lines of the surrounding buildings in a new perspective, lending a marvellously light and spacious air to enclosures that are normally to be seen in smaller compass. The obliteration of roofs cuts down the height of boundary walls. The whole place looks lower on the earth, capped and crushed, hidden and slightly humbled. The tall Tudor towers look stunted, even the proud pinnacles of King's Chapel assume a vaguely

M

veiled reticence. Everything rococo, on the other hand, is enhanced in grace by the silver pencillings of frozen snow along swags and leafage and encrusted mouldings. The Senate House becomes a dream-palace in a fairy-tale, the home of the Snow King's daughter. The gothic, and especially the pseudo-gothic, comes into its own, upholding sheeted spires and loaded crockets in sharpest definition. In the Backs, the frosted foliage of elm and lime and poplar hangs beside the untrodden lawns in still curtains of silver-point. The little ditches that divide the lawns are black mouths fringed with white beards. On the half-formed ice under the river-banks, small families of ducks stand around, waggling their shuddering tails and lifting their cold feet in turn from the freezing shelves. A few still paddle slowly along the liquid lanes, as if to stay the binding of the waters by their forlorn patrol. Others take sudden flight down to Queens' and the Mill Pool, either to keep warm or to see whether the skating has begun in the meadows towards Grantchester. In those rare winters when the river freezes over and the water-meadows beyond the University bathing sheds will bear it, the skaters throng the rink from Magdalene Bridge to the Mill, and all across the pastures beside the upper reaches.

Then may be seen that rare and majestic spectacle: dons on skates. Men who customarily are only to be seen stalking at two miles an hour along King's Parade may now pass you by with knees bent and sawing arms, flashing past like speed-boats with an urgent appointment at Grantchester or Clayhithe. Mathematicians gravely pirouette with folded arms and twinkling toes, combining business with pleasure as they square the circle. Bald heads that still retain the bronze of summer suns in the Tyrol or the Midi are tinged with sunset fire as the sky reddens over Barton and Comberton. A solitary exponent of the Dying Swan hovers in the middle of the Mill Pool, arms akimbo, toes nibbling, bald pate gleaming like a russet apple. Daffyd Evans, having described three successive circles about the solitary artist at a respectful distance, rejoins his friends at the bridge. His brain reels at the proximity of the transatlantic visitor whom he habitually salutes as 'the greatest living literary critic'.

"Boy," he moans ecstatically. "Boy! On the same rink with greatness!"

The swan dies. Resurrection swiftly follows. The greatest living literary critic has spotted the second greatest living literary critic gliding down from Queens'. They pass each other at speed, the greatest living literary critic swerving sightlessly at the last moment, as if irresistibly attracted by the prospect of collision. The second greatest living literary critic staggers, cuts a frenzied caper, and slides about fifty yards on his back-side. He picks himself up as if this were all part of his complicated design, and sails slowly back to Queens'.

"Highly symbolic," says Daffyd Evans.

The lights go in the flooded field beyond the bathing sheds. Four girls, with Newnham scarves streaming behind them, sweep past with linked arms, the front rank of the swelling battalions on their way to the evening carnival of the meadow-rink.

"Time to go," says Daffyd, as he squats on the bridge and takes off his skates. "I've got an essay to write before Hall."

Heaving his skates into his bicycle-basket, he looks his last towards the lighted rink and then pedals slowly back up Mill Lane. His essay is on Matthew Arnold, and he reflects sadly that even Arnold has what his supervisor would call 'a meagre belle-lettristic relevance to the human condition. . . .' He mutters to himself the lines that he had once thought beautiful, lines that Cambridge-English has taught him to regard as 'merely poetic':

> And we are here as on a darkling plain
> Swept with confused alarms of struggle and fight,
> Where ignorant armies clash by night . . .

Daffyd has learnt all the swear-words: 'beautiful', 'poetic', 'stylistic', 'emotive'. He has all the O.K. terminology at the tip of his tongue: 'significant', 'disciplined intelligence', 'ethos', 'major poet', and 'minor talent'. He knows there is nothing worth reading between Donne and Hopkins. He is full of 'awareness', armed cap-à-pie against the 'stock response', and brimming with 'trained sensibility'. The only trouble is that he can't any longer enjoy literature. The new revelation lies heavy on his stomach like unleavened bread. That is why he goes skating, or for long walks round Coton and Grantchester, or along the Roman Road over the Gogs. There are many like him, lean and hungry figures, striding over the familiar 'grinds', talking every inch of the way in hot pursuit of certainties. To talk it out, preferably to someone reading engineering studies, or Natural Sciences Part I, someone who will not answer back too readily: this is a wonderful way of convincing oneself, at least. 'It is certain my conviction gains infinitely the moment another soul will believe in it,' says Novalis.

It is in this last hour of a winter's afternoon, when the sun lies cold and red on the Royston hills, when the footfalls ring like iron on the homeward road, and when the lights begin to twinkle in the distant city, that many a thoughtful soul imagines itself to have come to the moment of truth. The eights are ice-bound in the boat-houses, the playing-fields are bare acres of frost-bound earth, and man is reduced to the simplest and cheapest form of locomotion. The blood is stirred, yet the brain remains clear. The life of the earth is at its lowest ebb, the sap withdrawn to the depths of the trees, the birds huddled silent in the hedges, the streams struck into glaciers. Mind shrinks to a pinpoint within the tingling skull. It pierces to the heart of a world stripped of all irrelevance. For a moment it thinks it knows why it is here, and what the world is, and what it is not. It even thinks it knows what Cambridge is, and what it is not, what it can give, and what it cannot give. For a moment only. The frosty stars, the distant lights, the running beads of a train as it shrieks at the Foxton level-crossing, the promise of a roaring gas-fire, and the savour of tea and toast and dinner in Hall, these things encompass great thoughts with a local habitation and a name. Cambridge is with us again, and the soul hot for certainties must make do once more with dusty answers, provisional gusts of revelation. The object of the exercise was truth. Its achievement, harvested only in a life-time which is as yet barely begun, is an ability to remain content with half knowledge, to rest in uncertainties.

Goldsworthy Lowes Dickinson used to talk of what he called 'the peculiarly Cambridge attitude about truth'. The societies of the young at Cambridge, he thought, generated 'a peculiar clean white light of their own', a light which remained with their members long into later life. It was, he believed, 'our only safeguard . . . against the wild superstitions always fermenting below and always breaking out in times like these'. He was writing in 1932. The societies of which he spoke consisted, and consist, not only of undergraduates crowding around gas-fires after Hall, but of the two's and three's perambulating the field-paths and the humble hills on afternoons in winter. For, here too, young men learn to sit loose to opinions, to admit uncertainty as a condition of a truthful confrontation of life. Those who deplore the increasing triumphs of authoritarian creeds among undergraduates in our time might do worse than to revive and encourage the old Cambridge habit of walking and talking on winter afternoons. Countless souls have been saved alive on Coton footpath, the Grantchester Grind, and the road across the Gogs.

Spring Morning

It's cold still, but there are daffodils and primroses and undergraduates ...
  Goldsworthy Lowes Dickinson, In Spring

This particular don knew his luck. He lived, a philosophical bachelor, in his rooms in Gibbs Building at King's College, through all the best years of his life. He was a highly civilized example of 'the resident don'.

There are not many of them left, now. Ever since the year 1882, when celibacy ceased finally to be one of the conditions for holding a Fellowship, Fellows of colleges have been getting married. Forfeiture at marriage, which had hitherto been the rule, was presumably based on the assumption that the Fellows of a college, like the monks and priests who were their medieval predecessors, owed their primary duty to the fraternity and should live together in a conventual society. 'Socius' is still the Latin name for a Fellow, as inscribed on tombstones or on the pieces of plate they are in the pleasant habit of presenting to the colleges from time to time. They are a Society. They are ceremoniously admitted to fellowship, on their election, by the Head of the House and in the presence of the Fellows. At this ceremony they make suitable declarations and promises. In them, as a body, is vested the government of the college, under the college statutes as approved by the Queen in Council. As a body, too, they hold the college property, and individually they receive an annual college 'dividend' which they formally vote themselves after passing the college accounts at the annual Audit meeting. It is assumed, and generally with truth, that they are a close-knit Society. And yet, the ancient physical basis of this solidarity is gone. They may dine together, sit in Combination Room together, confer together as a Governing Body; but they no longer live together in the ultimate sense of the expression. At the end of the day, they pedal off on their bicycles to the local donnery in Grange Road, or Barton Road, or farther afield, where they enjoy the lawful embraces of waiting wives and the filial chirrupings of the donlings, male and female, who swell their domestic nurseries. Their real home is no longer the college, but a suburban villa or flat. The surest way to get a young don married, it is said, is to elect him to a Fellowship and offer him his statutory right to rooms in college and meals in the Senior Combination Room. Within twelve months, and often less, he will seek out a nice young woman (rarely a donness), and set up house in one of the aforesaid dormitories. The other Fellows will protest that their hopes of securing a resident Fellow to live among the young men have been dashed again. But they are obliged to confess that they knew it would happen. It happened to them.

The unmarried don, the confirmed bachelor, who either likes living in college, or is prepared to tolerate it (for after all it has many material advantages), is really in a position to get the best of a number of worlds. He can, if he cares to make a fuss about it, preen himself on maintaining the ancient way of life of the Fellows of a college, that true community of the resident Fellows, even if the community consists of himself and the chaplain and a couple of research Fellows. He has a set of rooms, not merely a study, or offices: study, dining-room, bedroom, and the usual offices, rent and rates free, with heating and lighting and service (normally) provided at the college expense. He has first call on a gyp and a bedmaker who will tend to become his exclusive personal servants, again at college charges. He will (like all other Fellows) get his dinners in Hall free, all the year round, and other meals, delivered at his rooms at his own charges if he cares to order them. He will have taken no vows of poverty, chastity and obedience, like his monastic counterparts in less fortunate ages and societies. He need not, in fact, be either poor or particularly obedient, and he will be as chaste as any other bachelor, according to his tastes and discretion.[1] He will normally have all these things until the retiring age (generally sixty-seven), and no one will be able to sack him unless he shall be guilty of 'disgraceful conduct rendering him unfit to be a Member of the College', and even then it is generally provided by Statute that he shall be admonished until it is evident that he is thoroughly contumacious. His last ditch is the college 'Visitor' – some high dignity of Church or State, whose arbitral intervention is rarely resorted to in these days, though it was in former days quite frequently called into action. 'Appeal to the Visitor' may be said to be the last infirmity of ignoble minds.

'How does one get into this racket?' young Mr. Plummer has been heard to ask. If he gets a First in the second part of the Classical tripos, as he got it in part I, and if he turns thereafter to scholarship in the form of research studies, and if he is thereafter invited to deliver a course of lectures in the Faculty, and especially if at the same time the college thinks he would make a good tutor, and even if it does not, Mr. Plummer may some day discover the answer. After that, the racket will become the establishment, and he will become one of its strongest, even if sardonic, defenders. This fortunate don, the resident Fellow, with or without tutorial responsibilities, knows himself to be (despite his strenuous denials) one of the best placed men in the world. One might imagine that such a man – Silas Stock, for example – would offer up thanks to his Maker for his good fortune every morning in the year. Actually, Mr. Stock, at the age of fifty-five, is not at his best first thing in the morning. Port-wine and tobacco and the puerilities of Alan Skinner in the Senior Combination Room, followed by whisky and soda and a late session over *The Times* crossword, have left him with a dull wooden feeling at the top of his head and a taste of burnt string on his tongue. Little Smithson, the ex-Newmarket jockey, coming in with a cup of tea, three aspirins, a Turkish cigarette and a box of matches at seven o'clock, soon puts this right.

"Lovely morning, sir," Smithson chirps, just disturbing the curtains sufficiently to show the sunshine, as Silas Stock has patiently taught him

---

[1] "Young man", said one such bachelor to a delinquent pupil, "I get my ——ing done in London." It was as if he spoke of his laundry. But this was in Victorian times.

to do over the years (for Smithson's inclination is to dash them back and let in the day, as if the view were Newmarket Heath at exercise). "Wonderful weather for the time of year, as you might say."

"Might I?" growls Mr. Stock, squinting painfully in the streaming light. "What time is it?"

"Seven just gone, sir. What do we wear to-day?" Smithson is at the wardrobe door, hissing softly between his teeth, an irritating occupational habit of which Mr. Stock has failed to break him. It makes him feel like a horse. Indeed, little Smithson always calls the gentlemen for whom he gyps his 'runners'.

"The grey," he says, and then wonders whether he is right. It sounds too like a horse. "No, flannels and sports-jacket." After all, everybody in sight will be wearing flannels and sports-jacket on this sunshiny spring day, the day of returning youth and the peeping primrose. Everybody except Alan Skinner, who imagines a man can't be a tutor unless he wears a three-piece suit and an overcoat.

"The grey, I think, sir," Smithson insists gently. "There's the Body, sir."

"The College Meeting," Mr. Stock corrects him. "You know as well as I do that the College Meeting is not until this afternoon. I'll change after lunch."

"Very good, sir."

Smithson swings out the hanger with flannels and sports-jacket and goes away, still hissing. 'The Body!' thinks Mr. Stock. Not even 'the Governing Body.' Just 'the Body'. Still, perhaps even that is better than the 'G.B.' Skinner is everlastingly referring to 'the G.B.'

Silas Stock sips his tea, swallows his aspirin, and lights his cigarette. He always smokes a Turkish cigarette before he gets up. It is the only cigarette he ever smokes. For the rest of the day, and half the night, he will smoke his pipe. He has finished it when Smithson comes back with his well-brushed garments and his polished brown shoes.

"Bath on in five minutes, sir," Smithson announces as he goes away again.

But Silas Stock does not move. Not for another quarter of an hour. He resents the way Smithson takes charge of his time-table. If the damned bath gets cold he will have it filled again. If a man can't take life at his own pace at dawn of day he might as well be an office-boy or a dog. Silas Stock is always protesting against the conspiracy of college life to turn him into a drudge or a dog's-body. So he props himself up against the bedhead and muses on the limitless shores of time. He can hear the bedmakers chattering downstairs, the knocking of brooms, the slap of dusters, the slosh of mops. Footsteps drift past over the cobbles of the court. Sparrows quarrel in the gutters above the window. An awakening hum of traffic comes up from the London road. Bells chime in distant disputation over the hour of seven-thirty: first the mellow strokes of Trinity, then the more feminine strokes that Trinity clock lays on for St. John's, then a staggered chorus of tinny notes from the towers of the town churches, and above them all, cheerfully infallible, the swinging quarters of the 'Catholic'. In his mind's eye, Silas Stock sees the alien, Puginesque steeple of that late Victorian edifice towards the station. He sees the vane swinging from the south, and he tells himself that the wind is in the south-west.

Silas Stock swings himself out of bed, tears back the curtains, and stares out at the sunlit court. The fountain is already at play in the midst of the well-shaven grass. He wonders why he has failed to hear its sweet splashy sound until this minute. There was a time, many years ago, when Silas Stock would lie abed on summer nights listening to its endless music and telling himself that he would hear its music softly in his heart until his life's end wherever the world might call him. And here he is, at fifty-five, reflecting on the cruel effacement of the commonplace.

Close at hand, far too close for his liking, the chapel bell begins to clash its brazen tongue, and many (far too many) white-surpliced figures begin to parade across the court. Silas Stock's undergraduate life belongs to the 'twenties, and he can't for the life of him make out why the youth of the 'fifties are always crawling in and out of chapel. "Religious revival, my foot," he growls as he makes for the bathroom.

To bath, to shave, to dress, these operations occupy him for an hour, for he is determined not to hurry lest Smithson should take it into his head to start ordering breakfast for some unearthly time like eight-thirty or a quarter to nine. The little man won't get his own breakfast until he has settled his master at the table in the dining-room with *The*

Times and the marmalade. Let him wait, is Silas Stock's maxim. He sits down to table with his back to the window, not only that he may the better read the paper, but because he hates to catch sight of late-rising undergraduates haring across to Hall breakfast. Only when he has mopped up the last of the toast and coffee, and got his pipe going, will he look forth again into the court. Even now there are a few youthful figures on the move out there. Forgetting all about his resentful attitude to young men who cumber up the court at times when the place should be a beautiful oasis dedicated to the musing gaze of the Senior Tutor, he is cheered by the spectacle of those sparse drifting figures. The way the court generally empties at nine o'clock, as the young flock away to labs and lecture-rooms and libraries has come to depress him, in recent years, with fresh evidence of Skinner's success in turning the place into a kind of High School. In Silas Stock's youth, in the blessed 'twenties, there were always plenty of young men idling about the place at every hour of the morning. They were, he liked to think, educating each other, instead of swallowing 'tripos gen' (as they now call it, in their illiterate way)[1] spooned down their gullets by hacks. These reflections are a trifle disturbed by his closer identification of the gentlemen at leisure. There is the college Fascist ('we have at least one of everything,' Mr. Stock is fond of telling people), a lanky youth in coal-black, tight-fitting trousers and sweater, loping along and probably looking for a Jew to push on to the sacred grass. There is the mountainous Bug-face (his real name is unknown to Mr. Stock) who walks like a police-constable, very slowly and ponderously, one of the Master's mathematicians. The sight of him always makes Mr. Stock's blood run cold, for the fellow is so evidently a future don. There are the two staircase-men, one very old, the other very young, crossing from the kitchens to the gyp-room on M staircase with a pot of coffee and a jug of milk, travelling at about one mile an hour in order to waste the college's time and money until twelve o'clock, when they will start thinking about lunch. There is – yes, quite unmistakably there is – Skinner, hurrying across the grass in the direction of the tutorial office, and with a sheaf of papers in his hand. It is Mr. Stock's

[1] Silas Stock is always a little behind the times, and prides himself upon it. 'Gen' is out. You now (1960) 'get clued up'.

private opinion that the second tutor couldn't cross the grass without a sheet of paper in his hand. It is the tutorial passport. In another minute he would be taking the stairs to the tutorial office two at a time, humming softly to himself like a bee, or more likely a hornet, glancing on every other stair at his wrist-watch. The Senior Tutor refuses to attend at the tutorial office in order to conduct his business. He insists that a lady-clerk wait upon him at his rooms each morning at ten-thirty.

His letters occupy Mr. Stock until eleven. He is slow and hesitant at dictation because he dislikes the standard jargon of official letters, and tries to express himself in a personal style. He writes all really personal letters in his own carefully cultivated small Italic script, and he regards as personal all letters to people he has ever actually met, from the Headmasters who have visited him at Cambridge down to the least of his old pupils. At eleven o'clock Smithson brings him his coffee, and Mr. Stock always insists on his secretary drinking a cup before she goes back to the tutorial office. He suspects that she would greatly prefer to take eleven o'clock tea with the other clerks, but he thinks that coffee with the Senior Tutor is good for her further education. Fortunately she does not smoke, so he is usually free of her by eleven fifteen. To-day, he knows, he really ought to occupy himself until lunch with the agenda of the college meeting. However, he decides to do that over his lunch. On this beautiful morning, Silas Stock will take a walk through the Backs. He hasn't walked in the Backs for six – seven – eight years. The prospect of the meeting in the afternoon always depresses him. An hour or so of fresh air and sunshine may help him to keep his head above the waves of nausea which are bound to assault him between two-thirty and five o'clock. There is just a chance of meeting Skinner as he leaves college. "Going for a walk," he will announce and watch the clerkly eyebrows go up in horror.

He is still fooling with the catch of his outer door when the telephone bell begins to ring with that savage persistence of which only machines and small children are capable. Just in time, thank God, Mr. Stock mutters, as he swings the door to lock itself behind him. The insane staccato of the bell fades to the chirrup of an imprisoned grasshopper as he goes down the stairs. It pursues him faintly into the court. Passing

beneath the windows of his set, he hears it once more shattering the
upper air with the hovering clamour of some infernal flying-machine.
Someone must want him very much or they would have rung off by
now. A pupil in the hands of the police, or in hospital after a street
accident? The Master wanting to pre-arrange some item of the afternoon's agenda? The Minister of Education . . . ? Those idiots at the
Porter's Lodge would switch the call to the tutorial office in a minute,
and then Skinner would take it. . . .

"Dog's-body, dog's-body, damn' miserable dog's-body," Silas Stock
groans, and climbs the stairs again.

When he gets into his room – falling over himself to reach the blasted
instrument now – it is still keeping up its shindy.

"Stock, here," he announces blandly into the receiver.

"Gentleman asking for you, Mr. Stock, sir," comes the voice of
Alfred Carrington, the head porter. "I asked him to step round to your
rooms, sir, but he found your outer door closed."

This is the aggrieved accusation which reaches Mr. Stock's ears
from the lips of Alfred Carrington some seven times a week: the
inaccessibility of Silas Stock, outside his official tutorial hours. Silas
Stock tries a fresh variant upon his standard form of remonstrance.

"Has it still not occurred to you, Carrington, that I may have
occasion to leave my study for a short time in the course of the
morning?"

"Oh yes, sir. Of course, sir. Very sorry, sir. That is why I hung on,
sir, because I thought you were unlikely to be away long."

The telephone cable, entering the room from a point beneath the
window-ledge, suddenly afflicts Mr. Stock's fevered imagination with
the similitude of a twisted pin searching out the soft flesh of a winkle, a
silver wire thrust into a Gorgonzola cheese, a tape-worm, a ferret, a
scalpel, a dentist's probe, each and every one of them wielded by the
thick fingers of Alfred Carrington in that beastly little box at the college
entrance for the torment of an overworked, underpaid, eternally in-
carcerated tutor. He covers the mouthpiece of the receiver, groans
'dog's-body' three times, and conjures up his best brand of tutorial
tolerance.

"Thank you, Carrington. What is the gentleman's name?"

"Mr. Charles Hughes-Browne, sir. Old member of the college, sir. I'll put him through, sir."

Mr. Stock covers up again, groans, and waits for the voice from the past. It comes, plummy, exultant.

"Charles Hughes-Browne speaking. How *do* you do? You will perhaps remember me. . . . My boy is with you. . . ."

"My dear Charles, how delightful to hear your voice. Come right round. . . . Yes, H staircase. We never change, you know. . . . Ha-ha, you will know your way. . . . See you in a moment. . . ."

Silas Stock replaces the receiver. This means Combination Room lunch for two. Not another spare moment before the meeting at 2.30. Dished. Done. Trapped. Dog's-body. Toad under the harrow. In fact, a typical don's day.

The Changing Don

'Remote and ineffectual Don, where have you gone, where have you gone?'

Silas Stock's day is not really typical. Nor is Silas Stock. There are a number like him, men in advancing middle life, bachelors, encased in their colleges like winkles in their shells, lamenting the dying day of an older Cambridge, watching with defiant despondency the onset of newer forms of life. Such men are essential. They supply the *vis inertiae*, the rocks and shoals of resistance which ensure that the running tides of change shall prove themselves in the foam and flurry of battle. They also supply the young with justification for their ambivalent attitude towards dons, that reciprocated attitude of love-hatred which makes Silas Stock set up his imaginary machine-gun at the top of his staircase at the opening of every fresh academic year and then pour out lashings of sherry for his unharmed victims. It can safely be said that under-graduates feel a good deal of affection for Silas Stock and his like. Undergraduates find them the kindest and most imaginative members of the race known as 'senior members'. The world, too, has long since accepted them as its favourite image of what a don should be, an image which is long overdue for replacement by something closer to reality. For Silas Stock is definitely a survival, as Alan Skinner is always saying. If there were a typical Cambridge don in these middle years of the twentieth century, he would be much more like Alan Skinner than he would be like Silas Stock. Of course, there is no such thing. All that can be said is that there are more Skinners than Stocks.

The New Model race of dons which now pullulates at Cambridge (and at most other places which bear the name of universities) consists of married men who go to their work, on bicycles; who read the *Daily Telegraph* rather than *The Times* because it is shorter, and the *New Statesman* because they acquired the habit in their 'pink' youth in the thirties; who send their children to the local primary school first, and then (by dint of crippling themselves with examining for the G.C.E. every summer) to some school surreptitiously 'public'; who buy their houses through building societies; who play squash rather than tennis or golf to keep down their weight at the cost of the least possible expenditure of time. The odds are in favour of this kind of man's being a man of science, not because the number of undergraduates reading science exceeds the number reading the humanities (they are still in a slight minority, even at Cambridge), but because the specialized sub-divisions of science necessitate a very large teaching and administrative establishment. He will belong to a department, and most of his working time will be spent there, and in laboratories, so that his college life is likely to be exiguous in the extreme. He is much more likely to be in some sense a 'religious' man than Silas Stock, especially if he is in his thirties rather than his fifties, and more especially still if he is a scientist. Dons in general participate little in the current 'religious revival', but those who do, it is frequently observed, are more likely to be men of science than otherwise. The scientist, after all, like to have things 'taped'. Then he can get on with his work.

This kind of don, specified by Mr. Stock as 'a damned office-boy' or 'a jumped-up housemaster', – the kind who cycles into his college or his department from the suburbs, and keeps office hours, and appears at High Table when the Sunday joint has reached the rissole stage or his wife has gone to a hen-party out on the Huntingdon Road – whose conversation is of house-mortgages and small gains made on the Stock

Exchange – whose politics are pale pink and whose religion resembles a thin brown varnish: he is really that universal type of the twentieth century, the petty bourgeois, in academic dress. He works hard. He is probably engaged in a fairly routine piece of research, perhaps as a member of a research team in a laboratory. When he lifts his nose from the pursuit of his 'specialty' (the second 'i' is generally missing, even at Cambridge, nowadays) he has little to say on any topic apart from money, and possibly cricket. His ubiquity shows itself in the decline of 'general conversation' in Senior Combination Rooms and at High Table, where little huddles of specialists talk their particular 'shop', and in drawing-rooms where hostesses play Bach Partitas on the gramophone in despairing efforts to fill in the silences. And, after all, perhaps it is better that people should not talk at all, or should talk 'shop', rather than venture upon more general topics about which they know nothing. A great issue like the Suez crisis caused a flare-up of moralistic passion in Cambridge Combination Rooms, but one heard singularly little historico-political sense talked about it. Anything vaguely 'religious' or moralistic will pop and fizzle like fun, for here there is little call for knowledge beyond one's speciality, here one only needs to 'feel', and Cambridge religion to-day is largely a matter of feeling, scarcely at all concerned with theology. All this is scarcely new. The transformation of Cambridge by 'the organising and the researching don' was descried and denounced by E. M. Forster many years ago. 'Stuffy yet raw, parochial yet colourless – what a city was this! What a hole! Schoolmasters paraded its streets, specialists riddled its walls, governesses, married to either, held their lugubrious courts in its suburbs. Here the east wind blows forever, and the mist never lifts off the mud.'

Forster was giving utterance to the depressive view of Goldsworthy Lowes Dickinson, as he surveyed 'the new Cambridge' in the early years of the present century. 'The spectacle of learning gets more depressing to me every year,' he was apt to lament. Nor is his lament to be confused with *parti pris* against the growing domination of Cambridge by the scientist, the massed battalions of the laboratories. It was rather a protest against the tyranny of the man who is merely an expert, the man who knows everything about something and nothing about everything, the man who has forgotten – or who never knew – that learning, like life, is ultimately a matter of 'the eternal commonplaces'. We can be fairly certain that when Ortega y Gasset spoke of 'the peculiar brutality and aggressive stupidity with which a man comports himself when he knows a great deal about one thing and is totally ignorant of the rest', was not thinking especially of men of science. It is perfectly possible for a man to be no less stupid and brutal for knowing nothing but the number of members of the House of Commons who held shares in the East India Company in the year 1772, or the precise structure of the King's Household Offices in the reign of Edward II. There are plenty of historians who spend their time warning the young against books written by persons without 'professional standing', so that their pupils never read a page of Gibbon or Macaulay but know Professor Crackpot's article on rack-renting in the Isle of Man between 1681 and 1682 by heart. The Arts Faculties swarm with dons who treat their pupils not as young men and women reading history or literature, but as future professional historians or future professional literary critics. It is essential that there should be experts, and research is both admirable and necessary. Professional standards among scholars are the prime safeguard of academic honesty. But it is not necessary for experts and scholars, in either the arts or the sciences, to wash the dirty linen of their academic expertise in lecture-rooms for the delectation of undergraduates. The scaffolding of the temple of learning has tended to do duty for its pillars. The scholar and the teacher have come to think it their duty to 'show their working' in every line they write. Sciolism threatens scholarship, the minutiae of criticism destroys imaginative recovery, the natural generosity of the young is discouraged in favour of what Thomas Hardy called (in Leslie Stephen) 'lessening judgments'.

Yet things are never quite as bad as the prophets of woe would like us to believe. Pedantry was ever the occupational disease of scholars. Even the New Model don is sometimes to be seen at Fenners. The fact that he is nearly always a married man makes for his salvation. He is, on the whole, far less crabby than his celibate, college-haunting ancestors. The classic period of the Angry Old Men was the eighteenth century, when dons were for the most part shut up in colleges with very little to do. Those were the days when dons really were 'remote and ineffectual'. The New Model of our time is, in more senses than one, *engagé*. The closed-circuit specialist, the dumb ox who drives hostesses to despair of general conversation, is only half, or less than half, the story. There is also the devoted servant of intellectual communication, the don who has become a familiar figure in the life of the everyday world. He it is who sits on, and often presides over, government committees of inquiry, who is consulted on anything and everything connected, however remotely, with his work at Cambridge. He appears regularly in the public prints. His face and voice are known in a million sitting-rooms. He is the respected expert of the Quiz. He is the Brains Trust in person. He is the most valued public relations officer of the twentieth century, the child and the champion of 'communication' in the latest age. And then again, between the dumb ox and the fluent communicator, there is the great multitude of patient scholars who simply get on with their work as dons have always done, men of good conversation and unswerving devotion to the daily round and common task.

The don's world of Cambridge is, like nature and the British Constitution, never wholly old or wholly new. It is, indeed, the macrocosm in microcosm. A society, at any one time, gets the dons it deserves. It is useless to demand of them the function of 'resisting the bent of civilization in our time – of trying to move against the stream'. What can fairly be expected of them is that they shall be a little ahead of the average thought of their time. 'I am growing magnificent ideas about what a university ought to be', wrote Lowes Dickinson in 1889: 'it ought to lead thought, as it did at the Reformation, and not skulk behind and talk of vested rights. And there never were places with such chances as Oxford and Cambridge.' Their superior 'chances' were, and still are, given to them by the large measure of independence they enjoy, to decide what they shall teach and how they shall teach it. They receive large sums of money in the shape of Treasury Grants, but they may still be said to receive these grants without strings attached. The Universities Grants Committee is not a political institution. Its membership consists of university representatives under an independent chairman. Society may need more scientists and technicians, and government commissions may say so, but the State does not impose a quota system on the universities in order that they shall produce them. Instead, it is expected that they will respond, freely and intelligently, not to the concrete requirements of an industrial society, but to its changing intellectual modes. They will not simply conceive it to be their duty, by virtue of their independence and their cultural traditions, to 'check and control the blind drive onward of material and mechanical development, with its human consequences'; they will, as growing and changing organisms, cease to employ terms like 'material' and 'mechanical development' as inevitably pejorative concepts, even while trying to cure their 'drive' of its blindness.

And this problem of self-adaptation to the changing world of science and technology presents itself at Cambridge, more often than not, in terms of the changing don. During the last fifteen years, the development of the applied sciences – engineering, agricultural science, veterinary medicine, and many more – have brought into the service of the university large numbers of men who, although they are 'senior members', are not in any traditional sense 'dons' at all. They are, many of them, first and last employees of the university, and not 'college men'. They are men to whom the ancient college life of Cambridge is practically unknown, to whom the celebrated 'college system' means little or nothing, to whom it is likely to appear an antique survival, if not a positive obstacle to the purposes of a desirably 'undifferentiated university'. To the died-in-the-wool 'college men', however, these university characters are liable to appear as 'displaced persons'. With the best of intentions, they make efforts to secure their absorption within the college system, offering them college membership, dining-rights at High Table, even (where eminence is unmistakable) Fellowships. But Fellowships are limitedly available, and there are also limits to the capacity of High Tables, and it is not unknown for 'displaced persons' to regard the invitation to accept limited 'dining-rights' as a form of unsolicited patronage. In so far as they seek community life beyond the walls of their departments, they tend to find it at the University Combination Room, a recent institution founded at least in part to serve the needs of non-collegiate senior members, although many college men share gladly in its amenities, too. Although there is, at present, little reason to believe that they share anything like a common attitude of disparagement of the college system, the displaced persons, by their very presence, certainly constitute a standing criticism of its growing inadequacy to serve the common life of the university. It would be absurd to talk in terms of 'the Two Nations', but the shadow of bifurcation grows longer every year.

This is undoubtedly the most urgent and difficult problem that the modern university has to face. It is all very well to say, as crusted characters like Silas Stock have been heard to say: 'Let 'em go somewhere else . . . this place was never intended to be a Technical Institute. . . . Let 'em have their science and technology at Sheffield, or Birmingham, or some God-forsaken hole else. . . .' The fact is that 'they' are here. Their handsome and expensive laboratories adorn the sky-line, no less appropriately than the pinnacles of King's Chapel and the towers of Tudor Cambridge, each according to their several generations. It is good for Cambridge as a university that they should be here. They represent the challenge of history as history continues to be made, and unless Cambridge can face this challenge she must confess that she has failed her own life-principle. Even dons must change, and to hypostasize Silas Stock or Alan Skinner would amount to a surrender to the sentimental satire of a Belloc.

The Changing Undergraduate, or Cambridge Revisited

Being a Memorandum of a Conversation between Silas Stock, Senior Tutor, and Charles Hughes-Browne, an old pupil; which Conversation lasted some three hours, thus preventing the Senior Tutor from attending to the Agenda for the College Meeting at 2.30 that afternoon.

C. H.-B.: How delightful to be sitting in this room again after all these years!

S. S.: How remiss of you not to have come long ago, my dear Charles.

C. H.-B.: I have tried to catch you on several occasions when I have been passing through Cambridge, but I always seem to have struck an unfortunate time. I know how busy you are.

s. s.: Why don't you come up for Association Dinners?

c. h.-b.: You know how it is. When one first goes down, one is so terribly busy getting on in the world and all that. And then, when one has the time, and the money, one feels so out of touch . . . I did come up to an Association Dinner, once. But I found there were so few people of my year, and the ones who came were the wrong ones. . . . No, I fear I am not a very good 'old boy'. . . .

s. s.: I know, my dear Charles. It is always the same. These gatherings of old members are infested by the professional 'old boy' types. The people one would like to meet again never come and the people one spent one's undergraduate days hoping never to meet again come every year. The result is congregations of bores. . . . Of course, we make the mistake of having a general gathering each year. If the college invited old members according to years, the thing might be tolerable.

c. h.-b.: I don't want to sound disloyal but do you think it is really a very healthy sign for old members to clutter up the place at every available opportunity? Isn't it better for a man to have his three years and forget about it?

s. s.: As long as he doesn't forget the Building Fund, yes. I couldn't agree with you more, my dear Charles. Of course, we know it's impossible. A man can never forget the place where he spent three of the most impressionable years of his life, though it would be cant to say the happiest. But he might at least try to resist the temptation to keep running back to it. It's quite a recent phenomenon, this organized Old Boy cult. It argues a certain arrested development, infantilism, back-to-the-wombishness, and all that. It's certainly a sign that we are, as a people, getting old and tired. The young and healthy don't waste much time looking backwards.

c. h.-b.: If you'll forgive my saying so, Silas, that is what we all liked about you, when we were undergraduates – I mean your refusal to dwell on the past.

s. s.: You were wrong there, my dear Charles, as undergraduates are nearly always wrong when they generalize about their elders. I live in the past. Who, after all, would wish to live in the present? Of course, the past – to me – is the past as Voltaire and Gibbon saw it, and nothing to do with the travesty presented to us by our present practitioners.

c. h.-b.: I wouldn't know about that. I haven't opened a history book since I read for the tripos, nearly a quarter of a century ago.

s. s.: That just shows you, doesn't it? The stuff you had to read when you were up obviously cured you for life.

c. h.-b.: Actually, I rather enjoyed it, at the time, in spite of Bishop Stubbs and Archdeacon Cunningham.

s. s.: Ah, those impossible old parsons. *Il n'appartient point à un prêtre d'écrire l'histoire,* as my dear friend Voltaire once put it.

c. h.-b.: I keep promising myself the pleasure of reading Churchill, when I get time. But I don't suppose the Cambridge historians nowadays would call that History. At least, young Philip tells me so.

s. s.: That's their loss. What does young Philip call History? Toynbee, I suppose? And Namier? God help them.

c. h.-b.: They are names he mentions quite often.

s. s.: And hasn't read a word of them, I'll bet. The young seem to spend their time, in these days, swopping names, instead of reading books. Their teachers, I'm sorry to say, encourage them. You haven't got to know exactly what Namier says about anything, only what Namier stands for. They know the outsides of fashionable books, and the detailed contents of half a dozen grisly little articles in a learned periodical, and that's history.

c. h.-b.: If what you say is true, it hardly seems to be a subject worth reading.

s. s.: The whole thing is relative, my dear sir. Compared with most other subjects, history, I will allow, gives men the *entrée* to our world. You know the old rhyme? 'Geography is about Maps, Biography is about Chaps.' So is History. As long as history continues to be about Chaps it will remain the nearest thing to a general and humane education that Cambridge can provide. It has, to my sorrow, taken over the function of Classics in this respect, but it is a worthy successor. I am glad young Philip is reading it. But try to get him off the historical fashions, and all this blah about the history of history. Make him read Gibbon, and Macaulay, and Clarendon.

c. h.-b.: He's talking about switching over to English. That's one reason why I came to see you. He's made friends with a youngster called Evans – 'Daffyd' he calls him, and it seems that Daffyd has succeeded in converting him to the view that English is the only thing worth reading. I'd greatly value your opinion, my dear Silas. I'm going round to tea with the pair of them, this afternoon, and I want to know what to say.

s. s.: Tell them from me not to be a pair of donkeys. I'll talk to young Philip for the good of his soul to-morrow. If I'd known what was afoot I'd have had him on the mat from the first rumour of this nonsense. It's all very well for young Daffyd Evans. He's Welsh, as I daresay you've guessed, and he won a major scholarship in English. After all, it's a foreign language to him, and must involve a discipline. English should never be taught in an English university except to foreigners. For a decent young Englishman like Philip it would be like catching mumps.

c. h.-b.: Surely it isn't all that bad. I gather there are some very distinguished men teaching it.

s. s.: That's the trouble. No doubt it's an excellent occupation for adult minds. But it's poisonous for the young. They turn it into a theology. It's all adulation or damnation. They traffic in opinions. What the young need is drudgery, and plenty of it. They're not entitled to opinions until they've learnt something. Swallowing other people's opinions on an empty stomach makes them light-headed – bilious, and abominably conceited. Tell young Philip from me to get himself stuck into Stubbs' *Select Charters* and stop playing the fool.

c. h.-b.: If he's anything like I was at his age he'll go his own sweet way and call you and me a pair of bloody old fools.

s. s.: It's nice of you to put it in the plural. . . . All the same, he's quite capable of getting a decent second class if he sticks to a decent subject. He's not cut out to be a cobweb or a butterfly, a skimmer of other people's cookery.

c. h.-b.: If he is to get a decent second, he'll need to work a good deal harder than I did.

s. s.: They all work a good deal harder than we did, my dear Charles. That's one of the main differences you'd notice if you came back to Cambridge in these days. I don't say they work to any better effect. It's just that they are much more anxious about the future than we needed to be. And, after all, a much larger proportion of them are here on public money, which gives them a greater sense of being hand-picked and dedicated men. They are much more anxious to do well by their universal father, the 'State', than we were to justify the financial sacrifices of our poor old papas. They are altogether more sober and serious citizens. They are also much better-mannered. Did you come here on foot?

C. H.-B.: I walked around the town a bit before I came to the college. Why?

S. S.: Were you pushed off the pavement more than once?

C. H.-B.: Not once . . .

S. S.: In our time as undergraduates, you'd have had to step into the gutter a dozen times between here and Petty Cury. We really thought the place belonged to us. And, of course, it did. We were 'the gentle-men', and Cambridge existed to wait on us, hand and foot. Do you remember how we used to turn the cinemas into bear-gardens every night in the week?

C. H.-B.: That was in the days of the silent films.

S. S.: Nominally silent. We used to supply the sound-tracks ourselves. Hooting and whistling, hand-clapping and stamping. It was hideous. . . Undergraduates seem to have a good deal more respect for other people's pleasures nowadays. Perhaps it's because they are themselves more like other people. The old Town and Gown distinctions are not what they were.

C. H.-B.: They certainly seem to dress very much more alike. I mean, undergraduates seem to dress as young men dress everywhere else. Of course, I spotted a few of the old Pitt Club types – curly-brimmed trilbys, fancy waistcoats, drain-pipe trousers, and all. But there were far more of the leather-jacket brigade.

S. S.: On the whole, the standards of undergraduate dress have de-clined. Quite a few of them try to look like what they revoltingly call 'the Beats' or 'the Sicks' or the 'Angries'. It's mainly a matter of hair-do. Did you notice their disgusting habit of brushing their hair straight forward, without a parting, like medieval serfs, or unfrocked monks trying to cover up a tonsure? The young women do their best to look like urchins. I gather they actually call their present hair-do an 'urchin cut'.

c. h.-b.: And yet, one can tell at a glance that they aren't Teddy Boys or urchins. They're obviously in fancy-dress.

s. s.: Yes, I must say they show a certain amount of taste even in their distasteful appearance.

c. h.-b.: I'm told they're all keen on religion nowadays. In the 'thirties we were all politicians. Hardly anyone went to chapel. Is there really a religious revival?

s. s.: No, thank God. A lot of them are *interested* in religion. They go to church or chapel a lot more than they used to. But that's not the same thing at all. I suppose they feel that politics has let them down. . . . You know how the young are always hot for certainties? It used to be Karl Marx. Now it's just as likely to be Thomas Aquinas. Whoring after false gods is an occupational disease for undergraduates. When one lets them down, they soon take up with another. They have to work their way through the lot. That's what they're here for. What was it that John Keats said about the ability to rest in half-knowledge, without irritable reaching out after certainties? It doesn't matter much what they persuade themselves they believe in while they are here, as long as they grow up sufficiently to disbelieve in belief. That's education. . . . That's why you must insist on Philip sticking to history. Historians don't fall for superstitions so easily. A proper look at the past of mankind should cure you of any faith in easy answers, or short-cuts to salvation. You come to realize that it's all happened before.

c. h.-b.: It sounds like a school for cynics, the way you put it.

s. s.: No. Critical sense. A necessary scepticism. A prophylactic against superstition. Not a way of life, but a way of making life bearable.

c. h.-b.: Why not liquor? I gather they do drink a good deal, anyway. So did we, I suppose. Is there really much difference?

s. s.: In quantity, no. In quality, a great deal. We used to swill beer. The present generation has a taste for wine. From the parties I have been invited to in recent years (and that's another thing – they invite their seniors to their parties more often than we did), they show a great deal of better taste in drinks than our generations. Of course, the Rugger boys, and the Boat Club, still stand by the firkin. But there is undoubtedly a preference in gentler circles for French and Italian wines over our native home-brew. Some say it began with National Service. But they travel abroad much more than we ordinarily did, in any case. I think this change in taste is a good thing, on the whole.

C. H.-B.: Do they get tight very often?

S. S.: They do precisely what we did. They make a great deal of noise on nothing. A couple of half-pints, and they howl as if they've drunk the town dry. Genuine drunkenness is rarer than it ever was.

C. H.-B.: What you say about wine-drinking surprises me. How do they afford it. *We* couldn't.

S. S.: By economizing on book-buying, I imagine. The present-day undergraduate never buys a book if he can possibly help it. Oh, I know books are far more expensive, nowadays, but that's by no means the whole story. Go into the average undergraduate's rooms nowadays and you'll find half-a-dozen text-books and a few paper-backs. It varies a bit with what subject a man's reading. Scientific works are so appallingly expensive and go out of date so quickly that you can't expect people to buy them if they can borrow. But the fact remains that the expenditure of undergraduates on books has just about halved since the war.

C. H.-B.: I gather that they spend far more on wireless-sets, gramophones, and records.

S. S.: Oh yes. These things are regarded as indispensable. And why not? You will agree that you and I were comparatively barbarous where music was concerned. I'm all for this switch in expenditure. But the decline in book-buying is presenting some headaches for librarians. College libraries are becoming much more text-book agencies than they used to be.

C. H.-B.: And what about the everlasting topic – I mean, sex? We used to be crazy about it. I rather gather there's more of it. . . .

S. S.: Not really. They are far more sophisticated than we were. They grow up a lot quicker. And they are far more accustomed to female company from an early age. A much greater proportion of them come from co-ed. schools and take the female of the species for granted. You see them going around the place on easy terms. After all, both sexes wear these appalling nether garments. I often find it difficult to tell them apart.

C. H.-B.: All the same, I find it difficult to believe that a change in early environment and in dress can make all that difference.

S. S.: Believe me, my dear Charles, they really have. Oh, I know you will read so-called 'Cambridge novels' about young men and women who spend the greater part of their time hopping into bed with each other. I've dipped into one or two myself, and pretty boring they are. I'm no puritan. I regard myself as a displaced person of the eighteenth century. But I find the present fashion rather revolting, very tedious, and quite alien to life as it is lived here by 99.9 per cent. of the population.

C. H.-B.: And what about the homos? We always knew there were a few of them around. The general idea was that they should be chucked in the river pretty regularly.

S. S.: Of course, there are always a number of them. Why not? A certain proportion of the human race are made that way, and a university is pretty representative of the human race, or it should be. Practising homosexuals are few and far between, here as everywhere else. What is common is affectation of homosexual characteristics. Your undergraduate is a great poseur. He is the slave not of passion but of fashion. It's the same with this cult of religion, or the 'beat', or the 'sick' or what-not: something different. It makes a change.

C. H.-B.: If I may say so, Silas, I think your attitude rather savours (as we used to say) of ivory-towerism. I mean, you seem to me to be shrugging things off rather lightly.

S. S.: Perhaps. But you must remember, my dear Charles, I have seen so many of these cults come and go. Dons are often rudely described as 'remote and ineffectual', but there are few better points of vantage for observing the behaviour of the young than a college window. The resident don quite soon appreciates the truth of the old saying: *plus ça change, plus c'est la même chose.*

C. H.-B.: In other words, the changing undergraduate is something of a myth?

S. S.: I wouldn't go as far as that. Fundamentally, he is very much the same kind of human being that he has always been. All young creatures are rather silly, and rather boring: I mean, they are so busy learning their way about the world that they are bound to think their discoveries are interesting and exciting. One allows for that. Where they are definitely an improvement on our generations, I think, is in their tolerance, their greater sophistication, their superior honesty and frankness. I like them far more than I like the memory of myself as I was at their age. I speak as a human being. Of course, as a professional don, I hate their guts.

End with a Bang

Lent Term ends with a bang, not a whimper. It is the term of the dinner-parties: club dinners, Old Boys dinners, college society dinners, feasts. The Protestant University pays scant respect to lenten abstinence, although there is generally boiled cod at High Table (as an alternative, only) on Ash Wednesday. There are indeed excellent reasons why this orgy of eating and drinking should set in in the Lent Term. Michaelmas Term is too early, Easter Term is too late. By late February or early March the typical activities of winter are at an end. 'Cuppers' in the field sports have been decided, and victories must be celebrated. The first contests of the eights on the river, known as 'the Lents', are likewise fought and won, or lost. College societies of a quasi-learned character, meeting weekly or fortnightly throughout the winter months, have reached the end of their serious programmes; there will be little time for such frivolities in the Easter Term. Schoolboys, having had the best part of two terms to turn into undergraduates, are ready to get together in Old Boys' Clubs and invite the Headmaster to visit them for a convivial meal. Dons . . . Dons never need excuse for a large-scale 'exceeding night', though they generally find one. There is always something on hand: a great benefactor to be remembered, the annual Audit, the anniversary of the foundation of the college. Every term has its occasion.

The annual dinner of the quasi-learned college society is the most typically English of these occasions. Nowhere else on earth, it is to be presumed, would twenty or thirty young men organize a sumptuous meal, with wines and cigars, as a prelude to listening to a learned guest of honour read a learned paper. To have the paper first and the dinner afterwards would, one imagines, be too obviously suggestive of making the visitor sing for his supper. So, in college dining-rooms towards the end of Lent Term, the strange spectacle may be seen of small groups of young men in dinner-jackets,[1] full of roast duck and green peas, sherry trifle and Burgundy, trying hard to keep their eyes open while a visiting professor drones on for a long hour about . . . who, afterwards, can say what? The president, in proposing the toast to the guest of honour, has already attributed to him certain brilliant works which (as he mildly points out in his reply) he did not write. The secretary, after proposing the toast to the Queen, has already steered one or two of the weaker brethren away to their rooms in the interests of public decency. The guest of honour is becoming every moment more desperately aware that he is reading the wrong paper, having imagined that a society bearing the great name of Maitland, or Porson, or Newton must require of him the most learned effort of which he is capable, whereas it now appears that he might as well, indeed better, have come armed with a few quips about the great man's private life. All the same, there are those present who will go away uplifted and inspired by the experience – as young Mr. Evans would say – of being, for a time, 'in the same room with greatness'. This experience of a fleeting contact with the great, or even the semi-great, is one of the immeasurable gifts that college societies of this kind bestow upon the impressionable young. Even if the experience contains an element of disillusionment, it has an educative value. Nor is the mundane experience of being responsible for the organization of such an occasion without a certain value in coming to terms with the world and its ways.

Rugger, Soccer, Hockey, let alone Rowing club dinners are a different affair altogether. They are Homeric, bacchanalian, orgiastic. They celebrate the end of more or less spartan training, the conclusion of a series of hard-fought battles in mud and rain and biting wind. For weeks past, the knock-out competition known as 'cuppers' has whipped up enthusiasm to a frenzy. College teams have stormed their way between roaring touchlines through the short winter afternoons to the grand finale. For the culminating contest between the two surviving

---

[1] Lounge-suits have increasingly come to be the form for dinner parties since the war.

teams, or finalists, everyone is expected to turn out on the touch-lines, from the Master down to the humblest gyp, in order to swell the chorus of encouragement, derision, or mere advice. It is rumoured that Dr. Skinner keeps a book in which he marks the Fellows of the college for attendance, or otherwise, on these occasions. Flags and banners, honking bands, klaxon and rattles and sometimes bag-pipes, process to the scene of battle. Mild, middle-aged, round-shouldered men in spectacles have been known to take leave of their senses and dance like screaming dervishes for a goal or a try. All over the town there are mystic runes chalked on ancient walls:

JOHN'S FOR CUPPERS

or:

SIDNEY FOR CUPPERS

and within a few hours SIDNEY has been replaced by KIDNEY and CUPPERS by SUPPER. This is taken to mean that St. John's propose not only to win the Cup but to sup on the Sidney men afterwards. The friendly ferocity engendered by Cuppers is something beyond belief. After the final blast of the referee's whistle, however, victors begin the cheering by cheering the vanquished, and after the Cup has been borne away with all the solemnity and half the reverence accorded to the Holy Grail, victors and vanquished alike have recourse to song and dance, in college Halls and courts, long into the night.

An Old Boys' dinner, with the Headmaster, or sundry Housemasters, present, is a much more circumspect affair, at least until the visitors have been conducted back to their lodgings. Wholly circumspect, also, are the revels of the Strafford, the Burke, and those elegant associations which profess no other purpose than the discussion of food and wine, pure 'dining clubs' of the older sort, direct descendants of the eighteenth century. The apex of this great gastronomic structure, however, is undoubtedly the College Feast, decreed by dons for dons, and their guests. And the very topmost point of the apex is the feast to celebrate the anniversary of the foundation of the college. Next to, but not inferior to, the City Companies and the Inns of Court, the Cambridge College on a true 'exceeding night' might justly say (if it were ever vulgar enough to say anything): 'Here's richness for you'. The long tables are laid in the great Hall at dusk. By eight o'clock the candles are lighted, the ancient silver gleams among the bowls of flowers and the snow-drifts of napery, and the butler conducts his prelude among his assembled waiters with a folded napkin for baton, while the increasing roar of hungry men resounds from the adjacent Combination Room as the guests assemble and drink their first sherry. The kitchen-manager and his chefs and scullions stand by at the hot-plates and the service-hatches, watching the clock like jockeys watching the gate. A last flick of his napkin across the seat of the Master's chair, a quick glance at his wrist, and the butler disappears through the doorway behind the dais. Threading his way carefully among silken gowns and scarlet hoods, he picks out the Master where he stands on the hearth-rug with his eye cocked ready for the sign to go.

"Dinner is served, Master."

The going is hesitant, once the Master has gone with his principal guests. Men hang back for each other, drifting, teetering, steering each other with a hand on the back, slyly repudiating the soft impeachment of greed. Until the drift becomes a flood, a torrent, a brisk debouchment into the silver splendours of the candlelight beyond. At the tail-end of the flood come the scholars, those privileged undergraduate members who, by virtue of their scholarships at the college, are 'on the Foundation' and thereby entitled to places at a Foundation dinner. To-night, Dr. Skinner has been trying matily to make them feel at home in the Senior Combination Room. Now he counts them into Hall, shepherding them to the Scholars' table with nods and becks and wreathed smiles. These things he does in the interests of the far-famed college spirit, the spirit of solidarity and local attachment, while privately objurgating the Senior Tutor's greed and indifference as he makes his way to his place at the High Table. All over the room men are peering down at name-cards beside plates, seeking their appointed places with, or without, the table-plan in mind. A short space of shuffling silence, a single gong-note, and the Chaplain's mellow voice recites the immemorial Grace. A harsh scraping of chairs, a silken thunder of gowns and hoods settling down, a scamper of waiters, and the feast is on.

"Man, how's this for Apartheid?" Daffyd Evans murmurs in the ear of Frankie Thwaites as they settle down at the Scholars' table. "What's the betting they'll give us second-class citizens' food?"

"Doesn't look like it to me," Mr. Thwaites replies, and pretends to read from the menu. "Lancashire hot-pot, Welsh Rabbit, and – of course – Norfolk dumplings."

He adds this last item as he catches the eye of Peter Plummer, who scowls with the weary tolerance of a Major Scholar whose experience of Foundation dinners is now three years old. It is Peter who takes upon himself the role of Master of Ceremonies when speculation begins at the Scholars' table as to the identity of the college guests on either side of the Master, for no junior member ever gets near enough to the table-plan to satisfy himself in advance on this matter.

"The tall, grey-haired guy, sitting between the Master and the Stinker, is Lord Tantamount, about the best-known classical archaeologist in England. Not a bad chap, I'm told."

"Who's the little fat man sitting between the Master and old Silas?" Mr. Thwaites would know.

"That's Sir Stafford Plant, managing director of Plant and Plant, the construction engineers. Stinking rich, I understand. They're trying to soak him for the Building Fund. He was here about fifty years ago. Old pupil of Silas, I expect."

"Just a matter of getting him tight enough to unbelt to the tune of fifty-thousand?" Daffyd Evans reflects. "Boy, I'm all for soaking the rich in a good cause. . . ."

"What a crude fellow you are, Evans," Peter Plummer reproves him, at the same time drowning his portion of smoked salmon in a flood of mayonnaise. "Actually, you are witnessing a notable example of bridge-building. Communication is being established at this very moment between science and the humanities. If it costs the engineering tycoon fifty-thousand, it will be well worth while from the cultural angle alone."

"From the look on his face at this moment," Daffyd observes, "it is costing him every penny of it."

"Not to worry. The Stinker has just asked the company whether anyone can tell him what a machine-tool is. It's his latest conversational gambit and it has the virtue of stopping conversation. Observe how shifty they are all looking. Most of all Sir Stafford."

The truth is that Sir Stafford Plant has just expressed his aesthetic delight in the recent re-decoration of the Hall. Sir Stafford Plant is the tall distinguished grey-haired man identified by the Senior Scholar as the great archaeologist, Lord Tantamount, while the fat little man on the other side of the Master is not Sir Stafford but the Mayor of Cambridge, a wholesale green-grocer. The Mayor is invited annually, and *ex officio*. Lord Tantamount is never invited for the simple reason that he doesn't exist beyond the ample bounds of Peter Plummer's imagination. Opposite the Master, like a totem-pole crowned with a fuzz of cotton, sits the Senior Fellow. The expression of mild dismay on the faces around the High Table has nothing to do with embarrassing questions about machine-tools. It is the normal expression to be seen on the faces of men who sit within ear-shot of Cyril Tompion, at college feasts. The Senior Fellow has just reacted to Sir Stafford's ecstatic appraisal of the redecorated Hall with a high-pitched scream.

"Awful, isn't it? Perfectly *dreadful*. I'm in favour of pulling the whole thing down and building a new one. Eh, Master? What, what?"

"There are unfortunate features," the Master concedes with a wan smile, "but I, for one, should be very sorry to part with our historic Hall *in toto*."

"I shouldn't," the Senior Fellow yells. "I would pull it down, stone by stone, with my bare hands, if I were twenty years younger. It's absolutely disgraceful. I'm perfectly sure Sir Stafford is longing to build us something better."

Sir Stafford smiles and waves his hand deprecatingly and is at once engaged in earnest conversation by Dr. Skinner, who looks as if he may burst at any moment.

"I am sure I shall have your assent, Mr. Mayor," says Silas Stock, "when I claim that our Hall is the finest piece of architecture, of its period, in the whole of Cambridge."

"You're right," says Mr. Mayor. "There's not another one like it anywhere, to my certain knowledge."

"Of course, certain features were added in their present unfortunate style very much later than the rest," Mr. Stock continues. "I imagine that you have noticed that."

"Oh yes, indeed," says Mr. Mayor, who has been gazing up at the ceiling as if he expected it to open upon the Elysian Fields at any moment. "But I wouldn't say they was half bad. Not for their period, as you might say. No, not half bad."

"They're awful," screams Cyril Tompion, and raises his glass to Mr. Mayor in a gesture of complete agreement. "Horrible. Don't let the Senior Tutor deceive you, my dear sir. His taste is deplorable. Simply deplorable. Eh Silas? What?"

"I wonder, Mr. Mayor, whether you have ever read the life of Herbert Spencer?" Mr. Stock inquires archly.

"No, I haven't, not to my recollection," Mr. Mayor confesses.

"Well," Silas Stock informs him, "among other delightful items in that most entertaining volume, one discovers that the distinguished philosopher was wont to carry about with him a pair of ear-plugs which he would bung into, or pull out of, his ears whenever the conversation bored or distressed him. Charming idea, I always think. I am sure you will agree."

"A bit rude, I'm thinking," Mr. Mayor observes, even while entering heartily into the humour of the idea. "You're not going to suggest . . . ?"

A sharp but friendly dig in the ribs from Mr. Stock's elbow and a secret scowl in the direction of Cyril Tompion together serve to deflect Mr. Mayor's reflections to a more suitable channel.

"I'm thinking we could do with a few sets of that article for council meetings at the city hall. It's an idea. . . ."

The Senior Fellow is now engaged in wrestling with a portion of roast turkey and appears to have lost interest in the conversation.

After dinner, the Fellows and their guests retire in small groups to college rooms for further refreshment, which will occupy them until late into the night. The Master collects the more distinguished guests for a long session at his Lodge. He takes the three tutors with him, too, because it is hoped that at this stage Sir Stafford may come clean on the subject of financial assistance from industry for college building schemes. Sir Stafford, however, seems determined to keep the conversation on a properly academic level. He is particularly interested in the question of compulsory Latin for university entrance.

"Of course, you know your own business best," he concedes, "but if I may say so, any decision to drop Latin would come as a considerable shock to people like myself. Not to put too fine a point upon it, it would seem very like a betrayal of all that the university stands for."

"In what sense – a betrayal?" Dr. Skinner would know. "Surely, rather a recognition of reality."

"If I might attempt to interpret Sir Stafford's meaning," says Silas Stock with a superior smile, "I imagine he refers to the almost universal feeling of disgust experienced by civilized persons at the spectacle of the guardians of humane learning throwing the traditional tongue of western culture to the wolves of technology. I agree with Sir Stafford that it is a tragedy, an unmitigated tragedy."

"I am not sure that I meant to put it quite so strongly as that," Sir Stafford protests mildly. "I can quite see that it may be, as Dr. Skinner says, a concession to reality. After all, the world changes, and we must, no doubt, change with it."

Having thus contradicted himself sufficiently, the man of business sits back and sips his whisky and soda, waiting for the men of learning to contradict each other. They proceed to do so with alacrity, and at length. Once an issue has been before the Senate, men feel really free to be frank with each other.

Dr. Skinner asks Sir Stafford whether he has ever seen a Latin paper as set for Little-Go?[1] Sir Stafford freely admits that such a thing has never come his way since the far distant day when he took the examination himself. Dr. Skinner informs him that it has become a farce. He wants to know what benefit a young man could conceivably derive from mugging up Latin at such a childish level that he can translate a childishly simple passage with the aid of a dictionary, more especially when he is going to read a subject at the university in which he will have no further use for it? The thing has killed itself. All the Senate can decently do is to acknowledge the fact.

"All the same, my dear Alan," the Senior Tutor reminds him, "if the standard of Latin for the Previous were raised, you would roar with rage, would you not?"

"I have always held," the Master intervenes, "that we should take our decision upon the desirability of Latin as a compulsory subject in

---

[1] The Little-Go: old-fashioned slang for the Previous examination, or university Entrance.

the Previous examination, not upon the propriety of the sort of Latin papers that have been set in recent years, but upon the inherent value of Latin as a discipline. I can conceive of no finer test of clear thinking and the capacity for economical and precise expression than the rendering of a passage from Caesar or Tacitus into decent English."

"Oh, I can," declares Cyril Tompion, who, having insinuated himself into the party in a fit of absent-mindedness, has been on his best behaviour until now. "I would set them a passage from *Ulysses*, preferably from Mrs. Bloom's soliloquy. The only disadvantage, of course, would be that it might not be wholly unseen."

The Mayor, who has been feeling rather out of things, pricks up his ears at the mention of *Ulysses* and enters a caveat against encouraging lads to read dirty books. To which Cyril Tompion retorts that they all go to bed with *Lolita* under their pillows, and that there is plenty of unclean fun to be had from the Latin authors, not to mention the Bible and Shakespeare, if one knows where to look.

"All the same," says the Mayor, "it's up to us to show the lads an example."

"We do, we do," the Senior Fellow assures him with a ribald cackle.

The Master replenishes his Worship's glass and remembers his homework. He has lately been reading a book on 'Technology and the Universities', with an eye to entering into the interests of the guest of the evening. He expounds the main thesis with cautious approval. He is convinced of the importance of technological subjects being taught in the universities, not only in order to ensure the general education of the technologists, but in order to promote the technological education of the humanists. He talks a great deal about 'cultural bridge-building', 'cultural communications', and 'intellectual cross-fertilization'. During this exposition Sir Stafford is to be observed nodding sleepily. It is fairly evident that he doesn't know what the Master is talking about. And when Dr. Skinner backs up the Master's exordium by taking the offensive and demanding whether anyone present can define a machine-tool, he looks both sleepy and shifty. For the fact is that he has scented 'shop', and thinks it is time to go.

"If you will forgive me, Master," he announces, as he polishes off the last of his whisky and soda, "I think it is time I retired. I really cannot tell you how greatly I have enjoyed this charming conversation. It is so rarely that one gets a chance to escape from one's own shop and listen to someone else's. . . . Good-night, sir."

He wrings Silas Stock's hand with particular affection, for it is Sir Stafford Plant's conviction that a man like the Senior Tutor is the very prototype of what he calls 'the good old Cambridge don', and that the world would be a better place if all dons modelled themselves on his old tutor. Then, he tells himself, we should know where we are.

"I trust that we shall see something of you when you come up for the opening of Churchill?" Silas Stock asks.

"Churchill?" Sir Stafford yawns politely. "Oh yes, the new college. . . . No, I don't think I shall come. I'm not really interested in that kind of thing. I gather they are going to have about seventy per cent. men of science? Absurd. Who will want to go there, do you suppose? I shall always prefer men who have lived their university years in a college where scientific training is on an equal footing with everything else. No, no, I don't think I shall come. . . . Good-night to you."

As Mr. Stock strolls back across the grass in the moonlight with Dr. Skinner, he cannot forbear to thump the Doctor of Science between the shoulder-blades.

"Machine-tools my foot, my dear Alan," he crows.

"Really, Silas, you are the world's prize wrecker. . . ."

"Yes, yes, I know," the happy Silas assents. "I'm a positive Luddite. Up the machine-wreckers! That's what I say."

At that moment, the college clock begins to strike twelve, and coincident with its first note a gun goes off high overhead. A dozen young men, stripped of their dinner-jackets, who have been touching their toes in a line at the chapel steps, start off on a headlong sprint round the court.

"We will leave our scholars to their revels," Mr. Stock proposes. "I am glad to see that they keep up the old college customs on Foundation nights."

"All the same, I'm going to find out who fired that gun," Dr. Skinner announces between his teeth. "Here – you – Thwaites – "

He snatches at a flying figure as it passes, and young Mr. Thwaites spins to a standstill, glaring at his tutor with a horrid mortification, for he has set his heart on becoming the first freshman to win the annual race round the court while the clock strikes midnight.

"Who fired that gun?" Dr. Skinner demands.

"What gun, sir?"

"It sounded as if it was fired out of a top window. . . ."

Scanning the lighted squares beneath the dark roof-line, the tutors discern a black-headed figure looking down at them without any attempt at concealment.

"It's only old Zog," little Thwaites assures them with a grin.

"That damned Greek," Silas Stock murmurs. "I always said he was a Turk."

"Come down at once, Zogropoulos," Dr. Skinner calls up.

Mr. Zogropoulos's heavy head is observed to be turning from side to side in a motion of apologetic negation.

"It was only a blank cartridge, sir," he calls down. "It would be entirely alien to my intentions to employ live ammunition while I am at Cambridge."

"It's true, sir," Mr. Thwaites assures Dr. Skinner. "We soon cured him of that."

"Thus they educate each other, my dear Alan," says Silas Stock as the tutors resume their homeward way.

All the same, Mr. Zogropoulos will have to see the Dean in the morning. He does, and his education is carried a stage further.

Interlude - The Boat Race

By far the most famous occasion of the Cambridge year does not even take place in Cambridge, indeed it causes scarcely a ripple on the surface of Cambridge life. For the Boat Race is a national occasion, and everyone (more or less) feels personally involved in it, whether by sentiment or by family or by local attachment, or simply by reason of a shilling in a sweepstake. Next to the Derby in June, the Boat Race in April has the power to stop the life of the nation, or at any rate to produce a flutter at the heart of millions of people to whom the two ancient universities are no more than names signifying two shades of blue.[1] For a space in the middle of a spring-time Saturday, traffic is halted over some four miles of one of the world's greatest waterways while sixteen young giants propel two dwarfs and hundreds of pounds' worth of finely wrought timber and steel and canvas from Putney to Mortlake. That is what it amounts to in terms of flesh and blood and dead matter. In terms of the spirit, it is the annual *Iliad* of England.

It has been going on for well over a hundred years, ever since that day in 1829 when the gentlemen of the Cambridge University Boat Club sent a challenge to the gentlemen of Oxford to 'row a match at or near London, each in an eight-oared boat during the ensuing Easter Vacation'.[2] To-day that first contest, and many that followed, would appear strange indeed. The boats were like dug-out canoes of savage tribes, and the gentlemen who dug out the courses in the river Thames would appear to be bearded warriors wielding barge-paddles. The evolution of the modern 'shell', that miracle of craftmanship, was to be a long and delicate series of operations. Likewise, the evolution of modern styles of oarsmanship was the life-work of a succession of great coaches. These efforts for the perfecting of both men and materials have culminated in the racing crews that now take the tideway for the most beautiful display, unsullied by the alliance of the internal com-

---

[1] The light blue colours of Cambridge originated with the Boat Race. It was a gentleman of Christ's who purchased a bit of Eton ribbon and stuck it on the bows of the Cambridge boat just as the 1836 race was about to start.

[2] They still do, or at least last year's loser sends a similar challenge which renews the contest for a further year.

bustion engine, that the mind and eye of man can imagine between wind and water.

Still officially known as 'a private match', the Boat Race is nevertheless the cynosure of millions of pairs of eyes every year. Yet it is given to comparatively few to see it in flesh and blood. The thousands who go to the banks of the Thames see very little: scarcely more than a pair of water-beetles distantly paddling between the bobbing heads of the first line of the river-bankers. The expensive throng at Duke's Meadows sees more, for a little while, and the privileged mortals in launches following the wake of the crews see most of all. But science has come to the aid of vast multitudes who watch the spectacle on Television. Of all the great public occasions that are now brought into peoples' homes, the Boat Race is perhaps the most effectively displayed. The watchers at the hearth, or in the saloon bar, the office and the shop-window, really and truly 'see the Boat Race' from start to finish, and they are the only people who do. They pay for their ease and comfort and wider vision only in terms of the absence of the physical excitement evoked by the milling crowds at the river-side with their flaunting favours and roaring voices. It is still worth while not only to see, but to go to, the Boat Race. More especially is it worth while for the undergraduates themselves. For an hour, decked in scarves and blazers and rosettes, the present generation derives a vicarious taste of pride and glory. Any man can legitimately hope to be mistaken for an Old Blue, just for once.

Back home in Cambridge it is difficult to detect any sign of what is happening down there on the great river, sixty or so miles to the south, except for the fact that interference on television screens, which normally causes Cambridge citizens to curse the laboratory workers, has a merciful habit of stopping for about twenty minutes. It is vacation. College courts are deserted. Dons are mostly watching on someone else's television screen, or on the college screen in the Bursar's office. The few remaining undergraduates are gathered round the set in the Junior Parlour, or wherever such an alien contrivance can be quartered. The great mass of undergraduates are watching at home, scattered over the length and breadth of the land, and trying to look as if the result of the race is a foregone conclusion. As it generally is. Cambridge has got into the habit of winning the Boat Race,[1] and if Oxford should by some fluke manage to win it, Cambridge men nod their heads and express their pleasure that the race has become a race once again.[2] But they feel in their bones that the race is theirs all the same. What they feel at Oxford is scarcely a subject for speculation. After all, as they say at Cambridge, 'the other University' always gets the publicity, and ought to be content with that. In any case, Oxford can take it. The old distinction of manners still lives. The Cambridge man knows that he owns the earth. The Oxford man always manages to look as if he doesn't care a damn who owns it.

[1] Oxford had an unbeaten series of nine victories from 1861 to 1869, and another run of nine between 1890 and 1898. Since 1920 Cambridge has won 27 times to Oxford's 8 and holds the record for a sequence with 13 victories between 1924 and 1936.

[2] Not that either University glories unduly in unbroken triumph. Oxford has sent coaches to help Cambridge out of a ruck of disasters as often as Cambridge has done likewise for her sister. 'Our feeling has always been that our favourite science, rowing, ought to be the first object of our love', a famous Cambridge coach wrote when he offered his services to Oxford in 1853; 'to exhibit to the world rowing in perfection....'

EASTER TERM

April - The Cruellest Month

April is the cruellest month. . . . Already the daffodils have done dancing in the Backs, and the rooks are rowdy in the tall trees beside the Queens' Road, and the dead land beside Burrell's Walk is breeding lilacs. Any morning, now, there will be a cuckoo shouting from Madingley and swallows dive-bombing under the Downing porticos. The calendar calls it the Easter Term, though Easter is over before it starts. Ordinary men call it the May Term, because it looks forward to May Week, which, oddly enough, is in June. It looks forward also to certain preliminary examinations which are generally, and more accurately, known as 'the Mays'.[1] It also looks forward to tripos examinations, which spill over into June but are not known as 'the Junes'. It would be a pity to misappropriate the name of the loveliest month in the Cambridge year.

'The Tripos.' The word is on everyone's lips with its stealthy rustle of menace. It hovers in the springtime air over the river and the fields, an increasing shadow between the soul and the sun. And yet the word derives from a joke. Long ago, before written examinations were invented, men were examined on their ability in verbal disputation. The Senate House was a scene of oral contest, the learned lists of 'tongue-fence' or tournament in ancient languages, a kind of classical quiz. Originally, candidates were required to dispute, or wrangle, on propositions announced by the proctors. By the fifteenth century it was the custom for 'an ould bachelor' to post himself in front of the proctors and engage in argument with the disputants. He sat on a three-legged stool, or as we might say, a tripod. This old gentleman presently came to be known as 'Mr. Tripos'. He took his name from the stool, and the examination was to take its name from him. 'Mr. Tripos' was in the habit of conducting his part of the learned discussion in the form of verses, known as 'tripos verses', which he read out. When, in course of time, 'Mr. Tripos' himself ceased to function, 'tripos verses' still

[1] But, nowadays, it is to be regretted, as 'Prelims'.

continued, and by the middle years of the eighteenth century it was the custom to print the lists of successful candidates on the backs of the sheets of tripos verses. The lists came to be known as 'the tripos', and in the end the name was used for the examination itself, any examination leading to an Honours degree.[1] *Viva voce* examination, or examination by 'the living voice', barely survives at Cambridge to-day. There is nothing to prevent examiners calling up candidates for further elucidation of their written papers if they so wish. Examiners are free agents, and, within the general regulations laid down by Ordinance, can conduct examinations howsoever they please. Men and women reading medicine are required to undergo oral examination in some branches of their studies, and of course there are searching 'orals' in examinations in languages. A candidate for the further degree of Doctor of Philosophy will normally be examined orally on the work he has done in preparing his thesis. But since the later years of the eighteenth century, written or formal examination has steadily come, first to supplement, and then to replace, verbal 'exercises' and 'disputations', until to-day a tripos examination presents the vision of many hundreds of young men and women seated at desks in the Examination Schools, the Guildhall, and scores of places specially hired for the purpose in all quarters of the town, covering thousands of sheets in a succession of three-hour periods during the last week of May and the first weeks of June.

'Examinations for honours leading to the B.A. Degree are known as Tripos Examinations.' Thus the *Student's Handbook*.[2] There are nineteen triposes to choose from, and many of them are divided into two parts. A part of a tripos, if it is so divided, may take one or two years. For an Honours degree, it is normally necessary to take two parts, although not necessarily of the same tripos. Thus the system allows more, or less, specialization in a particular subject, as a candidate (strictly under tutorial advice) pleases. The extent to which he specializes in one subject will generally depend on his notions of what he intends to do in life. A

[1] The above account of the history of the term 'tripos' is based on the account given by Sir Sydney Roberts in the opening chapter of his classic little work *Introduction to Cambridge*.
[2] 1959–60 edition, p. 121.

man of science will nearly always stick to science all through. The 'arts man' will often choose his two parts from two different 'arts subjects'. A future lawyer will sometimes take the two-year part of the historical tripos (i.e. part I) and then go on to part II of the law tripos. Outside the more technical subjects, specialization in the interests of a future vocation is not, or should not be, common. The traditional notion of a Cambridge education is not vocational. With the increase of 'professionalism' in all walks of life, however, there is nowadays a great deal more specialization in a single subject than there used to be. There are even those who suppose that to read both parts of the economic tripos is going to help them to be more successful business-men. On the other hand, there are men and women who are going to be school-teachers who avoid specialization in order to have more than one subject to offer for teaching purposes. Even in 1934, when he wrote his excellent *Introduction to Cambridge*, Sir Sydney Roberts found it necessary to remind his readers that 'while the choice of a Tripos will obviously bear some relation to the choice of a career, the course of study for an honours examination in Cambridge is not primarily vocational. Success in a Tripos is not in itself a qualification for entry into one of the learned professions, though it is a valuable help to that end.' It should be noted that even to-day such vocational studies as Estate Management, Agriculture, Numerical Analysis and Automatic Computing, and Medicine, are not, in themselves, re-warded by an honours degree.[1]

For very large numbers of young men and women, however, the Easter Term is haunted by the overhanging shadow of 'the tripos'. It is now that they think of the things they ought to have done and have left undone. Now is the time when the mild air of penitence takes on the countenance of despair in the small hours. This terrible conjunction of present delights and prospective judgment gives April in Cambridge its name for sadistic torment. 'Examinitis' takes many forms. Strong

---

[1] Diplomas are awarded for proficiency in a large number of such subjects. Medical students commonly reach honours standard for the B.A. degree by reading for part I of the Natural Sciences tripos. (*See* Chapter IX of the *Student's Handbook*.)

men dream of 'aegrotats' and Doctors' Certificates.[1] The wiser brethren seek the shadow of the red rock which is the University Library. There won't be a seat to spare by early May. Others go to the cricket for relief, and find it: there won't be a seat to spare in the ring-side at Fenners until tripos week in late May.[2] It is possible to do both, mixing memory and desire, as it were, if you possess a bicycle. The thing is to have a good time-table and stick to it, as Peter Plummer maintains. The third-year man, who has had to face this problem twice before, is worth listening to, now.

The place for the third-year man's homilies, tips for tripos strategy in April, is the Espresso bar at the very portals of the Arts School. There, on the highest stool, the ineffable Plummer sucks his pipe at a one-man Brains Trust.

"Go to the ant, thou sluggards," Peter advises, showing no sign of going himself. "If you want a decent Second, I mean."

A decent Second being neither the height nor the depth of any male person's ambition, his audience loses interest. It is only when he states what he calls 'the indispensable minimum' that anyone asks any questions.

"Eight hours a day, every day, including Sundays," he announces. "Four in the morning, two after tea, two after Hall."

"What about rowing?" says Duncan Macleod.

"No one expects a rowing man to get a good class."

"All the same, they often do, you know."

"Only when there's an old rowing Blue on the Board of Examiners."

"How can you tell?"

"They publish the examiners' names. Keep your eye on the *Reporter*, Kiwi. It pays."

Mr. Zogropoulos, who has been giving this subject considerable thought throughout the year, smiles a happy smile.

---

[1] The attention of such dreamers should be drawn to p. 120 of the *Student's Handbook*, which quotes a passage from a report of the Council of the Senate on the treatment of cases of 'nervous breakdown', more especially nervous breakdowns induced by the belief that honours degrees can be obtained through the good offices of doctors and psychiatrists.

[2] The seats at Fenners, like those at the University Library, are free, except when visiting Test teams play the university. But voluntary contributions to the box taken round by a member of the team are invited.

"The names of our examiners were published last term," he observes. "I have attended their lectures, and in every case I have studied their interests."

"I shouldn't put my money on that, if I were you," Peter recommends. "You never know who is going to set any particular paper. Dons go on the assumption that any don is capable of setting any paper on any subject."

"Not in Natural Sciences, they don't," interposes little Frank Thwaites. "Too blasted specialized."

"All the better for you, Frankie boy. Anyway, you're bound to get a First with the Stinker on the Board. I'm told they don't even bother to read the papers in your bloody tripos."

It is now the turn of Albert from Africa. He has been listening, round-eyed with wonder, to Peter Plummer's exposition of this academic game of catch-as-catch-can. To his simple soul it seems a betrayal of those western values which he has been trained to admire.

"When I took the G.C.E. in Lagos," he says now, "we were forbidden to write our names on our papers. Each candidate received a number, and thus it was impossible for the examiner to know whose paper he was marking. Are you saying that this is not the system at Cambridge?"

"Bless your heart, of course it isn't," says Peter airily. "It's taken for granted here that examiners are gentlemen."

"All right, all right," coos Mr. Shalimar ecstatically, to whom the gentlemanliness of dons has proved a never-failing help in time of trouble. "For my part, I would trust an English gentleman with my purse."

"And much good may it do him," says Peter. "By the way, what about that coffee you owe me?"

"Certainly, certainly, my dear Peter. How decent of you to remind me of my debt."

Mr. Shalimar goes off to the counter to collect two more frothing bowls, returning just in time for Peter's coda.

"All this balls about tripos tactics is beside the point, really. A man gets the class he deserves, take it from me." No one having ventured to remind Peter that he has already one First under his belt, and another

to come, he concludes: "There's only one answer to the tripos problem.
Work to a time-table. Eight hours a day, including Sundays, – four
hours in the morning. . . ."

Presently, he slings his gown over his shoulder, relights his pipe, and
goes forth. His parting words sound half way between a threat and a
promise.

"You won't see me here again until after the tripos."

India and Africa go off together in the direction of the Law Schools;
little Thwaites has already departed for the Downing site; only Duncan
Macleod and Mr. Zogropoulos remain.

"Have another coffee?" Duncan suggests.

Mr. Zogropoulos, who reads Geography when he reads, assents
listlessly.

"I find Plummer very depressing," he sighs, after wiping the froth
from the seventeen hairs of his moustache. "Very depressing
indeed."

"Oh, don't take any notice of old Peter," Duncan advises. "You'll
find him in here again to-morrow morning, just the same. He works
at night. I live next door to him, so I happen to know."

"I do not refer to his working habits. They are his own affair.
Temperamentally, I am incapable of imitating him in that respect,
anyway. No. I refer to his remarks about the habits of our examiners.
Please give me your honest opinion. Is it possible, do you think, that
an examiner will not set the paper in the subject on which he lectures?"

"I wouldn't put it past him. I wouldn't put anything past dons, as
a race. Anyway, why worry?"

"Because, as I have already said, I have attended with complete
regularity the courses of lectures of all the examiners in the Preliminary
examination for part I of the Geographical tripos. I have noted most
carefully their opinions and their interests, so that I am confident that
I know, with a high degree of accuracy, the kind of questions that each
one would be likely to set. And now I am to understand that I have
been wasting my time. . . . I tell you, it is very disheartening, most
disheartening."

"Not to worry," says Duncan. "My supervisor says study the back
papers, not the examiners. In fact, he says they always set the same

questions, every year, only they wrap them up in a slightly different way."

"He says that? And he is to be depended upon, you think?"

"Sure. There aren't any flies on Nosey."

"No flies on his nose, eh? I understand. . . . Ah, if only I had decided to read history. You are very fortunate, Duncan."

Mr. Zogropoulos spends the next three days copying out the examination questions for the past ten years in parallel columns on large sheets of paper. Every man has his own method in the May Term.

Daffyd Evans's method is to lie on his back in a field between Brooklands Avenue and the Long Road, reading the works of Pyecraft. Philip Hughes-Browne goes to Fenners where he has been selected for a trial game with the Probables against the Possibles. He manages to get to early lectures with Duncan Macleod, all the same, for it is his opinion that lectures attended in the May Term are likely to stick until the proximate Day of Judgment. Quite a large number of other people seem to think the same, and the Severn Bore, opening his folder at the first lecture of the Easter Term, gazes sardonically over his spectacles at the unusually crowded benches.

"As I was saying, gentlemen, when we last met – or, at least, when some of us last met – estimates of the population of England in the eighteenth century tend to fluctuate somewhat erratically. Here is a demographic table which some of you may perhaps care to commit to memory. . . ."

Down go some two hundred heads over virgin pages, and the noiseless flow of ball-points leaves the auditory world to the quarrelling of starlings in the gutters and the swearing of Messrs. Eaden Lilley's vanmen in the furniture repository next-door.

When the survivors of the gallant two hundred get into the adjoining lecture-room at ten o'clock, Philip Hughes-Browne makes his get-away before the arrival of the Tar Baby, Duncan having agreed to lend him his notes. The trial teams will be assembling at Fenners, regardless of whatever may be happening to Frederick Barbarossa and Henry the Lion.

The Tar Baby doesn't bother to introduce himself, now. He simply holds out his arms, with the wings of his gown dependent in the style

P

of Dracula stooping to his prey, and smiles upon his captive audience.

"The Emperor Barbarossa was so named, we are given to understand, because his beard was red – an error in taste which I, for one, find it somewhat hard to forgive. . . ."

"Oh God," groans Duncan Macleod, "Less than six weeks to go, and he's making jokes. . . ."

Lecturers' jokes in the May Term tend to be minatory, sardonic, teasing, the kind of Jokes that Torquemada would crack with his victims while turning the rack. Twisting the knife in the wound. Splashing the water under the chin of Tantalus. These unpleasing activities are benevolent when compared with the tricks that are played in the Arts School, or the Mill Lane lecture-rooms, or the theatre of the Anatomy School, in the month of May.

"A star question in the Mays, gentlemen," cries Boanerges from the rostrum. "A question very well worth while the attention of the weaker vessels looking for a hole in the hedge."

And, as the weaker vessels are perfectly well aware that Boanerges is setting the paper – has probably set it already – has probably got the accursed thing in his pocket, ready to drop in at the University Press on his way back to college, they make a special note of it, only to spend the rest of the day debating whether Boanerges had really meant to be helpful, or whether he was bluffing, or whether (ghastly thought) the man is capable of double-bluff. Worst of all is the situation of the man whose supervisor is an examiner. He will be told to pick his own essay-subjects in the May Term. Then he has to scrutinise the man's face, and weigh his every word of comment, in hope of detecting some sign of his intentions. If he says nothing, it may mean (a) that he doesn't think it worth your while to bother with that one, or (b) that he daren't trust himself to say anything on a question he has set for the examination. If he says a lot, it may mean either (a) he wants to help you, or (b) he is trailing a red herring. And when you scan your paper on the morning of the examination you will probably find that not one of your laborious selections has come up, and that you might as well have spent your time in getting to know something about the subject. Far better, in fact.

Undergraduates have always tended to turn university examinations into sporting contests, occasions for the matching of wits. "I think I've tricked them," you may hear them say when they come out of the Examination School, after doing battle for three hours of a fine summer afternoon. Examiners are always 'them' or 'they', the enemy. This midsummer warfare, however, is conducted according to well-understood rules, and the rules are nearly always respected. After all, the object of the exercise, to the undergraduate, is not to deceive but to delude. There is a fine distinction. Deception is knavery, a form of swindling. Delusion is foolery, a form of advertising. The undergraduate's object is simply to make a little go a long way. It is very fortunate that this is his object, because examiners see through it with an ease that would dismay its practitioners if they only knew.

First examiner: Thin. Much cry, and precious little wool.
Second examiner: I agree. The man says nearly nothing in fifteen pages. Probably idle.
Chairman: A third, surely?
First examiner: Well. . . . He's not a scandal. There is something there. Not much, I agree. But something.
Second examiner: If we give him a two-two he'll carry a lot more. I'm all for giving more thirds.
Chairman: So am I. But we must take the man on his merits, slender though they may be. I mean, we should not go out of our way looking for victims. . . . Will anyone propose that he gets a two-two?
First examiner: Could we not leave him and come back to him later? See how he looks alongside some of the safe two-two's?

They leave him. They come back to him later. He gets a third. The 'safe two-two's', it is agreed, have more substance. This is a pretty plain case of clever waffle.

This is the kind of scene, the kind of decision, that is preparing all through the merry month of May. And in the middle of June, the President of the Immortals (probably a Fellow of Trinity) will finish his sport with a good fat two-two class, chiefly composed of strategists It really is advisable, in the May Term, to get down to some solid work, and most people do.

The near-obsession with examinations has come to something like a climax with the increased interest of public authorities in the university performances of the multitude of young men who now receive some form of financial aid out of the tax-payers' purses. It is part of the price to be paid for the provision of a career open to talent. What else can the Ministry of Education, and the County Education Authorities, go on? Nor can one blame the young for thinking in terms of Class Lists in a world where competition for remunerative employment at the end of a university education is desperately keen. Too many tears can be shed far too easily over this. One hears a good deal of nonsense talked about the degradation involved in the cult of 'triposathleticism'. A great deal more than ability to 'unload against the clock' is tested by the three-hour examination sessions which conclude a Cambridge academic year. Intellectual stamina, the long-breath, swift selectivity, readiness and relevance: these are no inconsiderable qualities. Moreover, these are about the only qualities that can be judged within the given conditions of public examination. If the university were looking for men of genius something different would have to be devised. Fortunately, both for themselves and for the university, men of genius generally go elsewhere. When, by some odd chance, one of them does get into the place, he generally gets a second class, or gets sent down for writing his papers in blank verse. The university is devised for l'homme moyen intellectuel, and it finds him out with a pretty sure touch.

The common-sense view of examinations is to get some solid work done, put your faith in God, and keep your powder dry. Remember, also, that though you may think you can trick the examiners, it is not their intention to trick you. They don't want to catch you out, but to find out what you know, a much simpler task in all respects. Their intention should be respected.

The Women

It is in the Easter Term that the women come forth, if not 'sprig-muslin

dress'd', at least in bell-bottomed skirts and billowing hoops, or whatever the present delightful fashion may be. Quite suddenly, with the
first sunny morning, Trinity Street and King's Parade are bright with
a radiance that rivals the tulips. Of course, the women have been there
all the time. It is now that elderly dons notice them, and that scales fall
from the eyes of the young men.

For Cambridge is, after all, an overwhelmingly male world. The
men outnumber the women by about ten to one. Men made the place,
men govern it, men set its standards and men dominate its social life.
There are, of course, what Lowes Dickinson unkindly called 'the
governesses' dispensing tea in the suburbs: in fact, dons' wives doing
their social duty. There are odd young women who set themselves up
as 'salonesses', scintillating over coffee and sherry for the benefit of the
more callow undergraduates and certain languishing elderly dons. And,
apart from the Union Society, which still excludes them from membership, there is scarcely any university organization of a social, political,
or cultural character in which the women are unable to play their full
part if they so desire. They are especially active, and welcome, in
dramatic societies, except the *Footlights*. And yet, one gets the impression that the women undergraduates exist in the interstices of the
university, flowers growing in the shallow soil of ledges; not wall-
flowers, but gentians. The original fear, prevalent in the days – little
less than a century ago – when they first appeared in the place, that
they would swarm and proliferate all over the place, like the willow-
herb in the ruins of a noble world overthrown, was always fantastic.
Girton and Newnham are still restricted to a maximum student population of five hundred, and New Hall[1] provides places for a mere
additional handful.

These, of course, are not all the women of Cambridge, though they
are all the undergraduate women of the university. There are in addition the populations of Hughes Hall, the teachers' training college for
women graduates, and of Homerton College, which is not a university
foundation but a college for training women to teach. The former has
a population of between sixty and seventy; the latter some three hun-

---

[1] Technically, a 'Third Foundation for Women', and described in the original proposal
for its establishment as 'A Third Foundation for women of moderate size. . . .'

dred. There is also the Cambridge County Technical College, which caters for a very large number of young women (and men) from all over the world. Beyond these, there is a periphery of cramming establishments and English Language Schools which enormously swell the numbers of young females around the place. The amount of impure English that floats up from the punts on the river in May is enough to make the loiterer on King's Bridge dream of the Seine and the Blue Danube, if not of the Euxine and the Bosphorus. Girton and Newnham, and New Hall, with their rather less than six hundred young ladies, provide only the undergraduate nucleus of this monstrous regiment. Their small population has to take its chance against a multitude of rivals in these days. For it is all the same to the young men whether the female of the species comes from Roedean, Birmingham, or Giggleswick; from Paris, Rome, Bonn or Belgrade. Or is it? The girl who wears the short black gown of the women's colleges is still one of the *élite*, and she knows it, and the men know it, too, when they are in their right minds. She is on the inside. She belongs. She has been selected on a rigorous intellectual test from among many thousand able young women throughout England, to enjoy, or at least experience, the best that university life in England has to offer. For three years she is to live in a society where the mind is still thought to be worth exercising for its own sake. She must be pretty good, her brothers will admit, to get in at all, where applicants are so many and places are so few. And she is good. She needs to be.

Life at Cambridge is bound to be more complex for her than it is for her brothers. It is untrue to say, as has been said far too recently, that 'women are interlopers in the cloisters of Cambridge, grudgingly recognized as full citizens in the university state'. The woman's problem has little or nothing to do with the way the men regard her, nowadays. If she is sensible, she accepts the obvious fact that she exists in a man's world and abjures the temptation to turn herself into a man. Her problem is to discover, by the tact of experience, how to make the best of it, and of herself, without either flaunting or flouting the differences that she knows to exist with the inevitability of hard fact. For one thing, she is used to hard work. That is, largely how she comes to be where she is. At Cambridge she must learn how to learn at leisure. Her great temptation is to cram with examinations ever in mind in order to justify occupying 'a place' where places are so hard to get. To know how, and when, to 'let up' is not women's strong point in intellectual labours. There are few tactfully, and even fewer tactically, 'lazy' women. It is said to have been in a women's lecture note-book that the words 'Will somebody please open a window?' were found. In any case, there is reason to believe that the inhabitants of the women's colleges are generally over-taught out of anxiety. And apart from 'work' she has to find her way in society. It is not difficult for her to strike the happy mean between the prude and the wanton. The men, she will tell you quite soon, are 'all right', although they are nowhere near so interesting as they think they are. Anyway, she is a lot older than they are in everything but years, and really they are sweetly schoolboyish when they write in *Varsity* about their views on 'Women'. No, her problem is chiefly how to live with other women. She has none of the male undergraduate's cherished escape-mechanism. She has to live within the walls of her college for all three years. Her room will probably be a mere cubby-hole of a bed-sitter. Her means will, more likely than not, be straitened. There is the temptation to live largely on hospitality accepted without much prospect of being able to return it. Yet, with all this, she feels the need for more, and more varied, clothes than her brother in his perennial sports jacket and flannel trousers. To learn how to be an economist without meanness, a worker without cram, an interesting person without affectation. . . . The requirements of Kipling's *If* are child's-play to those of a woman undergraduate.

Out in the town are all those girls with horse-tails and jeans, scarlet nails and duffle-coats, and (it always seems) bottomless purses, learning how to speak the English tongue over pots of beer on the wall by 'The Mill' or endless mugs of coffee in the Espresso bars. Should she envy them? Is it really true that

> Men don't make passes
> At girls who wear glasses?

When in doubt, probably the best way is to go and find out. The

results are generally encouraging, if not really surprising. A simpler way
is to go and look at the photographs of the pioneers of the college, in
the entrance hall. Most of the names have 'Mrs. ——' in a bracket
underneath.

The coming of the women to Cambridge has made far less difference
to Cambridge life than it was once imagined it would. Dire prophecies
were rife at the time of the foundation of the two women's colleges
(Girton, on its present site, 1873; Newnham, 1875), and of their
recognition as colleges of the university whose members were admis-
sible to tripos examinations on the same conditions of entrance and
residence as men (1881), though not to full membership of the university and its degrees (which was not finally achieved until 1947). It
was not so much the mere presence of women students in, or near,
the place that roused alarm and despondency. They could, and they
did, creep into the vicinity of the men's colleges by a process of peaceful
penetration, aided and abetted by liberally minded senior members like
Henry Sidgwick, James Stuart, and (for a time) Alfred Marshall. On
the whole, this process was tolerated or more or less politely ignored.
What aroused the fiercest feelings of repudiation for many years was
the notion that women should be admitted to degrees. The first major
contest over this fell proposal took place in 1897. It was voted down
in the Senate, amidst scenes of the utmost excitement by 1,707 to 661.
Nor were the members of the Senate alone in their apprehension. An
undergraduate poll organized by the editor of *The Cambridge Review*
produced an adverse vote of 1,723 to 446, for what it was worth. The
anxiety of the young men, it is said, was over the prospect of
'effemination' of the place and the maintenance of sporting supremacy
over Oxford where women had already been admitted to degrees, with
fatal consequences to athletic prowess. The uproar lasted for many
weeks and was known as 'the Women's War'. Headlines and posters
concentrated on the theme: THE UNIVERSITY FOR THE UNDERGRADUATE.
The women were referred to as THE INVADERS. It was declared to be
vital to MAINTAIN THE INTEGRITY OF CAMBRIDGE. Even when, in 1921,
the proposed admission of women to full membership was defeated
by 908 votes to 694, a mob went out to Newnham and defaced the

memorial bronze gates commemorating the indefatigable first principal, Anne Jemima Clough. So, for a time, women had to be content
with *titles* of degrees.

'We are being asked to adopt a tiger-cub, on the ground that it is
such a little one and can't do any harm.' This was one of the mildest
of the expostulatory legends of 1897. There was abroad a terrible fear
of the 'strong-minded' woman. And certainly 'strong-minded' the
pioneers of women's education at Cambridge had to be, and generally
were. Not that they were without their own peculiar scorns and contempts for the masculine world into which they sought to enter. Emily
Davies, first mistress of Girton on its present site, was always reluctant
to settle her young ladies in close proximity to the source of infection.
She organized the nucleus of the community that was to become
Girton College twenty-six miles away, at the salubrious town of
Hitchin. When the move to Cambridge was mooted she wrote:

We have been asked with hands held up in horror, were we going to Cambridge? We had two visits from brothers in Hitchin, and although everyone
concerned behaved with the utmost propriety, we felt thankful the brothers
did not live within thirty miles.

The distance of Girton from Cambridge is about two miles.

Much of the trouble from the masculine angle, oddly enough,
appears to have arisen from the fact that the women were women, and
insisted on looking like women. Three out of the first five proto-
Newnhamites brought to 74 Regent Street,[1] Cambridge, by Miss
Clough, on their way to their permanent home, in 1871, were voted
'extremely beautiful'. Henry Sidgwick, seeking to edge the girls into
the masculine system, thought it 'very distressing that the women
could not slip through unobserved. It was,' he added, 'all the fault of
their unfortunate appearance.' By which he meant the opposite of what
his rather ill-chosen words might imply. Undergraduates at that time,
and for some time to come, appear to have been singularly deficient
in either eyesight or taste. 'Miss Shabby Hag, the Newnhamite', was
to remain the type-character of the woman undergraduate for many
years. As late as the nineteen-thirties there were still male university

[1] Now (1959) the *Glengarry Hotel*.

lecturers who took pleasure in driving women students from their lecture-rooms by, to say the least, ungallant language and allusions. No doubt the habit of the late Sir Arthur Quiller-Couch of addressing his audience on all occasions as simply 'gentlemen' was merely playful. Not so the world's greatest authority on Stubbs' *Select Charters*, who would refer with a snort and a sigh to the island in the Antipodes populated exclusively by men, until the women arose in a body and walked out.

"No hurry, my dears," he would call after them. "There isn't a boat until Thursday week."

Facetiousness, banter, sly allusion, all have passed away now, and the women's presence in the overwhelmingly male world of Cambridge is taken for granted, without comment, though happily not without consciousness. No doubt the greatly increased number of men from co-educational schools has a good deal to do with it. The changed attitude of society in general has still more. If the women at Cambridge have their critics they are nowadays to be found in their own ranks. Surely it was a woman contributor who concluded 'Women's Page' in a recent edition of the *Varsity Handbook*, proffering advice to women undergraduates, with the admonition: 'wash, wash, wash.' It is unlikely that Miss Davies or Miss Clough would have been easily persuaded of either the necessity or the propriety of this admonition. Their homiletics were of a different order altogether. 'No levity', said Miss Davies to Miss Garrett who was laughing about a woman having to serve as a chairman. 'Your jokes are many and reckless. . . . They do more harm than you know.' For, in those early days, a high seriousness was essential. Far too many people outside the new establishment were prepared to take higher education for women as a joke after the manner of *Princess Ida*. The mood within the establishment was, and had to be, 'serious, uplifted, and a trifle defiant.' Early Newnham had a discussion group, devoted to the discussion of 'Things that Matter', which debated fiercely such questions as 'Is Pleasure the only Good?' Things that matter explicitly excluded both Sex and Religion, but included Contributory Pensions. These things were approached, we are told, in an atmosphere of 'Exalted Humanism'.

There is still exaltation. The lop-sided red-brick tower of Girton, out on the Huntingdon Road, still hangs lofty and remote beyond the town, the landmark of an ideal. The pink brick and white paint of Newnham, squatting beyond Queens' Road and the fen, still speaks of a life that belongs to Cambridge and yet is not wholly absorbed therein. Lady-dons sail forth in academic dress to lecture to overwhelmingly male audiences, to take their full share of administration, examining, and all the manifold duties and privileges of university life. The young women under their care likewise go forth, to lecture-rooms and laboratories, and often enough to supervision by men supervisors. It is not long since women attending supervision by male persons were required to attend in pairs, and to write their tripos papers under the eye of a knitting chaperone. Long passed away are the days when a woman, entertaining men friends in college, must leave her door open and remain on her feet through the proceedings. Men and women entertain each other in their colleges with complete freedom to-day. Entertainment to meals in Hall, however, remains beneath the ban, although one hears every now and then of some infringement by means of disguise. This restriction can prove embarrassing, as when some distinguished lady-don visits a men's college to read a paper to an undergraduate society. The idea of entertaining ladies at High Table is still strongly resisted in most colleges. Senior members of the men's colleges are sometimes entertained at High Table (or at a table suitably nearby) in the women's colleges. Their chief impression, they say, is of the deafening din created by a hall-full of young women talking at their natural pitch. The lady-dons retire to their Senior Combination Room after dinner where, it seems, they drink port, although it is generally denied that they smoke pipes.

Any fine day, now, the Head of a Woman's College may become Vice-Chancellor. It is said that postponement of women proctors[1] must wait upon a solution of the problem of what to call lady bull-dogs.

---

[1] This has, of course, already happened at Oxford. But it was decreed that a woman proctor, while undertaking all other proctorial duties, would not be required to walk the streets.

The Sights of Cambridge

It is at this time, too – when the sunshine has begun to warm the pavement – that the odd birds appear, figures that would be stared at, and even hooted at, if they appeared in public places anywhere else in England, with the possible exception of Oxford. Where they come from nobody knows, though one suspects that they have been hiding all winter in those tall dark houses in St. Paul's Road and Brookside. They are, it seems, shy, valetudinarian, or semi-relegated dons, old Fellows of colleges. The standard of eccentricity for Fellows, as Winstanley observed, was always high. And the best of it is, as Winstanley failed to observe, that they don't know it, or anyway they don't care.

First don: (black sombrero, khaki shorts, brown ankle-socks and brogues) I wonder why one no longer sees the queer old academical characters that one used to see in the streets of Cambridge?
Second don: (yellowing straw-boater, sun-glasses, and ankle-length overcoat) I have often wondered the same thing . . .

Their ladies come out, too. They proceed in pairs, carrying ebony sticks and string-bags, and generally followed by fat little dogs. They wear clothes very like the ones they are to be seen wearing in the early photographs of Girton and Newnham college groups at the end of the nineteenth century. The younger generation takes them for bedmakers or washer-women. They are not to know that they are in the presence of women who sat at the feet of Alfred Marshall or Henry Sidgwick, women famous in their day for their championship of academic causes in battles long ago, the mothers of victories that made possible the enjoyment of both hooped-skirts and honours degrees by the little girls who now pass them by with a smile. The Cambridge young are on the whole tolerant of these relics of the Cambridge past. They will step off the pavement to let them pass. They will pick up their bicycles (for many of them still ride unsteadily through the hazards of Market Street and the Cury), or even run after them with strayed parcels or wind-tossed boaters. But they do not know they are touching the fringe of history. It is May Term, and they are in a hurry. Unlike Oxford,

Cambridge is not a town of two categories, the quick and the dead. Its life is shared, tolerantly, and honourably, by the half-dead, not to mention the half-baked. The half-baked are not so numerous as once they were, though there are still enough of them to maintain the old Cambridge aspect of an academic village complete with idiots. Jock, with his beret, his beard, and his made artist's face, still claps his hands and breaks into a horn-pipe in Tennis Court Road. The Man in a Hurry still trots in from Shelford with his mysterious suit-case, smiling and perspiring and whispering to himself as he anticipates some wonderful bargains among the Cambridge bookshops. But, alas, the Mad Shepherd with his long Newmarket coat, his deerstalker, and his crook, no longer haunts the streets with his lost and wistful look as he did in summers long ago.

Now is the time, when all the world is on show, to bring up one's parents. Early May is certainly the best time. It makes a good excuse to knock off work for a long week-end, and it forestalls their arrival in May Week, when there is so much more to do than showing people round. Of course, the third-year man will have to have them up for Degree Day, anyway. For the rest, early May is ideal. There are plenty of good hostelries. Choose one which makes for a minimum of wear and tear in terms of shoe-leather and weary feet, and bear in mind that the flat Cambridge streets are far more exhausting to the sightseer than are the climbing thoroughfares of more hilly regions. For mothers and sisters in particular, stiletto-heels on flagstones and cobblestones have been known to kill the splendours of King's Chapel and Trinity Great Court stone-dead. Centrally situated hotels, however, are very expensive. There is a lot to be said for getting the porter or the landlady to recommend some private house which does bed-and-breakfast. Best of all, perhaps, and not only from the parents' point of view, is to encourage your visitors to come up on a day-trip by road, parking the family car in the Queen's Road, and taking odd meals at pubs and restaurants. The Union Society's dining-room is a favourite rendezvous. There, parents will feel that they are really in the university.

Economizing time and foot-slogging on these occasions calls for some little advanced planning. It is much better to determine what one intends to show off, rather than to amble haphazard. If it is a matter of showing off the colleges, two or three good short itineraries can be readily picked from one or other of the numerous, and generally excellent, Cambridge guide books. These are good for initiation. But, if there is time, or if the visit is not simply initiatory, it is best to work out one or two good 'walks round', taking the colleges as centre-pieces only. Thousands of visitors think they have seen Cambridge when they have seen King's and Trinity and St. John's, with one or two little gems like Clare or Queens' thrown in. These favourites are all very much in a line of about half a mile's length. Such an itinerary, while it takes in some of the finest buildings, is like picking the icing off the cake. Cambridge itself is made up of vastly more varied components. The visitor will not have seen Cambridge, as distinct from a group of splendid buildings, until he has gone out of his way to see the outlying beauties of Jesus College, and Magdalene, and Downing. And even then, he will still be stringing pearls instead of exploring the complex of greens and courts and lanes and alleys where the life of this ancient place has circulated through the centuries. Of course, it is always a matter of time: time to amble and penetrate and poke around. For the undergraduate showing his visitors the place, it is often also a matter of ignorance. He has been so busy going about his daily occasions within a time-table, that he is most unlikely to know what there is to see beyond his customary routes between college and lecture-room and library and playing-field. Here are two recommended routes that will enable him to share in the sense of 'the unknown' along with his guests. After a few terms' experience of outwitting those in authority with an air of assumed knowledge, he should have little difficulty in persuading fathers and mothers, aunts and uncles, that he knew them all long ago.

The first begins at the Castle Mound on the top of Castle Hill, and within the grounds of the Shire Hall. From this eminence, the chief impression to be gained of Cambridge is that of a town of trees. The greenery, in spring and summer, obscures the college landmarks, with the exception of King's Chapel and St. John's tower in the right foreground, and the roofs of Magdalene almost at one's feet. It is possible, however, to form some idea of the fundamental layout of the place: the crooked spine of the main thoroughfare snaking along past Sidney and Christ's and Emmanuel to the distant Gog-Magog hills where the Via Devana points towards Colchester; the crossing where Chesterton Lane and Northampton Street meet, which carries the traffic from Ely and King's Lynn and East Anglia in general, to the western road over Madingley Hill to Bedford, Bath, and the west. The answer to the question: Why Cambridge? is evident when one looks down at this crooked cross north of Magdalene Bridge and the river. And here, at Castle Hill, one is at the heart of the earliest Cambridge, the settlement of the Mercians north of the river. Descending to the main road again, one can explore the oldest haunts of Cambridge life, a life that thronged here before ever the scholars came to the place. Crossing the road, and turning into Kettle's Yard,[1] make the circuit of lanes around St. Peter's Church, taking a look at what good twentieth-century rebuilding has done to the tumble-down cottages on the side of Pound Hill – one of the happiest examples of homes for old folks that it is possible to imagine. The remainder of Pound Hill is still ugly and uninteresting. Returning by St. Peter's Street to Kettle's Yard once more, go through the tiny churchyard to the tiny church of St. Peter itself. There has been a church here for nearly nine hundred years. Since the twelfth century, its proportions have shrunk to its present diminutive measurements of fifteen by thirty-six feet. By the middle of the eighteenth century, St. Peter's by the Castle, or Beyond the Bridge, was unused. Soon it lost its roof and its windows. Only in 1781 was it rebuilt on its present scale. Recently, it has been restored and repaired once more, and it is now used for children's services. White-washed within, bare and empty of all but its ancient font and simple altar, it still holds up its tower and spire, a small and wonderful witness to triumph over time and change.

At the foot of Castle Hill, on the right-hand, is Northampton Street. The corner is occupied by the *Old White Horse Inn*. This somewhat shabby old house now contains the bygones of the Cambridge and County Folk Museum. Northampton Street itself is a perfect example of what Cambridge must have looked like for many centuries. It was along here, at the end of the eighteenth century, that Richard Kidman,

[1] Nothing to do with tinkers, but derived from such common old Cambridge surnames as Ketel and Turketel.

the celebrated Cambridge cracksman, aroused suspicion about the source of his prosperity as a builder. This ingenious character, a supposedly respectable clock-mender and glazier, was the leading spirit in the great college plate robberies of 1796-99, when Caius, Christ's, King's and Trinity all suffered from his activities. Having built himself comfortable quarters in Bell Lane, Northampton Street, he was sufficiently foolish to start issuing 'Bell Lane Sixpences' and silver shoe-buckles. Bow Street Runners found the tools of his trade in his house, which led to his transportation.

Behind Northampton Street is the oldest secular building in Cambridge, 'the stone house of the scholars of Merton'. It is thought to go back to the later twelfth century, and was the manor-house of the estates of the Dunning family, which provided Cambridge with its first mayor. The Dunnings sold the property to Merton College, Oxford, in whose possession it has remained ever since. It may be that Walter of Merton invested in this house, as in other properties in Cambridge and the neighbourhood, as a refuge for his scholars at the time when Oxford became too hot for them in the town-and-gown warfare of the thirteenth century. The house acquired the name of 'the School of Pythagoras' from antiquarians in Elizabethan times, and it is still thus miscalled. Its connection with the university of Cambridge is remote and vague. In its day it has been a manor-house, a school for boys, and a temporary abiding place (1872-4) for the society which was to become Newnham College. Excluding churches, this is the most venerable piece of building in Cambridge, a stone-built medieval manor-house, to match the tiny medieval church of St. Peter on the hillside above. These two remain as the surviving memorials of the earliest Cambridge to the north of the river. Unfortunately it is only possible to see 'the School of Pythagoras' by peeping into the yard of *The Merton Arms*, in Northampton Street, a private car-park.

Leaving the yard of *The Merton Arms*, turn through the next gap in Northampton Street to the east, and explore the new courts of Magdalene College behind the shops and houses on the west side of Magdalene Street. Here are Benson Court and Mallory Court. Benson Court was designed by Sir Edwin Lutyens, and was built in the early 'thirties, to commemorate Arthur Christopher Benson (Master, 1915-

Rugger Boat in May Week Races

Pembroke College Chapel – the earliest work of Sir Christopher Wren

1925), whose meditative sketches under the title of *From a College Window*, were once known and loved by many thousands to whom life at Cambridge was otherwise unknown. Mallory Court, which faces it, belongs to much the same period. It was built in memory of George Mallory the Magdalene man who died on Mount Everest. But the really interesting and beautiful thing about these ranges of Magdalene College on the western side of Magdalene Street is the newest grouping of domestic architecture between the entrance to Mallory and the street entrance through the old entry to the inn-yard of what was once *The Cross Keys* (now a post-office). These charming and colourful houses were built between 1952 and 1956. They bear witness to the abiding influence of the architecture of the South Bank Exhibition. When one thinks of the dismal formalism of 'dons' architecture' perpetrated up and down Cambridge over the last thirty years, here is something to be thankful for. Magdalene has increased the sightseers' debt to college enterprise by stripping off the cement facing of the old court of her main building on the opposite side of the street, thus revealing the original brickwork, and by replacing the slate roofing with tiles. Between 2.30 and 3.30 in the afternoon visitors are admitted to the Pepys Library which is housed in the handsome, late seventeenth century, building which closes the second court, beyond.

This excursion around transpontine Cambridge may very well end with lunch, or tea, at the Union. The building itself (Waterhouse's best gothic), as the guide-books say, 'need not detain us', but visitors duly refreshed may fairly be expected to take a look at the Round Church next door.

An alternative area for exploration lies at the opposite end of the town, around what was once 'the Trumpington Gate'. This, the southern entrance to Cambridge, was situated in the neighbourhood of the Pitt Press building and Pembroke College. Guests staying at the *Garden House*, beside the river at the foot of Little St. Mary's Lane, should be encouraged to make this tour. Leaving the hotel, take a walk over the fen fields towards Fen Causeway. Here is fenland Cambridge tamed and drained into a most pleasant land of slow streams, poplars, pasture and ponies. Go out with the ancient and buttressed wall of the old Peter-

Q

house deer-park on your left hand, and keep on past the back of the engineering laboratories to the Fen Causeway. Crossing the road, follow the path behind the Leys School and then bear right to the swimming sheds. Cross the humped iron bridge over the river and go through the park on Coe Fen, emerging once more into Fen Causeway. Cross the Causeway behind the flats of Causewayside, and follow the branch of the river to the mill pool. Here is one of the pleasantest sights of a Cambridge spring or summer day: the pool with its fringe of willows, between the *Jolly Miller* and the *Granta Inn*. The pubs themselves are two of the ugliest in Cambridge, but beyond the pool is the Malting House, a warm brick and tile house, with a pillared portico and an oast-house wing with a delightful lantern. Then follow the pathway over the two wooden bridges to the main river and *The Mill* beside the weir. Looking back across the lower arm of the river and the mill pool, give a respectful thought to the house of Darwin. Over there, in those delightful houses whose backs look to the water, and whose fronts face on to lower Silver Street, lived many of the characters who populate Gwen Raverat's *Period Piece*. This little colony is now linked to the town proper by the new Silver Street bridge, a link at last worthy of a neighbourhood known not only to the Darwins but to Desiderius Erasmus who spent his Cambridge sojourn within the walls of Queens' College which adjoins its eastern end.

From the brick ramparts of the bridge and the weir in front of *The Mill*, go through Laundress Lane at the back of *The Anchor*, and into upper Silver Street. The grimy brick wall of Queens' faces you across the road, somewhat jail-like with its narrow barred windows. Do not be discouraged by this, but turn into Queens' Lane and walk through the college, Cambridge's neatest example of fifteenth century redbrick domestic architecture. The second court with its cloisters and its timbered and overhanging gallery (the President's Lodging), its paved and cobbled paths and its lawns, have all the intimate and peaceful charm of a private house. Beyond, as you come out over the river, you find yourself on the celebrated 'mathematical bridge', a humpbacked timber complex of intricate stresses and strains neatly calculated in the age of Sir Isaac Newton. In early spring, the peninsulashaped garden beyond the river is a paradise of daffodils. Going out into lower Silver Street, cross the new bridge and turn right into Laundress Lane again. Then continue beyond the front of *The Mill* and turn left into Little St. Mary's Lane. Here, on the left hand, are some neatly restored and charmingly decorated small houses that might well flank the village street of some tale by Mary Mitford or some drawing by Kate Greenaway. If Cambridge has a dream-lane, this is it. On the right is the Church of St. Mary-the-Less, formerly known as St. Peter outside Trumpington Gates. Bishop Hugh of Balsham gave this church to the scholars of his foundation, St. Peter's College, now Peterhouse, close by. Just inside the door, to the left-hand, is the memorial to Mr. Godfrey Washington, who was minister here and a Fellow of St. Peter's College. He lived from 1670 to 1729, and over his memorial you may see his shield bearing three stars and two stripes.

Following Little St. Mary's Lane into Trumpington Street, cross the main road and look back to the pleasant house of St. Peter beyond the church. Outside the topmost window nearest the street, in the high stone block looking north, there is an iron bar, or rail, affixed. This may be taken as a memorial to the poet, Thomas Gray, who lived in the rooms beyond the window, before he moved to Pembroke across the road. Gray was mortally afraid of fire, more especially as he lived over rooms inhabited by rowdy young men. He kept a rope-ladder ready to attach to this bar in case of emergency. It is said that a false alarm raised by his neighbours caused him to descend, early one morning, into a tub of water placed underneath and that this greatly precipitated his migration to the adjoining college.[1] Pembroke has a Christopher Wren chapel (his earliest work), with a pretty cupola perched on its roof, and this can be seen fronting the road opposite Peterhouse. Just beyond is the handsome Lodge of the Master of Peterhouse, the loveliest example of the Queen Anne style of domestic architecture that Cambridge can show. Turning back towards the town once more, go into Pembroke if only to see the portraits of its Masters and distinguished *alumni* in the dining-hall. Here you may see the naughty smiling face of Roger Long, the nonagenarian; the bust of

---

[1] The old story is *ben trovato*, but R. W. Ketton-Cremer in his *Life of Thomas Gray* declares the tub of water to be apocryphal.

Thomas Gray smirks from one corner, and the Younger Pitt turns up his marble nose from the alcove of the south window.

This perambulation of Cambridge at the Trumpington Gate end should include St. Catharine's and Corpus Christi. At Corpus, go through leftward from the first court into the small medieval court which adjoins the church of St. Bene't. Here, duly commemorated with a large stone plaque, is the lodging of Christopher Marlowe and John Fletcher. The exit into the street runs close by the Saxon tower of St. Bene't's, architecturally the oldest church in the shire. Across the road there is the inn yard of *The Eagle* (originally the *Eagle and Child*), one of the mere half-dozen Cambridge inns which go back beyond the nineteenth century. From here the Royal Mail once set out daily for London, and the house itself is shown on old maps as the Post Office. It was at *The Eagle* that the Mortlock family, in alliance with the Dukes of Rutland, had their headquarters for the control of the borough, and its parliamentary representation, in the Whig interest in the days of the Younger Pitt. Here the well-drilled squads of Cambridge 'freemen' were wined and dined with an efficiency which far exceeded the standards of Eatanswill. John Mortlock, the great oligarch whose manoeuvres brought all Cambridge, and not a little of the shire, within his sway, had his banking-house on the opposite side of the street, where Barclays Bank now stands. Within the Bank there is still to be seen the handsome port-wine glass which was used to regale William Pitt and his local cronies when the great man visited the managers of his constituency. The territory in the neighbourhood of *The Eagle* is well worth exploration. Peas Hill, it is called, though there is never a hill in sight. The best way to see it is by a bird's-eye view from the roof-garden of the Arts Theatre during an interval of a play. On foot, it is best seen by making a circuit along Bene't Street, leftward along Peas Hill itself, leftward again by the back of the Arts Theatre, and then righthandedly along St. Edward's Passage, round the churchyard of the Church of St. Edward, King and Martyr (once celebrated for the preaching of the Cambridge Protestant martyrs of the Reformation, Bilney, Barnes and Latimer), past David's bookshop and out into Peas Hill again beside the *Central Hotel* adjoining the Midland Bank. The *Central Hotel* at the corner, now a tea and coffee bar, is all that remains of the old *Three Tuns*, a house where Pepys once drank deep, and a favourite resort for aldermanic feasting.[1] Turning back again, along St. Edward's Passage and right-handedly at the Arts Theatre restaurant entrance, the way leads out into King's Parade. Across the Parade, and a little to the south, there is King's Lane. Here again one is on holy ground, for it was at this spot that there once stood *The White Horse*, known in Reformation days as 'Little Germany', by reason of the foregathering here of reverend scholars from King's and Queens' to discuss the new teachings from the land of Luther. By following King's Lane into Queens' Lane back into Silver Street, and then across into Laundress Lane and past *The Mill*, we are again at our starting-point at the *Garden House*.

As addendum to this inspection of the Trumpington Gate region of Cambridge, an afternoon should be devoted to the Fitzwilliam Museum. The outward aspect of the Fitzwilliam Museum, with its flight of steps, its huge Corinthian pillars and its statuary, gives the visitor no notion of the intimate and domestic charm of its interior. Its nucleus was the private collection of paintings, etchings, books and manuscripts bequeathed to the university by Richard, Viscount Fitzwilliam, in the early nineteenth century. Its expansion by the generous gifts of many patrons, great and small, and under the guidance of a succession of most loving and devoted directors, has not been allowed to destroy the personal and intimate character of its origins in a private collection. The Fitzwilliam is an institution, but it has very little of the institutional air that afflicts museums in general. Furniture, hangings, carpets, cases of manuscripts, ceramics and miniatures, all these things are disposed in a sweetly mingled array, so that the visitor to the main rooms can still feel that he is wandering at will in the private apartments of some great nobleman. Of course, there are also adjoining galleries which house more specialized collections, some of them of immense value; but even here, spacious rooms and excellent lighting hold off that oppressive air which is so often engendered by large numbers of examples of a single type of exhibit. Anyone who

[1] And the *Central Hotel* seems unlikely to survive the intention of King's College to erect a students' hostel on the site (1959). It is now demolished (1960).

comes away from the Fitzwilliam Museum with a headache must have taken it with him.

Sometime in the course of these parental perambulations there will occur personal encounters that call for a certain degree of *savoir-faire*. There is, of course, the point when parents have to be acknowledged in the presence of one's room-mate, and it is ten to one that your fellow keeper will be half-naked, or playing the wrong tunes on a guitar, or deep in writing an essay, when you show your parents your room. The best way to keep one's head is to get it firmly fixed in your mind from the start that John, or Ian or Peter has his troubles, too, and that he will be bringing them into this very room on some other equally ill-chosen day. And you can be quite sure that your parents will be delighted to come upon the species undergraduate *au naturel*, and that this particular specimen will bid them welcome with the utmost courtesy and shy good-humour. Moreover, there will be a far more difficult encounter to come. The odds are ten to one that you will run into your tutor, or your director of studies, or your supervisor, as you go out into the court again. Indeed, throughout your parents' visit you will probably find yourself developing the peculiar contortion of the features that is commonly known as 'undergraduates' mouth', a screwing up of one corner in order to form a funnel through which you can shoot out the ventriloquial grunting hiss of "Look out – here comes m'tutor. . . ." It is important to replace this swift contortion immediately by a rather tooth-achey smile and enter into the standard form of address.

"Mr. Stock, sir, may I introduce my father and mother?"

Mr. Stock will already have produced a frog-like beam. In fact, he will be so busy beaming with the correct degree of deprecating bonhomie that you will not need to do anything more than stand slightly to one side and blush. It is advisable to train your parents in advance for this encounter, so that they don't ask things like: "I hope he is doing plenty of work?" or "How is he shaping?" Most important of all, they must never, never, say: "We have heard so much about you from Henry. . . ." Let them praise the beauties of the college. This will give your tutor the opportunity to say what he always says: that the place looks its best at this time of year, and that they have chosen a beautiful day for their visit. This is all that he ever says, and it is best to get it over as soon as possible. Your parents won't notice what he says. They will be too busy thinking that they have at last had conversation with a real live don. On no account should evasive action be taken when these encounters loom up. For one thing, it deprives parents of very real pleasure. It also deprives tutors, and other persons set in authority, of an opportunity to parody themselves. In any case, tutors and other persons set in authority, will take their vengeance upon you at a later date for your pusillanimity.

Don: I saw you with your mother, yesterday.
Undergraduate: It was not my mother, sir. It was my fiancée.
Don: I think if you give the question a little thought, you will decide that it was your mother.

There is no answer to this one. Dons are always right.

The best encounters are silent, and purely observational, as when you find yourself walking behind a tweedy, stooping figure in a flat cap, and shoot out the whispered information: "That's Forster – right ahead of us"; or you walk right into the path of a Telly-don and find yourself confirming an incredulous question of recognition with a blasé: "Yes, that's him all right. He's quite often round the place." Showing around Cambridge has its rewarding moments, and they are not all architectural.

On the Eve – and the Day

If April is cruel, May is impossible. So much to do, so little time to do it. Hearts that were stout in November, or January, or even March, coolly counting on numberless days ahead when the undone tasks could be confronted and mastered, now quail and sink and flounder. Men ask themselves: is it worth it? Settling down has taken a week, term divides within another three weeks, and within a week after that – tripos agony begins. Lectures cease somewhere around the division of term. Supervisors wonder increasingly whether supervision will make any difference. "They've classed themselves already," they are heard to mutter to each other. "I've chosen my four questions," the prospective victims are heard to tell each other. Whatever appears on examination papers, those four answers will be offered up, and the examiners – it is to be hoped – will declare themselves 'satisfied'. Satisfying examiners, where they sit like so many versions of Cerberus in the purlieus of the Examination Schools, becomes more and more a matter of pre-digested sops. Men whose hours are numbered still expend some of them in adverse analysis of the absurdities of the examination system. It is wonderful what people will find time for on the eve of the Day of Judgment. Even this, most likely, has its educational value. 'Depend upon it, sir,' said Dr. Johnson, 'when a man knows he is to be hanged in a fortnight, it concentrates his mind wonderfully.'

And then, in the midst of the peak-production period, there comes music from on high. ASCENSION DAY, says the Diary; and moreover – SCARLET DAY. On this day, it is decreed by ancient statute, there shall be no official instruction given in the university. Lecturers can take a day off, and if by any odd chance the day falls during the examination period, the examinees will be compelled to take a day off, too. Not everyone, in these hectic days, observes, the ban, although Doctors who perform any public function on Ascension Day are obliged to dress in their scarlet robes. Those who resent the curtailment of instruction may derive consolation from the sound of the young voices floating down from the tower of St. John's College Chapel, where Ascension Day music is performed at mid-morning. Unlike the May Day singing on Magdalen tower beside the Isis, which is offered up in greeting to the dawn, Ascension Day singing at Cambridge is not accompanied by breakfast in punts on the river. Indeed, few people at Cambridge ever hear the singing overhead at St. John's, which is a pity. It is a more than satisfactory substitute for the melodies of the momentarily silent lecture-rooms. Lame dogs, desperately clawing at stiles in study and library, might take heart from the sweet sounds, recalled to the knowledge that there are more things in heaven and earth than are dreamed of even by tripos examiners.

Considering the amount of *angst* that broods over Cambridge in the

May Term, it is wonderful how gaily the public face of youth continues to shine. The river-side lawns along the Backs are littered with reclining figures on the warm afternoons. Punts go up and down with

*"If we'd worked reasonably hard in Michaelmas and Lent
we could have avoided this frantic last minute rush."*

a fair similitude to the thronging armadas of May Week. True, there are books, too: virtuous-looking volumes propped on knees, fluttering note-books spread on the grass. Conscience doth make cowards of us all. But the watcher on the bridge by Clare, or King's, or Trinity, is unlikely to sense an air of studious calm. Only the green cascades of the weeping willows wear an aspect of depression, and they are so elegantly beautiful in their narcissistic pose that one can only suppose them to be dreaming of the madrigals that will be sung on the river in June. Away from the river, where college windows look down upon the brightening lawns, every window-seat has its perching, shirt-sleeved occupant, turning the pages as the hours creep quietly towards tea-time. Really reckless men, or men who have compressed a great deal of leaf-turning into the weeks and months of winter, stand about in gleaming white at Fenners or on college cricket fields. The eights of the May boats are kicking their way past Midsummer Common, and every tennis-lawn is booked up from lunch to Hall time. Even at the University Library men and women creep forth into the prison-yard between the high walls for a stroll and a smoke as the long afternoon passes on.

'Thank God that some of them still regard their university years as an interim period in the slavery of life,' reflects Mr. Stock as he looks forth from his high window, *Times* crossword on knee.

'They'll have to pay for this, some of them,' Dr. Skinner snarls inwardly, as he spots two of his pupils swinging tennis-rackets as they cross his path to the tutorial office.

'*Mens sana in corpore sano*,' murmurs the Chaplain happily as he sets out for the tow-path.

'Just time for a quick one,' says Alistair Wynne as he cuts a corner across the sacred grass on his bicycle and pedals frantically in the direction of the university bathing sheds with the bursar's furious eyes boring into his back. On the way he overtakes several familiar donnish figures bent upon the same objective. They include the greatest living literary critic, and Cyril Tompion, and 'the laziest Fellow in Cambridge'. After his plunge in the stone-cold waters of the Cam, Alistair suns himself for a few minutes on the grass verge in company with some of the most distinguished academic flesh of the university. There are times when even a don may resemble a forked radish.

Jonathan Fowkes, punting his parents up to Grantchester, raises his pole in solemn salute as he catches sight of his near-naked tutor on the bank. This is the ideal situation in which to encounter a don when one has one's parents in tow – perched on the tail-board of a swinging craft, with twenty feet of water to starboard. No need, now, for a screwing-up of the mouth as one announces the distinguished presence.

"Don't look now," says Jonathan calmly. "I'll say when."

He gives the punt a mighty thrust forward and trails his pole to steady and straighten its course as his parents gaze with mild curiosity at the lawn strewn with recumbent effigies.

"The lanky one, third from the right. Green trunks and hairless chest. England's leading authority on Real Property."

Beyond the gasworks, stroking the second May boat towards Grassy, Duncan Macleod is staring into the sharp face of little Thwaites under the beak of its cox's cap, and marvelling at the man's progress in courtesy. Six months ago he couldn't stir hand or foot in a boat without uttering the most fearful imprecations. Blasting to hell was his mildest oath. Now he observes the cox's code of manners as if he were born with the rudder-lines in his hands. The Third Jesus boat, loitering ahead, is requested to make way.

"May I pass you, sir?" Mr. Thwaites calls out, with a long 'a' to his 'pass'.

"You may, sir," the Jesus cox replies.

"Thank you, sir," Mr. Thwaites says, and passes.

Really, Duncan reflects, there is education going on everywhere in this wonderful world. He proceeds to carry on his own, '*In* ... Out ... *One* ... Out ... The *Bill* of Rights ... *Clause* one ...'

No harm in reading history, as the great Steve Fairbairn would have said. Recite your dates as you roll your wrists. Between the *Pike and Eel* and Ditton *Plough* it is possible to cover the main constitutional cases in Gardiner's Documents of the Puritan Revolution, and a bit more.

Philip Hughes-Browne sits in the pavilion at Fenners, a loose-leaf note-book on his knees, waiting to bat at number seven. His lips move silently over the main facts about the Investiture Contest, like a priest at his breviary. He knows that he might just as well have left his note-book at home. Yet it provides something to hang on to while the butterflies flutter under his belt. Will another wicket fall before close of play? Will he have to go in as 'night-watchman' to play out time? A bit unfair on a freshman in his third match for the university. ... Number six is hanging on like a junior Trevor Bailey. Number two has been out there all the afternoon, and looks as if he may be there again to-morrow. The humiliation of the Emperor Henry IV at Canossa is as nothing when compared to the humiliation of Philip Hughes-Browne making a duck at Fenners. ... Number six gets an outside edge at last, and is caught at second slip. ... Number six comes slowly back to the pavilion. ... Number seven drops Henry IV into his cricket-bag, adjusts his pad-straps, tucks his bat under his arm, and goes forth fiddling with his his gloves. He passes Number six at the foot of the pavilion steps.

"Watch that spot on the off," Number six mutters.

"Thanks," Philip acknowledges the tip. "I've been watching it since tea."

Pope Hildebrand has been standing on that spot for hours waiting for unwary Emperors. The Protestant soul of Philip Hughes-Browne is roused. He plays out time, making twelve in a little under an hour. Good enough for a freshman at Number seven, he thinks. So does everyone else. Number seven goes back to college watched by the unacknowledged shade of Sir Henry Newbolt. After Hall, he finishes off Hildebrand.

Mr. Zogropoulos is still copying out back questions in the library. Albert of Africa is as calm as a mill pond as he methodically mops up useful facts about the English Legal System with Mr. Shalimar. Between bouts of 'hearing' each other, they play croquet in the paddock. The fashion for this ladylike pastime has taken a strange hold upon Cambridge undergraduates of late. It is said to be part of the Victorian revival, the movement that has put the girls into hooped skirts and brought the most hideous bric-à-brac to the adornment of undergraduate living-rooms, along with the cult of Betjeman, beards, and swelling congregations in college chapels. Dons approve of it. Stooping to their games of bowls in the Fellows' Garden, they smile happily to hear the quiet clock of mallets keeping time to the soft knock of their woods. And presently, as the spring-tide evenings lengthen out, the news goes round that the nightingales have come back to the copses around Madingley. Walking out to Madingley at the rise of the moon begins to rival in popularity the spring-time nocturnal visits to the orchards of Grantchester. People tell each other once more that the Cambridgeshire countryside is not uninteresting, after all, if you know where to go.

And yet, as the merry month of May enters upon its fourth week, all these delights are touched with the dawn-light strengthening in the windows of the *Conciergerie*, or the guttering candle-light of the Duchess of Richmond's Ball. Day by day, now, and hour by hour, the faces of one's friends begin to disappear. The crowds on river and lawn and playing field and library benches dwindle from sight. Fenners lies green and empty beneath the sun. The breathless hush in the close spreads to streets and cafés and college courts. Only at morning, and shortly after noon, the black-gowned multitudes swarm momentarily in the sunshine, parading in battalions to the Examination Schools, the Corn Exchange, the Guildhall, and the scores of labs and libraries and museums that serve for the nonce as improvised torture-chambers. Men come into Hall at evening, thoughtful, chastened, or defiantly gay. Bronzed faces begin to develop pale edges. For an hour or two the pulse of life quickens again. Then, as night comes down, life holds its breath once more behind lighted windows where, long into the night, the unready toil ill-advisedly over note-books against the advancing day. Here and there the lights tremble at the reverberation of manly voices raised in song where some fortunate beings celebrate the end of their labours. For tripos examinations are staggered, and those who stagger out before the rest are unmindful of those who have still to labour on. The dean has put up his customary notice begging 'gentle-men who have completed their examinations' to remember that there are others, less fortunate, whose rest should be respected. The struggle naught availeth. As things have been they remain. Only 'men at work' can deal effectively with men at play.

That rare bird, the man without an examination (left, by some quirk of regulations, with only the obligation to gain a certificate of 'diligent study'), skulks around the place like a pariah. All his laughing complacency during the past weeks has left him, now. He almost, but not quite, wishes that he made one with his fellows in the ranks at their desks under the eye of the invigilator, a dedicated scribe toiling in silence where the myriad penpoints crepitate over the square miles of feint-ruled paper. He wanders about looking in vain for some one with whom to share his melancholy solitude. From some high windows of the Guildhall or the engineering labs, he seems to hear the sad, sweet voice of his friend:

> Ah, Moon of my Delight who know'st no wane,
> The Moon of Heav'n is rising once again:
> How oft hereafter rising shall she look
> Through this same Garden after me – in vain!

There is only one thing to do, now. Go to the *Mill*, or the *Mitre*, or the *Baron of Beef*, and turn down an empty glass.

May Week

Men and women come out of examination rooms like sleep-walkers. Instead of candles, they carry very white-looking sheets of printed paper. They walk slowly, unsteadily, poring over these sheets in company with their friends, telling each other what they 'said' on this question or on that, disputing rather half-heartedly, listening reluctantly to 'right' answers propounded by the better-informed, rejecting scornfully 'wrong' answers propounded by the obviously ill-instructed. They complain, they ridicule, they rejoice – in moderation.

"What was it like, John?"

"Lousy. Not a thing one might have expected to come up. How was yours?"

"I think I've tricked them."

"That sod, the Tar Baby, has been wasting my time for the last six months. Red herrings all the way."

"Didn't I tell you not to go to lectures?"

"Still, they've got my four prepared cherries, and I hope it gives them the belly-ache."

"I had not believed it possible to set any question on Real Property that had not occurred during the last ten years. I have grossly underrated the ingenuity of our examiners."

"Anyway, they ought to give you *some* marks for showing you know *something*. . . ."

The fatal thing is to go and look it up after the event. Post-mortems, after that short walk back to college, are to be shunned. No decent supervisor will entertain them. Best go on the river, or get drunk.

Now it is the turn of the unfortunate examiners. The vast parcels of spoilt paper are unloaded at their doors, and for about three weeks the recipients will remain invisible by night and day, except when they are to be observed trudging wearily into each other's rooms for meetings. An examiner on the prowl is always to be identified by the sheaf of scripts with green string-tabs hanging out of the broken-sealed envelope under his arm. Young examiners like to be seen going to and fro with the fate of a still younger generation tucked under their arms. No one takes any notice of them. The young show their good taste by passing them with averted eyes. Time enough to take notice three weeks hence when the lists go up on the screens outside the Senate House. The young will never believe that it is a great deal worse to examine than to be examined.

Now is the time for a black-out, or a brain-wash. Almost everyone has been promising himself the pleasures of total idleness for weeks past. At the very least, one has looked forward to being able to read all the things one has been prevented from reading by the exigencies of 'work'. Daffyd Evans has had it in mind to retire to a suitable meadow up the river with Iris Murdoch. Little Thwaites plans to lie in bed until midday between Agatha Christie and Simenon. Mr. Zogropolous intends to lie in bed. Philip Hughes-Browne and Duncan Macleod are going to give a bottle-party to end all bottle-parties. Peter Plummer has arranged to wash his brain in the company of certain third-year classical scholars at the *Bridge Hotel* at Clayhithe. In the event, all these plans fall a little flat. Most people collapse into an armchair in their rooms, drink a few bottles of beer from the Buttery with kindred spirits equally deflated, and go to bed where they sit. Mr. Zogropolous, it turns out, is the wisest after all. Not until the third day after the end of the tripos do most people wake up to the possibilities of freedom. And then, like the English people as reviled by Jean-Jacques Rousseau, they proceed to show that they do not deserve it by the use they make of it. They at once deliver themselves over to new task-masters: boat captains, ball committees, play producers, impresarios of every kind. Their zest for hard labour will now exceed all that has gone before. From this time forth, the young will show themselves more luminous, more vocal, more *dévot*, more tireless of mind and body, than at any other time of the year.

These new tyrannies are not really new. College ball committees have been sporadically active for weeks and months past. Posters have been up since April. Tickets have been canvassed, and bought, at anything between three and seven guineas, all through the term. The harassed young don who serves as chairman of the ball committee, i.e. as financial watch-dog over the enthusiasts who want to get the best band in London, unlimited champagne, and the latest thing in flood-lighting, has been haunted by 'guarantees' of solvency from the first moment of his appointment. Nor is he alone in his anxieties. The Dean has had sixty-seven applications for leave to hold 'going-down' parties. The steward has entered upon his annual struggle with the kitchen manager and the butler over the serving of food, and liquor, for supper-parties in college rooms on the eve of balls, college concerts, the Footlights' revue, let alone the provision of a putative Bump supper for the Boat Club on the last night of the May Races. Silas Stock has delivered his annual threat to book accommodation at the *Bull* at Long Melford in order to enjoy a little peace and quiet – a threat which he never carries out, but which raises a good deal of fierce debate on the rights of resident Fellows to pursue the even tenor of their ways despite the dislocation inflicted upon college arrangements by the festive activities of the young. Everyone knows that on the night of the ball, Silas Stock will put on an ancient set of tails and a once-white tie, in order to amble round the marquee and the supper-tent for an hour towards midnight, and that he will beam like a superannuated frog.

But, first things first. Before the fairy-lights go on in the gardens and the bands strike up in the canvas ballrooms, the Free Foresters must be beaten at Fenners and the order of boats must be bumped out on the river. The last important match before the Eleven goes on tour, which ends at Lord's, is a quiet, friendly affair, something of an exhibition match after the keen contests with visiting County teams and the tourists. Distinguished amateurs who made their debut at Fenners, not so very long ago, have come back to play against distinguished amateurs of the future. It is the kind of match to which one may suitably take friends and relations for an afternoon in the sun. The time and the mood are ripe for instructing the American cousin on the precise meaning of a backward short-leg or a silly mid-off. The time and the mood are also propitious for Philip Hughes-Browne, released from the menaces of Hildebrand, to score a century and make sure of his Blue. Oddly enough, in the absence of papal and other pressures, he gets a duck in the first innings and five in the second. His average for the season sinks from twelve to nine, and the vision of a blue cap fades into the deeper blue of the afternoon sky above the roofs of Hughes Hall. Another freshman's dream is over. But there will be

The Old Mill, an engraving by Gwen Raverat

Degree Day – a characteristic scene

another year, and another after that, and Philip will continue to believe in his luck until Lord's.

The May Races begin on the first or the second Wednesday in June, according to the vagaries of the calendar at the hands of a moveable Easter. They go on every evening until Saturday, the day after Full Term ends. College balls begin on the following Monday, by which time rowing men will be out of training (and a good many men will have gone down). There will be balls at various colleges until the following Wednesday. This means that May Week, properly speaking, extends between two Wednesdays in June; one in term, and the other outside it. If you are going to 'keep a May Week' in the full sense, you have to stay up for at least three days after the end of term. Nobody minds this very much, with the possible exception of tutors and examiners, and they can be conveniently forgotten. Indeed, they have been known to forget themselves on occasion. Dancing all night after interviewing pupils and marking scripts all day is, at any rate, a change of work. And if an examiner turns up at an examiners' meeting in white tie and tails on Tuesday morning, after the First and Third Trinity Ball, it is always possible that he may take a less exacting view of borderline cases. It is just as well that an examiner should be more easily satisfied on some occasions than on others. Free ball tickets for examiners (though not for tutors) have often been mooted on college ball committees.

Mr. and Mrs. Frank Thwaites have come down from Lancashire to see young Frankie cox the Second Boat to victory. Frankie's boat rows in the third out of the seven divisions in the Mays. The idea is, the Thwaites parents are given to understand, that Frankie's boat shall catch, or bump, the third Jesus boat, immediately in front of it, and escape being caught, or bumped, by the second Downing boat which rows behind it. Mr. Thwaites frequently expresses the opinion that the system is crazy, and that there is bound to be a champion mix-up. Mrs. Thwaites holds her breath tight and prepares to invoke the Mother of God to save her son from being drowned when the crash comes. Frankie, swathed in a gorgeous scarf, a braided blazer, and a pair of hairy-looking flannels several sizes too big for him, settles his peaked cap well over his eyes, and makes off grimly for the starting-station – a spot conveniently down-river, beyond sight of the milling crowds of the tow-path. He has provided them with a large light-blue race-card which bears his name at the bottom of the listed crew of the boat, among a vast and perplexing array of others, all arranged in seven columns according to the Order of Boats. This card his mother will have framed when she gets back to Lancashire, with Frankie's name underlined. At present she uses it as a fan, for the day is muggy, with thunderclouds coming up from the south-west.

"Stay where you are," is Frankie's final command. "Keep on the hedge side of the path. For God's sake don't start running with the crowd. This path will be a blasted stampede once we come in sight."

"Promise you won't bump too hard, Frankie," his mother pleads.

"Leave the lad alone," Mr. Thwaites commands. "You give it 'em, Frankie, and we'll pull you out if need be."

Face to face with his father's Lancashire aggressiveness, cox suddenly becomes politely blasé.

"We shall catch them at Grassy," he announces, swallowing a yawn. "When you see the cox of the boat in front put his hand up, you will know that we have registered the bump. You will then see both boats come in to the bank. Don't expect me to come ashore. . . . See you at the boat-house. . . . Cheery-bye."

He is gone. The crowd thickens. Everyone seems to be moving from right to left. After an interminable time, a gun goes off distantly on the left, and a roar of voices swells up beyond the bend. Then, as the leading boat comes in sight, everyone seems to be moving from left to right again.

"Here they come," Mr. Thwaites announces.

They come. The Thwaites press, and are pressed, into the hedge, almost swept away by the thronging, yelling, running throng of the tow-path. Young men in blazers zig-zag through the torrent on bicycles, bellowing through megaphones. Men and girls run shoulder to shoulder.

"Oh, well rowed, Jesus!"

"Come on Lady Maggie! You've got 'em!"

"Don't dawdle. Did anyone see. . . ."

"Jees-us! Chri-i-st's! Emma – Emma – Emma! Hall – Hall – Hall! . . ."

Bells and rattles, megaphone voices, howls and shrieks and surging cheers. A length beyond Grassy Corner, the boat – the only boat on the river – thrusts itself in a final spurt to overlap its quarry by inches. The cox of the Third Jesus boat raises his hand, and a spent crew let their oars feather the water and drift into the bank.

Mr. and Mrs. Thwaites stagger out from the hedge-side and limp after the trailing crowd.

"Champion," says Mr. Thwaites. "Champion."

"Was it?" says his wife, nursing her corns. "I didn't see a blessed thing. . . . Was Frankie all right?"

"All right?" says Mr. Thwaites. "I'll say he was all right."

Indeed, Mr. Thwaites is by this time persuaded that the whole thing is all right. He will stay and see the other two divisions, far beyond Mrs. Thwaites' tea-time. With the re-appearance of Frankie, flushed with victory, and in the company of a young man whose name, she gathers, is 'Duncan Stroke' Mrs. Thwaites decides that it was well worth while to hold out until the end, after all.

That evening, Frankie disappears with the injunction that no enquiries are to be made for him until morning. Parents of victorious crews must dine alone on Bump Supper nights. When next they see Frankie his parents find him rather pale and silent. Mr. Stroke looks somewhat chastened, too. From information later received, it appears that Mr. Stroke expended enormous energies on the previous evening by performing a frenzied Maori war-dance on the High Table in the appreciative presence of the Master, the dean and the Senior Tutor; while little Mr. Thwaites left most of the skin of his knees and elbows on the roof of the chapel, where the morning light discovers a bed, ready made-up with sheets, blankets, and other necessary accoutrements. Alfred, the head porter, and several staircase-men, are busy dismantling it, and getting down to earth, when the Thwaites parents pass through the court on the Sunday morning after the night before.

"What tricks they get up to." is Mrs. Thwaites' comment.

"Champion," says Mr. Thwaites. "Champion."

They will stay for the college concert in the afternoon before driving back to the north with Frankie, and all Frankie's kit, stowed in the back. For every college has its concert, or its play, or both, at the end of the May Term. College courts and gardens are ideally suited to such performances. Providing the weather permits, King Richard the Second will descend over the leads of Queens' cloister, and Julius Caesar will die beneath the capitoline portico of Downing dining-hall. And on a grey evening of cold wind and spitting rain, all Cambridge, town and gown, will crowd on to King's lawn to hear the Madrigal Society sing sweet songs in their tethered punts under King's bridge.[1] The most memorable *moment musical* of May Week is the moment when the punts begin to move slowly downstream, bearing away the madrigal singers to the dying melody of *The Silver Swan*. Not the greyest of summer evening skies, nor the most persistent drizzle of June, can quench the triumphant loveliness of that wandering music in the Backs.

Elsewhere, the festivities of this crowning week are better able to take evasive action in face of the vagaries of the Cambridge climate. Braziers are posted in college courts, ready to go into action if the night of the ball turns unfriendly. Weather-proof pavilions with blazing lights; dining-halls ready panoplied for suppers and sitting -out; canopied paths from one sheltering roof to another; all these things ensure a modicum of happiness even on the wettest night in June. All that is lost by bad weather is the punt trip up to Grantchester orchard for breakfast in the summer dawn. The dauntless few will do it, even if it means draggled finery, rather than forfeit the proud sense of ultimate achievement. For the sisters and the girl-friends have heard of this, among so much else, as the magic hour of May Week, the hour when the partner of a night may turn into the partner of a life-time.

May Week is among the things in the Cambridge year that never changes. This is odd when one considers that the social world that flourished when May Week assumed its present character has changed out of all recognition, no less at Cambridge than elsewhere, and that a large proportion of undergraduates are, to a greater or less degree, 'state pensioners'. The cost of a double ticket for a May Week ball, a tail-suit (even if hired), and such incidentals as suppers, breakfasts, taxis, adds up to a considerable sum. 'May Week' has not yet become an acceptable item among the fees that public authorities are prepared to pay, and everyone knows that 'maintenance grants' are forever under

[1] But nowadays on Trinity backs.

fire as stingy and inadequate. Yet the May Week revellers are drawn from no exclusive social strata, and May Week on the cheap simply would not be May Week. The essence of the thing consists of making a splash or cutting a dash. No doubt dealers in the current cant attribute the whole thing to a plot on the part of the Establishment to turn outsiders into insiders, or at least into its lackeys. No doubt, once a man has put on a white tie and tails and been stared at by the ladies of the town as he descends at the college gates with his dazzling partner on his arm, he will never be the same again. No doubt a white tie is the mark of the beast. No doubt the women are to blame. Weak of social conscience, competitively vain, victims of the life-force, the poor creatures clutch at the chance of a lifetime to tame a savage, but remunerative beast, for the cause of hearth and home. The fact remains that they go. And at six o'clock in the morning they will have their photograph taken in a 'ball group' against the background of stately buildings that have watched their gyrations all night along without batting an eyelid. The men look devilish rakish in their white waistcoats by daylight. The women look as fresh as paint. For this, after all, is the moment of truth, and it will be recorded forever in a thousand drawing-rooms up and down England. Friends will be suitably impressed. A touch of snobbery makes the whole world kin.

The Turn of the Tide

By the second week in June, the tide is definitely on the turn. It recedes unevenly, almost imperceptibly. There is no mass exodus in June to compare with the mass inrush in October, January and April. Like old soldiers, undergraduates at the end of the May Term simply fade away. The earliest to fade are the freshmen, for 'last in first out' is the general rule. Not that freshmen any longer admit to the name. No one is really fresh at the end of May Term. It is the one time in the year when the whole university population is, if not middle-aged, at least adolescent. Second-year men take on the look of third-year men in the making. Third-year men set their teeth, or sigh with relief, or think of ingenious ways of hanging on for a fourth year. A favourite way is to enrol at the Education department (for there really is such a thing, strange as it may seem) for what is horribly, and incorrectly, known as 'Dip. Ed.'[1] But, whether you go early or late, there is still 'the final *exeat*'[2] to be got: that chit of paper which informs whomsoever it may concern (chiefly the head porter) that Mr.X is permitted to go out of residence. Moderate queues outside tutorial rooms are forming for this purpose at stated 'tutorial hours' all through the last days of full term. Here men greet each other, and sometimes see the last of each other, with false hilarity.

"Hi, John, you on your way out, too?"

"Thank God."

"Fleeing from the wrath to come? Or are you coming back for Degree day?"

"Can't afford to take it by proxy, can you?"

"Mine won't be worth it, anyway."

"Nonsense, you're safe for a starred first."

"Telling me. Mine's a Special."[3]

"Got a job on hand?"

"Sufficient unto the day. . . . What are you doing?"

"Dip. Ed. The last infirmity of noble minds. Even the professor doesn't believe in it, they say."

"I've heard that. Takes three years at this place to cure a man of any misplaced belief in education. . . ."

As between departing freshmen, the conversation goes somewhat differently:

"Have a good vac., Philip."

"Thanks. And you. Give my love to primary production, Daffyd."

"Not a hope, man. Local Government offices. Road Fund licences

---

[1] Teachers in training actually take a 'certificate of education'. The diploma, involving original research means a further year. However, the fourth year fledgling still says he is taking 'Dip. Ed.' – very much as *Varsity Handbook* decorates its cover with a design of graduate squares, with their characteristic long tassels. Ante-dating their seniority is an occupational disease of undergraduates.

[2] Literally: 'he may go'.

[3] A part of the ordinary, as distinct from an honours, degree. It is sometimes hoped that the name will impress backward parents with a suggestion of distinction. It impresses no one else. (*See* p. 30, note 2.)

and all that. That's the best a man is fit for after three terms in this place. Shop-soiled, that's what we are."

"Beat, are we? Or sick? Learn to play cricket and cultivate a healthy outlook."

"Gr-r-r-r-r."

"See you at Lord's."

More or less angry young men have been job-hunting since early spring. Those looking for vacation work generally find it near home, although 'See you at Butlin's' is still a fairly common form of *vale* between departing undergraduates. Those looking for a future have a variety of expedients. They pore over advertisement columns in the City library. They get their names on the books of scholastic agencies. They attend meetings held in college rooms by representatives of 'business'; gentlemen in charcoal-grey suitings and spotless collars, who expatiate on the delights of 'personnel management', salesmanship and advertising. The City, the Civil Service, even the Church, send recruiting agents down to 'talk to young men who may be interested'. The official university agency is, of course, the University Appointments Board, known unjustly to the young as the Disappointments Board, mainly because the young tend to expect more of it than it can possibly give. The Board consists of several secretaries, each covering certain fields of employment. It is a complex institution, combining the activities of selection board, advice bureau, employment agency, and Father Figure. When the initial form has been filled up, indicating inclinations and qualifications, the applicant goes to Chaucer Road for an interview with one or other of the secretaries. It is important to remember that the Board lives in the house that Lord Acton built for himself in Cambridge and that the entrance bears the inscription (in invisible ink): ALL POWER CORRUPTS. . . .[1] This is not intended as an alternative to ABANDON HOPE . . . but only to recommend modesty of aspiration. Remember also that the secretary who interviews you is hand in glove with your tutor, and probably knows far more about you than you know yourself. Unless you have determined unshakably what you want to do in life, this gentleman will help you to decide what you are fit to do, and there is often a great deal of difference. A

[1] The Women's Appointments Board is, appropriately, under the same roof.

very large proportion of budding graduates pass through the hands of the Appointments Board, and a considerable proportion of them have very little idea of what they want to do, let alone what they are fit for. This applies most notably to men reading arts subjects. Doctors and lawyers are predestined men, and men of science – more especially engineers – are scrambled for like gold-dust. Teachers, staving off the evil day with their mythical 'Dip. Eds.', are likely to be taken care of without much trouble. The rest – historians, modern linguists, economists, geographers, literary men – these are the main problem. For them there are undoubtedly round enough holes if they refrain from accentuating their squareness. The Board is in close touch with a vast variety of fields of employment. There is really no reason why a man with an arts degree should assume the style of Jimmy Porter and his sweet-stall. Give the Board a chance, apply early (in your second year, preferably), remember that you live in an age of technological prestige, and take what is coming to you with a smile. You can always change later. The Board keeps your file indefinitely, and is quite accustomed to men 'writing back'.

"What sort of class do you expect to get in the tripos?" the secretary is likely to ask.

Be careful, here, because your tutor will already have answered this one. It is safest to reply:

"Some sort of second. A two-one if I'm lucky."

The second class is very comprehensive, and in some Arts subjects it positively bulges with mediocrity. As for firsts, the percentage varies greatly between the various subjects. In Classics it is as high as 22 per cent, and in the Natural Sciences it amounts to about 13.6 per cent. In History the percentage is about a half of the figure in Natural Sciences, and in English it sinks to 5 per cent, or lower, while in Law and Economics it is lower still.[1] These disparities sometimes cause alarm and despondency, more especially among those who complain of being 'branded for life as a second' because, as they are careful to put it, they 'chose the wrong subject'. They lead to loose talk about the need for more 'co-ordination' (blessed word) among the

[1] Taking Arts subjects as a whole, and excluding Classics, it may be said that the normal percentage of Firsts is about half that in the Natural Sciences.

Faculties. Yet the fact is that these disparities simply reflect very real, and quite natural, differences between disciplines. It is obvious that examiners in different subjects are looking for different things. It is easy enough for the men of the 'humanities' (another sacramental expression) to say that the scientists are looking for good scientists while examiners in the humanities are looking for educated men. What else could, or should, scientists be looking for? Subjects with a high technical or scientific content are only to be taken successfully by men who have been very carefully selected after several years of specialization at school. When they come to their tripos they are examined on their special aptitude for a specialized type of work, and a fair proportion of their achievement can only be judged on a 'right-or-wrong' basis. To a great extent, this applies to Classics as well as to the Natural Sciences. The exactitude and precision required for the successful pursuit of classical studies will always ensure that a high proportion of entrants in this subject are of above average aptitude to read it at the university. On the other hand, a very large number of young men come up to read History and kindred subjects without any specialized, let alone technical, ability at all. They come up in search of what the old 'ordinary degree' was supposed to give: a general education. History, at least, will give them some knowledge of economics, law, and politics, together with a certain amount of training in straight thinking and clear writing. They will be tested not only on acquired knowledge, but on general qualities of mind. Beyond a very elementary point, there are few 'rights', and even fewer 'wrongs', that can be tested in 'arts subjects'. The stringent attitude of examiners towards the award of first classes in what the scientists like to call the 'more inspirational subjects' is a highly proper one. There is a great deal of difference between a first class mind and first class ability in a certain subject. It may be added that it is difficult to condemn a man in an arts subject as an outright failure.[1]

None of these considerations, however, prevent Dr. Skinner from working himself up into a red-nosed frenzy every June over the

[1] These, and other, considerations, are constantly prompting examiners in arts subjects to raise their sights. Perhaps, also, they account for some of the anxiety shown by some historians to insist that traditional distinctions between scientific disciplines are out-moded or unreal.

scarcity of first classes outside the Natural Sciences. He still wonders furiously why the half-starved literary subjects lag so far behind his own laurel-crowned lads. For many days before tripos lists are posted he accosts any senior member of the college he meets, who happens to be examining, with the encouraging demand, half mendicant, half accusatory:

"Got any firsts?"

At the tutorial office he employs a clerkly runner who posts to and fro between the college and the Senate House, bearing the news, grim or gay, to be embodied in the great sheet of statistics on his desk. The clerks run a sweepstake on the total number of college first classes for the year. Their master commends their enthusiasm. Their devotion to the interests of the college, he regrets to say, greatly exceeds that of the Fellows of the college.

"My dear fellow, you can't have it both ways," Silas Stock observes, as the lop-sided lists begin to come in. "If you will insist on filling up the college with your Natural Stinkers. . . . Anyway, I see young Plummer's done it again. Going on the basis that one first in Classics is worth ten in Natural Sciences, things are about even."

This is the kind of frivolity which causes Dr. Skinner to avoid the company of the Senior Tutor at this time of the year.

Letters and telegrams, of their various sorts, are going out from the college office every day, now, all signed by the Senior Tutor. Telegrams congratulating men on their first classes; letters merely informing men that they have been placed in the upper or lower division of the second class, or in the third class; other letters regretting that men have been awarded the consolation prize of the ordinary degree, or a part thereof, or that they have simply failed. Some of these last are told to hold themselves in readiness to return to Cambridge in case they are required to appear before the Master and Fellows when they hold their grand inquest on examination results on the eve of degree day. At that meeting, men who have distinguished themselves may be elected into scholarships or exhibitions; prizes, in terms of value in books, will be awarded; failures will be admonished and required to show cause why they should not be sent out of residence. Very few will suffer the extreme penalty. After all, once a college has taken a man to its bosom, it is reluctant to let him go without affording him every reasonable opportunity to proceed to a degree.

Most men hear the verdict at home, by telegram or letter. Tripos results are not published until about a fortnight after the end of full term. Third-year men, who will be coming back to take their degrees, may very well be around on the day when the lists go up outside the Senate House, and thereby are enabled to enjoy, or suffer, the experience of reading the news from the Screens with their own eyes when the clerk pins up the long galley-like sheets at nine o'clock in the morning. The age-old custom by which the chairman of the examiners used to read the lists from the gallery inside the Senate House is falling into desuetude. The days of riotous crowds thronging the floor and galleries to cheer and hoot and to lower the wooden-spoon for the last man on the list of the mathematical tripos, have long passed away. Now, it is a matter of treading on the heels and breathing down the necks of the people in front while craning one's own neck to read the writing on the wall, starting at the bottom.

Considering that so many men have gone down, it is astonishing how large are the crowds in Senate House Yard at nine o'clock on these late June mornings. Not only third-year men waiting for degree day, but men of other years who have contrived to stay on by one excuse or another; men from overseas who may be staying in England throughout the vacation; dons who have not received inside information; girl-friends, landladies, college servants, tutors' clerks, shopmen who have engaged to inform their customers by pre-paid telegram, journalists on the look-out for early news of intellectual achievements by rowing Blues, cricket Blues, and other persons of eminence. All through the morning, as the clear sweet chimes of St. Mary the Great quarter and count the hours, the crowds cluster like swarming bees before the Screens, thickening, thinning out, seeming ever to dissolve as men shoulder their way out with grim or smiling faces, and yet forever swelling up again as fresh contingents shoulder their way in with faces set in stoical anticipation. The low buzz of conversation is mainly ejaculatory.

"Peter's got his first, again."

"John's made it. Third time lucky."

"Look at our Stella, up there among the two-ones. . . ."

"Do they ever make mistakes?"

"Not in my experience, old boy. They've given me a second again."

"I say, it's an absolute bloody scandal. . . . They've got the thing upside down."

"Never mind, Roger. You'll always be a first by his standards. They always penalise his pupils. He says so himself."

Duncan Macleod, copying down names and classes to send off by pre-paid wire for his absent friends, is in a trance-like state. He has found his own name in the upper division of the second class, at least half a class higher than he expected, and half a class higher than Philip Hughes-Browne. From an adjoining list he gleans the name of Daffyd Evans from among the two-ones. Daffyd will be secretly disappointed, although he has said throughout the year that anyone reading English in the light of the true faith must be content to suffer the persecution meted out to the faithful by purblind examiners. Duncan is delighted to discover Frankie Thwaites in the first class of the Preliminary examination in Natural Sciences. He remembers the warm, hopeful, proud face of Mrs. Thwaites, and is glad. Turning away to hurry to the post-office, he overtakes the slow-drifting figures of India and Africa. He can tell even from their rearward view that they have both got two-two's. Disappointed men go off in a hurry, heads down, hands in pockets, whistling softly. These two are like himself, men to whom Cambridge has now become a happy home, men for whom the tower of St. Mary the Great, and the soaring pinnacles of King's Chapel, and the shouldering red roofs of King's Parade, have become the familiar furniture of every day.

"My dear Macleod," Mr. Shalimar beams, taking his arm, "Allow me to buy you a coffee to celebrate this satisfactory moment. Albert and I are on our way to *The Anchor*. All seconds together, yes?"

"Where's Zog?"

"Mr. Zogropolous is in bed. He could not face it. We have undertaken to bring him the news."

"Hadn't you better hurry?"

"No, I think not," says the gentle Albert, rolling his liquid eyes sadly. "A man can always wait for a third class."

"Poor old Zog," Duncan reflects, cheerfully enough. "And he knew all the examiners, personally, one might say. . . ."

Degree Day

It is all over within little more than a month, the grand climacteric of the academic year: tripos examinations, May Week, tripos results, degree day. At Cambridge, the final agony is not sustained, the final triumphs are not postponed. Examiners distrust afterthoughts. They place no faith in *vivas*.[1] To summon men, and women, back to the university weeks after they have written their papers, in order to *viva* them for a first class, is no part of their design. Perhaps this robs decision of some of its dramatic suspense. Perhaps the man, or woman, who lacks complete coherence on paper may gain something from the opportunity to meet examiners face to face. Perhaps the glib journalistic writer may reveal his true stature when put to the verbal test. At Cambridge, whose quiet courts are dedicated to poetry and commonsense, they let things alone. *Hypothesis non fingo*, wrote Sir Isaac Newton, Cambridge's greatest son.

'General Admission', says the Diary, against two dates near the end of June, a Friday and a Saturday.

Is this where we came in? Can it be that the whole show is beginning again at the beginning? But no. For those most intimately concerned with the ceremonies at the Senate House on these two days, 'Admission' means not the beginning but the end. These are degree days, when the minted products of three years of Cambridge life are admitted at the Senate House and receive the hall-mark of the university before being put into circulation in the currency of the nation's life. For a few hours on these two days, James Gibbs' lovely palladian palace takes on something of the aspect of a factory working overtime on the conveyor-belt system. The 'graduands', processing in their dark suits and their fur-trimmed hoods, with their college praelectors beside them like corporals trimming the ranks, enter the Senate House by the east door

[1] *See* p. 220.

in fours. They re-appear, one by one, out of the north door in Senate House Passage, as 'graduates', to receive a handshake from the Master of their college, and/or their tutor, whereafter they skip round the outside of the building to join their friends and relations on the grass in Senate House Yard. There they pose in suitably sophisticated or deprecatory groups while fathers or brothers or fellow graduates or professional photographers from the town, snatch this mortal moment for immortality. It is, for very many of them, the first and last time that they will wear the white-trimmed hood of a Cambridge graduate. Half an hour later, hired hoods by the hundred will be back in the tailors' shops, having brought the men of business seven-and-sixpence or half-a-guinea a-piece. Future parsons and schoolmasters will buy their regalia, now, or in the near future. So will gentlemen from the more outlying regions of the Commonwealth. A fair number of these will also sit for their academic portraits with the town photographers. Literally 'sit', at a desk or table, with a closed volume at their elbow, and possibly a bachelor's 'square' drooping a tassel beside their brow. For the most part, however, the newly-fledged graduate is relieved to get out of fancy-dress. Probably his college has laid on a tea-party in the Fellows' Garden for his parents, his sisters and his cousins and his aunts. Thither he will now wend, *en famille*, a little proud, more than a little thankful, and wholly unable to discern within himself any transformation of soul or general consciousness at the hands of the Vice-Chancellor.

This is scarcely surprising. So many young men and women pass through the Senate House during the two days of General Admission that the whole business has inevitably something of the sausage-machine about it. The praelector, or 'Father' of the college, whose duty it is to present graduands for their degrees, generally does his best – perhaps at a 'graduands' breakfast' on the morning of the great day – to make men aware of the meaning of the forthcoming ceremony, but the unfortunate man is generally preoccupied with form rather than spirit. Will graduands remember that they must (repeat must) appear in dark (repeat dark) suits? Flannels, sports-jackets, sweaters, brown shoes, sandals, are definitely *out*. Decent (repeat decent) under-graduate gowns must be worn. Graduate hoods must be slung properly from the shoulders, and not (repeat not) inside out. White ties and bands must be worn neatly beneath the chin, and not (repeat not) under one ear.

It is when the praelector comes to describe the actual ceremony, that the first hints of mass-production creep into his discourse. Graduands will assemble ('parade' is a word to be avoided) outside the college chapel, where there will be a brief inspection. Anyone unsuitably attired will there and then be required either to remedy the matter, or to retire from the proceedings. . . . Graduands will then proceed ('move off' is best omitted) in column of fours to the Senate House, not marching, but maintaining good order. When the college's turn for Admission comes (colleges being admitted in order of seniority of foundation), graduands will follow the praelector through the east door and on to the floor of the Senate House. The praelector will then extend four fingers to the four graduands in the foremost rank (alphabetically arranged), thus. . . . Each of these four men will grasp a finger, and the praelector will present them to the Vice-Chancellor where he sits in his chair of state. He will lead them along in three paces, bowing to the Vice-Chancellor with suitable cap-raising each time, assuring the Vice-Chancellor that each in his turn is suitably endowed, both morally and intellectually, to receive the degree of Bachelor of Arts. Then, each man will kneel in turn on the cushion at the Vice-Chancellor's feet, and place his hands in an attitude of homage, thus . . . between the hands of the Vice-Chancellor. Where-upon, if all goes well, the Vice-Chancellor will utter the ancient formula[1] admitting the supplicant to his degree. All that remains is for the newly-made graduate to rise (taking care not to trip over the tail of his gown), bow low, and withdraw from the presence by the door on the right. Now, is that perfectly clear? Are there any questions?

All that will be said on this solemn occasion in the Senate House will be said in Latin. Graduands under instruction by their praelectors rarely, if ever, ask for a translation. If he is experienced in his job, the praelector generally goes on to conclude his rehearsal with a few words on the future.

---

[1] *Auctoritate mihi comissa addmitto te ad gradum Baccalaurei in Artibus in nomine Patris et Filii et Spiritus Sancti.*

"In a little more than three years from now, many of you will be returning to proceed to the degree of Master. This, as you will already be aware, involves no further examination, but only a fee of five pounds. This, you will be told by the ill-informed, is a scandal, especially in view of the fact that graduates of some more modern universities take the further degree of Master of Arts by examination. It is as well that you should know what to reply to this unworthy charge. In the first place, you should know – although you would be well-advised not to say so – that three years at Cambridge are the intellectual equivalent of seven years anywhere else, with one possible exception. In the second place. . . ."

There then follows a somewhat complicated historical account of how the medieval *trivium* (occupying three years) was followed by the *quadrivium* (occupying four years), so that it took seven years to attain to the Master's degree, very much as the apprentice in any other trade took seven years to become a Master of his craft; how the Elizabethan Statutes, which required seven years' residence for the Master's degree, were evaded and re-interpreted until it was accepted that the Bachelors might equally well go out of residence and make themselves useful for the last four years in teaching school or the cure of souls, 'following their books in the country'; in short, how with changing conditions and the coming of the tripos system, the *quadrivium* ceased to denominate a course of study at the university and came simply to be a period of time: a period of time spent (it was to be hoped) industriously and fruitfully elsewhere.

"I am confident, gentlemen," the praelector concludes, amidst general applause, "that your time will be thus spent during the next three to four years, so that when you return to take your M.A.'s you will have advanced appropriately in both learning and wisdom. Some of you may think that your education is now complete. Let me assure you that it is only just beginning, and that it will go on all through life. . . ."

Graduands are getting restless; they have heard this one before, or something like it. Thankful applause resounds through Hall as the praelector sits down. The Master is glancing at his watch and stubbing out his cigarette. He will not detain them, he declares, truthfully, as he

gets to his feet. He wishes only to bid them God's speed and good
fortune in all their undertakings; to remind them that the name and
fame of the college is in the keeping not only of those who live within
its walls, but also in the hands of those who have gone out into the
world. If they will permit him to do so, he will quote Burke.
(Permission is never refused, and he always quotes Burke.) The college
is what Burke called the State: a partnership. Not a partnership in some
low material concern like a trade in pepper or coffee calico or tobacco;
to be taken up for a little temporary advantage and to be dissolved at
the whim of the parties. It is rather a partnership in all science, in all
art, in every virtue and all perfection; a partnership between the living,
the dead and the yet unborn.

"Your names, gentlemen, will remain on the college boards:[1] the
college will remember you, and you – I trust – will remember the
college."

With a brief reference to the Building Fund, the Master sits down.
Thunderous applause, and exodus.

Throughout these proceedings, Peter Plummer, Senior Scholar,
and President of the Amalgamated Clubs, has sat on the Master's right
hand. Peter has an unbroken record of first classes, not to mention a
hockey Blue, a policeman's helmet, and an unrivalled collection of
public sign-boards. He is, although he hardly suspects it, a man whom
the college is fast deciding to take unto itself. The Minister of Education
has agreed to extend his State scholarship for a period of research
studies. Within a year, the college will elect him to a research Fellowship. Within another two years, the Faculty Board will invite him to
offer a short course of lectures. Then, if all goes well (as it certainly will),
a university appointment, an official Fellowship of his college, and
(if Silas Stock has his way, as he certainly will) a tutorship. During the
past six months, Silas Stock has been making up his mind that Peter
Plummer is what he calls 'tutorial timber'. Seasoning, carving and
polishing, he knows full well, take at least six years, and often more.
But it is important to keep an eye on the problem of what colleges call
'the tutorial succession'. The appointment of a new tutor will not

---

[1] There are no 'boards' in any literal sense. Colleges in almost all cases retain the names
of their members on their books for life, unless a man asks for his name to be removed
or the college orders its removal in consequence of disgraceful conduct.

become urgent until Silas Stock comes within sight of retirement, for he has long given up hope that Alan Skinner will depart for pastures new and suitably distant, and Alistair Wynne has long given up hope of a professional career at the Bar. He envisages Peter Plummer as a spare-wheel during the last year or two of his own career as a tutor, a spare-wheel whose tread it will be within his power to mould to his own tutorial ideal.

When Peter comes to say goodbye to his tutor after breakfast, Mr. Stock treats him to his customary display of busy-ness, the customary growling-wail of "Come in" at the knock, the customary fiddle with an unfinished letter as he sits at his desk with his back turned to the door. Only, when he turns about and sees the cheerful young face grinning at him with respectful familiarity, he gets up briskly, holds out both hands, and steers him to the familiar chair.

"Too early in the day for sherry," he decides. "Never too early for claret."

"Could I have a glass of beer, sir?" Peter proposes.

"To-day being to-day, I am prepared to pander to your beastly tastes. Don't expect me to share them."

They have their beer and claret, nodding to each other over the brim. They chat of this and that: the extension of the State scholarship, the proposed subject of research, the absurdity of the Ph.D. (one of Mr. Stock's *bêtes noires*).

"Keep out of that racket, if possible, my dear sir. Unless, of course, you don't mind seeing yourself in the same list as lab. boys who have succeeded in measuring the reproductive cycle of stoats, or the rate of flow of a viscous fluid through an iron pipe."

"Is there any alternative, sir?" Peter asks, wondering how Mr. Stock had kept himself out of the racket, or whether he had ever been in it. "One must have a further degree, I imagine, if one gets public money for research."

"Nonsense. Write a book. You'll have a further degree when you take your M.A., anyway, and that's all a gentleman has any right to ask or expect."

"All the same, sir, I gather that university appointments, outside Cambridge, do rather depend on it. . . ."

"Why worry with 'outside Cambridge'? Stay put, if you possibly can. You'll get some college supervision to do fairly soon. Publish a few articles on your research subject. Keep your fingers crossed and try not to annoy the members of your Faculty. There'll be plenty of time for that, later."

Peter grins more broadly than ever. When he rises to go, the grin vanishes and he finds speech difficult.

"I want to thank you for everything, sir," he gurgles. "I mean, everything you've done for me. . . ."

"Rubbish. What do you suppose the college pays me for? Anyway, I shall be seeing you again in October. . . . Where are you going for your holiday?"

"My people always go to Yarmouth."

"Break them of it. No, better still, pack them off to Yarmouth, and go to Greece."

Mr. and Mrs. Plummer have come up from Norwich to see their son take his degree. The neat little local government servant and his lady sit in the seats of the mighty for a time, watching the final thronging scene of the academic year on the floor of the Senate House; the milling Masters; the endless ranks of graduands advancing from the east door; the praelectors bobbing and bowing and capping as they present their men to the robed and muttering figure of the Vice-Chancellor where he sits in his chair of state; and at last, in a haze of black and white and scarlet, shuffling feet and muffled Latin and muted trumpets – Peter making his bow. Mrs. Plummer wipes away a tear as she follows her husband out through the throng of departing parents to the lawn of Senate House Yard, to meet the new-made Bachelor with a kiss.

"I couldn't hear what he said," she tells her son. "I mean, when the Chancellor leaned forward as you knelt before him. . . ."

"The *Vice*-Chancellor, mother," Peter corrects her gently.

"What *does* he say, Pete?" Mr. Plummer also wishes to know. "Whatever it is, I should think he must get pretty tired of saying it. . . . Hundreds and hundreds of times. . . ."

Peter smiles the esoteric smile of a double-first in classics.

"Oh, he just whispered in my ear: 'My lad, you 'ave done well. . . .' "

The Chimes at Midnight

Even as the latest generation of graduates departs in June, tutors are concerned with the next generation of undergraduates which will arrive in October. Meeting at the Lodge under the chairmanship of the Master, they survey the shape of things to come.

"Altogether it looks like being a fairly typical freshman year," the Master sums up. "Total population of the college up slightly. Composition, in terms of subjects, showing once more a slight increase in favour of the Natural Sciences. Numbers from the Public Schools somewhat in excess of numbers from Grammar Schools. On the whole, a familiar pattern, I think."

"All too familiar, Master, I fear," groans Silas Stock. "If our numbers continue to rise at the present rate, we shall soon cease to be a college and become a mere totality of men. Once the Natural Sciences catch up with the Humanities, we shall be well on our way to becoming a technical institute. The only consolation that I derive from our situation is the fact that we still attract a large proportion of our men from the Public Schools."

"What the Senior Tutor seems not to realize," says Alan Skinner, "is that this college, like a good many others, depends increasingly for its solvency on its undergraduates. . . . Unless we go in for numbers – within reason, of course – we shall be bankrupt within five years. As for the number of men reading Natural Sciences, we all know that the country must increase its trained scientists or die. Personally, I am all for the Public Schools. We all know that they turn out the best men because they are the best schools."

"In other words we ought to imitate the action of the ostrich?" Alistair Wynne inquires. "We know perfectly well that in all other matters we talk of 'giving a lead to the schools'. Only in this matter of admissions do we disclaim all responsibility, or even interest."

"I fail to see that we can do anything apart from making it perfectly plain that we take the best boys offered to us, without fear or favour," the Master avows.

"But do we, Master? Can we? How are we to know who are the best? Too often, I fear, 'the best' means the lad with a good interview technique and nice manners, things he has acquired fortuitously from home background and Public School training. I find that the Grammar School boy, who so often lacks these advantages, generally catches up sufficiently in these respects during his first year here, and quite often proceeds to beat the Public School product to a first in the tripos. But I do deplore the unfair start that the Public School boy enjoys in the competition to get here at all."

"All the same it is up to us to take the best men we can get," the Master insists. "Just that, and only that. The question whether it is fair that some boys can go to a Public School while others can't, is, I maintain, no business of ours."

"Not the ostrich, but Pontius Pilate?" Alistair murmurs. "At any rate, I think we might try to improve our powers of judgment, so that we can see through the accidental to the essential in both character and attainments."

"That is precisely what we pride ourselves on our ability to do," the Senior Tutor declares. "At least, those of us who have had sufficient experience as tutors. Do you realize that the best man in the college over the past three years – I refer to my pupil, Peter Plummer – came to us as a Norfolk Dumpling from the household of a poor clerk in the Norwich Post Office? That rather raw Grammar School product revealed his potentialities to me from the start. He has taken three firsts in a row, and served as President of the Amalgamated Clubs with great distinction. In fact, I see in that young man the makings of a future college tutor."

"Is he as good as all that?" Alan Skinner wonders, aloud. "I find it hard to believe."

"Oh, I'm not denying that we have our successes," Alistair concedes. "I'm not talking about the brilliant exceptions, but about the good average rank and file, the men who make up the bulk of every college, and rightly. They are the people who present us with our main problem. And, as I see it, unless we tackle it a great deal more perceptively than we are tackling it at present, we shall find ourselves subject to some sort of public inquiry into the whole question of college admissions."

"Heaven forbid," the Master exclaims a little breathlessly. "We all know what that would mean. It would be the first step towards setting up a university Admissions Board, with powers to compel the colleges to take in pre-determined quotas. And then – what becomes of college autonomy, the very essence of Cambridge as a university?"

"All the same, Master, we know quite well that there are many among us, nowadays, who are beginning to think that college autonomy has outlived its usefulness, even its possibility as a working principle, for the mid-twentieth century. After all, it grew up in an age and a society which have passed away. The future, I can't help thinking, belongs to universities, not to colleges."

"Are you thinking of resigning your tutorship, dear boy?" Silas Stock murmurs hopefully.

"No, I love the college, and I like being a tutor. I am merely trying to face the facts. We do, as a race, rather tend to sweep the dust under the carpet and then bury our heads in it, don't we?"

There is a profound silence, the silence of outraged good taste. The Master looks wistful and grieved. Silas Stock looks froggishly tolerant of youthful folly. Alan Skinner looks as if he may burst. It is the Master who speaks.

"I think you will admit, my dear Alistair, that nearly all the great things that Cambridge has done in the world have been done through the colleges. Even those changes that the colleges have resisted, in the first instance – I am thinking of the way certain colleges resisted the institution of our present excellent system of university lectureships, especially – have been achieved the more wisely and effectively because they had to pass through the fire of college criticism, the criticism of truly autonomous bodies."

"More than that," Silas Stock observes, "the colleges have not only survived these changes in the university. They have emerged stronger and more respected than ever."

"In my view," Alan Skinner adds, "the whole question of university-college relationships is a purely academic one."

"Naturally," Alistair retorts. "How could it possibly be anything else?"

To label any issue 'academic' is the most familiar academic way of putting an end to its discussion.

"I sometimes wonder," Silas Stock remarks, as he strolls back to his rooms with Dr. Skinner. "I really do wonder, quite often, what induced us to appoint our dear Alistair to a tutorship."

"I happen to know, my dear Silas, that you quite often wonder the same thing about me."

"Come, come, my dear Alan, these are bitter words, indeed, and quite untrue." To his own surprise, no less than to the surprise of Dr. Skinner, he finds himself tucking his arm beneath the bony elbow of the man of science. "We may have our little differences, but at least we are both good college men. So is the Master, of course. Oh yes, I think the college system will last our time. . . . By the way, my dear Alan, about young Plummer. . . ."

They go on together across the immemorial grass. For the best part of an hour they pace to and fro in the evening light, secure within the borders of their inviolable sanctuary, sacred to the feet of Fellows, beyond ear-shot of all lesser mortals.

The last luggage-laden family car has hummed away along Trumpington Street and into the London road. The last train has puffed out of Cambridge station. A profound hush has settled upon courts and lawns and gardens. Silas Stock lies in bed and listens to the silence as the clocks chime on to midnight and the voice of the fountain prevails alone in the summer night. He is very tired, too tired to sleep yet awhile. His feet still ache from long perambulation among friends and parents at the college garden-party after the Senate House ceremonies. For the Senior Tutor has done his duty, as he always does, in that sunset hour of the academic year, the hour that precedes the departure of yet another light-blue flotilla into the great unknown. He finds it endlessly touching, that valedictory session under the trees of the Fellows Garden, where middle-aged men and women stand or sit about in small groups of polite expectancy, while their hosts circulate among the guests star-scattered on the grass. Touching, and often embarrassing, for even tutorial ingenuity is sometimes over-taxed by the problem of saying something kind and consolatory about John's failure to climb out of a two-two into a two-one, or Richard's unaccountable lapse from a first to 'a very good second'. Easy enough to deal with the case of Roger, that jolly young ruffian who has failed to make the honours grade. "An excellent influence in the college. . . . After all, examinations aren't everything. . . ." A rapid closure of thumb and forefinger on Roger's biceps and a firm pat on the back to stand substitute for a good kick in the pants. . . . Roger understands. He grins appreciatively and securely in the no-man's-land of parental protection. Thank God, Mr. Stock groans behind his kindly smile, this is positively the last appearance of Roger – at least, until he comes up to his first re-union dinner and proves himself to be the keenest member of the College Association; which, in Silas Stock's experience, the Rogers of this world generally do . . . all this is the commonplace of many years to the slow-stepping, silken-gowned, self-consciously-donnish gentleman with the benevolent and frog-like smile and the aching feet. Long before the last hand-shake, the Senior Tutor suspects that he is, after all, suffering from angina pectoris and fallen arches. Nice people, good people; but he wishes in his heart that they would all go away. He sees himself, longingly, sitting at his high window, look-ing out upon a sunlit, empty court. . . . To-morrow and to-morrow and to-morrow it will be the Long Vacation.

So, at the end of it all, he lies in bed and listens to the silence, the quiet bell-strokes, the sob of the fountain. Presently he hears the steady tramp of the porter on the cobble-stones as he goes round putting out the lights on the stroke of midnight.

"The lights are going out all over Cambridge," he mutters, as he turns over once more in search of dreamless slumber. "We shall not see them lighted again until . . . until . . . the Long Vacation period of residence, early in July . . . or what the ignorant little beasts insist on calling 'the Long Vac. Term'. . . . To-morrow morning, without fail, Master Duncan Macleod will employ that abominable locution when he comes seeking tutorial permission to spend July and a part of August in college. . . . *Memo:* tell Master Macleod that there is no such thing as a Long Vac. 'term', that there never has been, and never will be while a single tutor has breath left in his body. . . . Tell him, also, that his talk of 'coming up to do some work' is eye-wash, and that he is really looking for a chance to play some cricket, and that no civilized person ever came up in the Long Vacation for any other purpose. . . ."

And there swims into Silas Stock's fading vision the panorama of the playing-fields beyond the river, the screen of massy elms, the parched green grass, the blistered white face of the pavilion, the women in deck-chairs and the men squatting on the turf, while the far-flung men in whites move easefully at the tip of their lengthening shadows all through the long summer afternoon. . . . Men in whites? No, not all, for this is the annual game with the college servants, and here and there a gyp or a gardener sports grey flannels and gym-shoes and occasionally braces, and nobody minds. . . . The Master bowls the opening over, pitching the ball with professional mathematical precision in the hope of dismissing for a duck that stalwart clerk from the college office. . . . The majestic Alfred, head porter, stone-walls for a laborious ten in two hours, while little Smithson, wearing a jockey's cap and breeches, is wheeled to the crease in a barrow by an under-gardener, where he flails his bat for thirteen in five minutes. Keith Parker crouches in the slips, Alistair Wynne lounges elegantly in the deep, and Alan Skinner takes over the bowling with fiery bumpers until the Master whispers in his ear, when he resorts to slow leg-breaks. . . . This is the family at play, Silas Stock sighs. A college as it ought always to be, the true classless society, though not without a touch of the good old feudal spirit when the Master is out first ball and the whole fielding side insists that he take a second innings. . . .

The Senior Tutor would prefer to dream of this all night. But the scene darkens once more with the arriving throngs of 'conferees' in August and early September. . . . The Institute of Meat, United Steel, the Chartered Accountants, General Practitioners, Preservers of Ancient Buildings. . . . And, all the time, the Americans popping cameras up to their eyes, the French blacked out with sun-glasses, the Italians and the Scandinavians and the Portuguese. . . . And, even before the last Bostonian has stalked away, the swallows and daffodils of early October, crying each to each, in Petty Cury and along King's Parade, with the high-pitched voices of everlasting youth.

"Hi, John. Had a good vac.?"

"Not bad, Peter. And you?"

THE SHAPE OF THINGS
TO COME

The Shape of Things to Come

Will it really be like that? Will it all be starting all over again in October? 'Starting' is hardly the appropriate word. Cambridge life is a continuous performance. October marks the point in time when senior persons tell themselves 'this is where we came in . . .'. Cambridge life is lived according to 'the mode of existence decreed to a permanent body composed of transient parts'. New persons, and even new ideas, come in; old, and not so old, persons – and ideas – go out. But Cambridge itself remains 'in a condition of unchangeable constancy'.

This complacent sounding phrase is not necessarily a synonym for stagnation. It may be a witness of devotion to paramount and essential purposes. The constant and increasing purpose of Cambridge has been, and still is, the maintenance and exercise of the free mind, together with the insistence that the free mind may be exercised and strengthened in the study of anything, from Plato's *Republic* to newts' tails, so long as the study is conducted within the framework of larger purposes than Greek Philosophy or 'Half-subject Vertebrate Zoology', or, in other words, within the concept of education for life and not simply for a vocation.

The means by which such purposes may best be served are forever under debate, and at the present time the debate has reached an historic turning-point. There have been other such turning-points. At the Reformation the issue was the survival of the idea of the free mind itself. In the eighteenth century it was the development of college teaching to supplement a Professoriate that hardly taught. In the nineteenth century it was the absorption of the Natural Sciences into university studies on an equal footing with the humanities. Every turning-point has really been concerned, in essence, with the adaptation of an historic institution to a changing world while still preserving its abiding character. At the present time, this perennial problem of adaptation is fast reaching a climax because changes in the life of society at large have developed a turn of speed unknown in earlier times. The world of aristocracy and privilege in which the university was born and grew up has given place to a world of social equality, a world in which 'university education for all' has become a slogan, a world in which science and technology are paramount in the lives of men, a world which thinks that the 'disinterested' pursuit of learning means lack of interest. All these things – the demand for 'more places for more men', for more room within the university for the specialized concerns of science and technology, for more vocational or obviously 'useful' intellectual pursuits – are having an impact on the university which threatens to transform its whole character and to obscure its historic purposes. The problem has become one of preserving quality in a world of quantity, of keeping alive the concept of a liberal education in a world of intensive specialization.

Every problem with which the university is most acutely confronted to-day stems directly, or indirectly, from the increasing predominance of science and technology in the world in which we now live. An increasing proportion of the boys clamouring at the gates are boys who want to come to Cambridge as the great nursery of scientists. Their teachers, at school and at Cambridge, are the vanguard of the assault on compulsory Latin for University Entrance. The men who will teach them in the highly specialized Departments of scientific studies when they get to Cambridge make up a very large proportion of the senior members of the university who cannot be found Fellowships in colleges, men whose academic lives are perforce lived beyond the ancient societies of collegiate intercourse. The greater the pressure for places for undergraduates and Fellowships for their teachers, the greater the demand is likely to be for new colleges.

The Natural Sciences Tripos was founded in 1848. Long before that time provision was made for teaching various branches of science by Professorial Lectures. A man determined to read science at Cambridge could do so, although not until some years after 1848 could he be examined in it for an Honours Degree. The organization of scientific studies could hardly be achieved by Colleges. By their very nature, the sciences require a vastly more complicated and expensive structure and organization than the humanities. Laboratories, schools, research-centres, workshops, all involve not only very large sums of money but a very large and departmentalized staff of lecturers and demonstrators. Only the university as a whole could meet these requirements. In undertaking this great and necessary task of organization, the university has come to loom very much larger than the colleges on the mental horizons of large numbers of men. Employed and maintained by the university (although, of course, appointed by their Faculty), and sometimes without Fellowship, or even in a few cases without membership, of a college, they may be said to have brought a quite different outlook to university life and its problems from that of the traditional 'college man', born and bred. To the historian, this process may resemble what happened to the United States when Thomas Jefferson carried through the Louisiana Purchase, vastly extending the area of authority of the Federal government, nursing new subjects and new communities into life, and ultimately fostering vigorous elements in the national life that had little to thank the 'states' for and a great deal for which to thank the 'Union'.

The foundation of more colleges within the university, and the creation of more Fellowships within the existing colleges would transform the older universities beyond recognition. Many people would not find this altogether undesirable. The foundation of Churchill College, largely on funds put up by industry, did not produce anything like the opposition that might at one time have been expected. What opposition there was arose rather from anxiety that the new college, with its large proportion of scientists and its unusual style of building, might not conform in style and structure to the Cambridge tradition of what a college should be, than from opposition to the founding of a new college *per se*. The residual argument against adding to the number of Cambridge Colleges, or to increasing the population of the existing ones, is sometimes said to derive from the preference of the English, as denizens of a small island, for small things in general, including country cottages, terriers, and women. In fact it derives from something more than that. There is a very real, and very understandable, fear that Cambridge, with its highly domestic and personal mode of life, should become an unwieldy, amorphous and impersonal mass of 'students', undifferentiated and 'university-ridden'. It is often argued that new, young, and worst of all poor, colleges, would be likely to be susceptible to that perennial horror of the devotees of 'college autonomy' – pressure from 'the University' – pressure to take on University teachers as Fellows, simply *qua* university teachers. This horror was expressed in many quarters when the present system of University Lectureships was introduced, a system which makes it cheaper for a college to maintain as Fellows men who hold university appointments than men without them. Such fears are, and always have been, very real, and the provision of more colleges, possibly lacking the resisting power of long tradition, seem to many people a very real menace to the ancient and cherished principle of college autonomy.

Why this horror of the University, or the Great Leviathan? Why is Alma Mater so frequently suspected of eating her children? Love of the small unit, the House, college loyalty, has always been the basis of public affections at Cambridge. But the world has changed since the colleges developed their tradition of autonomy, and, just as the age of the small state is passing away, so may pass the academic age of the small and independent college. Much that has made Cambridge famous in the world would depart with it. The tradition of college tutorship and teaching, with its personal and intimate relationships between the young and the not so young, has had a unique value in the making of men. Few things in English life have made so valuable a contribution to the production of Englishmen with their roots in a beloved soil and their lungs in a free air. But these virtues can be transformed into vices at the hands of too intensive cultivation and too narrow an interpretation. Parish pumps have their usefulness. It is what goes into them and what comes out of them that matters. Probably the most necessary safeguard, at the present time, against dictatorial intrusion lies in a more rigorous and imaginative policy of college admissions. Alistair Wynne has something, although not everything, on his side when he pleads the cause of the Grammar Schools in a university which takes only about 40 per cent of its freshmen from their ranks in the year 1960.

Undergraduates reading Natural Sciences and their allied subjects at present compose about 45 per cent of the student body. They are dispersed unevenly among the colleges. One college has allowed them to preponderate to the extent of 52 per cent. They take their full part in college life, although their specialized studies occupy a very considerable proportion of their daily lives with the specialized and some-what segregated occupations of the laboratory. Of their teachers, and those who run their Departments, a large number have very slender contacts with college life indeed. The graduate staff of the university increased by 82 per cent between 1938 and 1954. By 1959 out of 944 posts under the supervision of the General Board of the Faculties, some 80 were vacant, and of the remainder 450 were held by Fellows of Colleges and 414 were not. Less than 40 out of the 414, however, lacked not only Fellowship but also membership of a College, so that the number of what may fairly be called 'displaced persons' – in the sense that they have no College privileges at all – are very few indeed. Nor is it true that even the most 'displaced' of displaced persons is necessarily a man of science. And, larger and more baffling than the problem of displacement, or semi-attachment, is the problem of com-munication (to use a somewhat sacramental expression). It is not simply that large numbers of senior members are leading a different kind of academic life from the traditional life lived at Cambridge for so long by the men of the humanist subjects. Life in a scientific Department has rewarding qualities of its own. What is disturbing (and this applies not simply to life within the universities, but to life everywhere in our world) is that men involved in diverse disciplines are coming to speak different languages. There are, as Sir Charles Snow has expressed it, 'two cultures'. Or, as Sir Eric Ashby puts it, the university is suffering from a split personality. Too often, the man of science and the arts man does not know what the other is talking about, and still more often he doesn't very much care.

This is the point of real danger: the transformation of what used to be arrogant incomprehension into a polite indifference. Each raises his intellectual hat to the other in a slightly cynical dumbshow, saluting 'the cultural value of the humanities' on the one hand, and 'the crucial importance of science in the modern world' on the other. It is pointless for either party to accuse the other any more of ignorance or intolerance. They are learning to live together in peace with a wall, or a smoke-screen, between them. Ladders are set up on either side of the wall, in the shape of lectures on 'Science for arts-men' or 'The History of Science', an activity which so far seems to have resulted in more

T

give than take. Slightly significant shapes begin to show through the smoke-screen: undergraduates find the history of science looming up in lectures for the Historical Tripos, while men reading the Natural Sciences have a non-compulsory 'half-subject' on 'The History and Philosophy of Science' in Part I of their Tripos. But communications are unlikely ever to be opened up effectively by syllabus or lecture-courses, more particularly when specialization within subjects is so severe, and the amount of sheer basic labour required for Tripos examinations is so heavy. But it is important that the universities should take the lead in facing the problem of the two cultures, or the split personality, even though they cannot be expected to solve it, short of a total recasting of our educational system in which they have their part. It is important that they should think, and act, boldly about the problem, for, to repeat what Lowes Dickinson wrote, many years ago: a university 'ought to lead thought, as it did at the Reformation, and not skulk behind and talk of vested rights. And,' he added, 'there never were places with such chances as Oxford and Cambridge. . . .'

It would be unwise, perhaps, to expect too much of the universities, powerful as they may be in shaping the minds of the men and women who shape the future. Generally speaking, it is true that a society gets the universities it deserves. It may very well be, as Sir Charles Snow evidently believes, that it is a matter of the whole of society, with government at its head, waking up to the gigantic problems of the age of science, and this awakening is going to be impelled by the urgency of an opportunity which, if we continue to let it slip, will be seized from our hands by the thrustful and positive communities of the East in the cause of universal humanity and its basic human needs. Seen in such terms, the little jealousies and small squabbles over the relative claims of arts and sciences in the university may shrink to the dimensions of the insectal *statis* of a Greek city of the fourth century B.C. Even the controversy over 'compulsory Latin' in the Previous Examination may fade into insignificance if scientific thought comes to supply the cement for a common European culture, as it was supplied in the Middle Ages by the Latin tongue and Catholic theology. The conflicting claims of the sciences and the humanities will lose a great deal of their relevance if technology becomes the core of a new

humanism of the twentieth century, as Greek became the core of the
new humanism of the fifteenth. And, if that is what the future holds,
it will hasten the day when the university will emerge once again as
the important unit, and the colleges maybe will become the homes of
intellectually displaced persons.

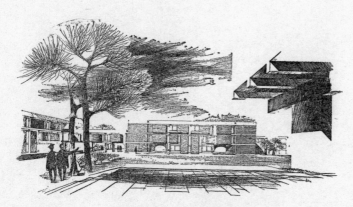

Churchill College - Architects' Drawing

APPENDIX

SOME CAMBRIDGE BOOKS

For factual information on day-to-day matters there is *The Student's Handbook to Cambridge*, revised annually and published by the University Press. Varsity Publications Ltd. issue *Varsity Handbook* annually, a highly practical and compendious guide especially for freshmen. Sir Sydney Roberts' *Introduction to Cambridge* imparts, within a hundred pages, not only essential information, but something of the life, spirit and history of the university.

The best and most recent account of the City, the University, and the Colleges is to be found in the latest volume of the Victoria County History, edited by Dr. J. P. Roach. This is the indispensable volume, authoritatively written and finely illustrated. The Royal Commission on Historical Monuments has recently brought out two magnificent volumes on the City of Cambridge, picturing and describing almost everything of historical and architectural interest.

The Cambridge past is chronicled exhaustively in Cooper's *Annals of Cambridge*. Arthur Gray's *Cambridge University: an Episodical History* supplies a shorter and more readable work. Henry Gunning's *Reminiscences* are the most famous source for Cambridge gossip in the later eighteenth and early nineteenth centuries. If everything in Gunning is not entirely true, one feels that it ought to be. There is a neat little volume of *Selections* from Gunning compiled by D. A. Winstanley. Winstanley's own books, *Unreformed Cambridge*, *Early Victorian Cambridge*, and *Later Victorian Cambridge* are the fruit of unrivalled learning in the history of the subject over two centuries. J. H. Monk's *Life of Bentley* (1830), tells the story of the most extraordinary academic career in the history of the University.

There are a great many minor works of reminiscence and historic miniatures which throw light on the past and present of the place: some of the best being Mrs. F. A. Keynes' *By-ways of Cambridge History*,

Sir Arthur Shipley's *Cambridge Cameos*, Leslie Stephen's *Sketches from Cambridge*, W. E. Heitland's *After Many Years*, and Gwen Raverat's *Period Piece*.

Important aspects of undergraduate life are treated in Percy Cradock's *History of the Cambridge Union Society*, and R. D. Burnell's history of the Boat Race, 1829-1953. Jean Lindsay's *Cambridge Scrapbook* makes a lively anthology of Cambridge life, and Bryan Little's finely illustrated portrait of Cambridge to-day makes a valuable contribution in succession to the older *Cambridge* by John Steegman. No one interested in the politics of university life can afford to miss the late F. A. Cornford's *Microcosmographia Academica: a Guide for the young academic Politician*.

Two recent essays of great relevance for the understanding of current Cambridge problems are Sir Charles Snow's *The Two Cultures and the Scientific Revolution* (*the Rede Lecture, 1959*), and Sir Eric Ashby's *Technology and the Academics*.

INDEX

Index

SELECT INDEX OF SUBJECTS

SELECT INDEX OF PEOPLE AND PLACES

PEOPLE

PLACES